For a Just and
Better World

For a Just and Better World

Engendering Anarchism in the Mexican Borderlands, 1900–1938

SONIA HERNÁNDEZ

UNIVERSITY OF
ILLINOIS PRESS
Urbana, Chicago, and Springfield

Cataloging data available from the Library of Congress
ISBN 978-0-252-04404-5 (hardcover)
ISBN 978-0-252-08610-6 (paperback)
ISBN 978-0-252-05298-9 (ebook)

For my one and only, Camila Chávez

Contents

List of Illustrations   ix

Acknowledgments   xi

A Note on Terminology   xvii

Abbreviations Used in the Text   xix

Timeline   xxi

Introduction: Reenvisioning Mexican(a) Labor History
across Borders   1

1   The Circulation of Radical Ideologies, Early Transnational
    Collaboration, and Crafting a Women's Agenda   25

2   Gendering Anarchism and Anarcho-Syndicalist Organizations:
    "*Compañeras en la Lucha*" and "Women of Ill-Repute"   56

3   *Feminismos Transfronterizos* in Caritina Piña's Labor Network   80

4   The Language of Motherhood in Radical Labor Activism   98

5   "Leave the Unions to the Men": Anarchist Expressions
    and Engendering Political Repression in the Midst of
    State-Sanctioned Socialism   111

6   A Last Stand for Anarcho-Feminists in the Post-1920 Period   131

7   Finding Closure: Legacies of Anarcho-Feminism
    in the Mexican Borderlands   145

    Notes   155

    Bibliography   191

    Index   211

Illustrations

Figures

1. Map of the Gulf of Mexico and Greater Mexican Borderlands   3
2. Map of Tampico and Villa Cecilia   27
3. Warehouse of the Huasteca Petroleum Company, Villa Cecilia   30
4. Oil tank cars on the loading docks, Tampico, ca. 1910–1920   30
5. Railroad yards from the bluff, Tampico, ca. 1880–1900   31
6. Nicanor Piña Hernández, Caritina Piña's father, ca. 1910   38
7. Zenaido Piña, Caritina Piña's half-brother, ca. 1911   39
8. *Magonista* Lázaro Gutiérrez de Lara with female soldiers, 1911   40
9. Librado Rivera and Enrique Flores Magón, ca. 1910–1915   44
10. Venustiano Carranza, Carrera Torres, and other *militares*, ca. 1910–1920   65
11. Caritina M. Piña, ca. 1920   81
12. Tampico street scene   84
13. Anarchist demonstration against the police in Tampico, 1925   103
14. Women workers in a Mexican public laundry   130
15. Market scene from station, Tampico   134

Tables

1. Population of Tamaulipas as reflected in urban and rural zones, 1910–1930   32
2. Population of Tampico, Tamaulipas, by sex, 1900–1921   33
3. Selected Confederación General de Trabajadores (CGT) affiliates, Tamaulipas, 1921   57
4. Selected list of labor organizations in Villa Cecilia, Árbol Grande, and Tampico, operating between 1912 and 1940   86
5. Liga Cultural de Mujeres Libertarias, Tampico (1922–?)   91

Acknowledgments

Three major events that transpired over the course of the writing and revising of this book significantly influenced me: the growing movement for racial justice in the United States, which reverberated in other parts of the world and in some ways felt as one; the feminist movement to combat gender inequity and antiwoman violence in Mexico; and the devasting and scary new reality that Covid-19 wrought on the planet. In all of these three huge moments with other smaller corollary moments, women—in some cases accompanied by their children—led and participated in marches, organized virtual meetings and gatherings, and sadly, also lost family and friends to Covid-19 or died after exposure to the virus.

I kept thinking of the longer genealogy of women's presence in global social movements and it remained the backdrop for understanding the women who take center stage in this book. Many of the women who are shaping today's movements, like those before them, are working class and engage in direct action, always critical of the role and power of the state in their lives and the lives of their families as well as the lives of millions of other people. That legacy of women's collective action is indeed long and rich. Along the Texas-Tamaulipas border a handful of women had participated in social movements at the turn of the twentieth century, and by the postrevolutionary period their presence in labor collectives and unions was conspicuous.

There were moments where I was so motivated, I wrote for long periods of time watching my nine-year-old daughter write her own chapter book composed of her experiences with virtual learning and drawings of Covid-19. There were, however, other times I was so heartbroken at what I witnessed in our world, in my own community, in my daughter's own reflections, that I did not want to write. I felt my writing at this particular juncture in our lives was disconnected, elitist, and not worth expending so much energy upon when there were things of greater concern going on. I witnessed the beating and killing of Latino and Black Americans, the indiscriminate manner with which the virus took the lives of scores of frontline workers, and the crumbling of a global economy. But the more I wrote and refined my ideas, the better I understood this new normal and the better I understood the response to such contemporary challenges. Finally, I better understood how hope and the desire for change can keep the human spirit alive.

The writing of a second book, in many ways, was more challenging than writing the first one. In the first I had the constant eye of my advisor, John Mason Hart, to whom I am deeply indebted for this book as well. But, this time around, the constant eye was not there. However, there were individuals who kept me going by inspiring me and pushing me to think more critically as I examined women's anarcho-feminist practices. I shared my ideas about the transnational network of labor activists as well as the history of Caritina Piña in multiple venues with numerous scholars and students as well as community members in the last several years. And, thanks to them, I was able to see and understand my subjects more clearly and distance myself from them, as too often I became so enamored with Piña and her colleagues, self-identifying with them as I attempted to understand them, that I lost objectivity.

I owe much gratitude to people who provided me with access to historical documentation and rare photographs. There are two people whose assistance was absolutely crucial. César Morado Macías, friend and historian from Nuevo León, and Marvin Osiris Huerta Márquez, *cronista* for Antiguo Morelos, both provided consistent support in the research phase and helped me locate Caritina Piña's birth certificate, a rare photograph of Piña, and other key information. César listened to my reflections on Piña while always reminding me of the larger historical and geographical context with which to better understand her role; Marvin shared many of his news stories on key Tamaulipas figures written to engage a more popular audience and, similar to the daily functions of Piña's labor network, he and I exchanged information about each other's work, but this time via social media. Special thanks to my good friend and colleague Diana Méndez from the Instituto de Investigaciones Históricas (IIH) at the

Universidad Autónoma de Baja California for her support throughout the years and for putting me in touch with Roberto Guzman from Tamaulipas who helped me locate other materials.

Throughout these past several years, the staff at the Archivo Histórico de Tampico, Archivo Histórico de Cd. Madero (formerly Villa Cecilia), and the Instituto de Investigaciones Históricas at the Universidad Autónoma de Tamaulipas (IIH-UAT) provided invaluable support and allowed me to scan or photocopy historical documents related to the rise of anarchism and unions as well as access to material not available digitally, particularly in the Archivo de Esteban Méndez Guerra. My most sincere gratitude to Juan Díaz Rodríguez from the IIH-UAT for his assistance. I enjoyed every one of my research trips to these centers that allowed me to piece together this history. Support from the Special Collections at the former University of Texas–Pan American was crucial, especially assistance with newspapers from McAllen and Edinburg not accessible anywhere else. The trips I made to the Archivo General de la Nación (AGN), the Hemeroteca at the Universidad Autónoma de México (UNAM), and particularly my time at the Centro de Estudios del Movimiento Obrero y Socialista (CEMOS) proved crucial in recovering key documentation on the labor movement in Tampico, especially the relationship between anarchist and communist organizations. The diligent staff at the Archivo Nacional de España in Madrid as well as librarians from the Archivo Histórico de Barcelona helped me locate materials needed to understand the larger transatlantic connections to the port of Tampico.

Besides the availability of partial or complete runs of anarchist newspapers in repositories in northern Mexico and Mexico City and in some repositories in Texas, two digital collections have been extremely useful in recovering Mexican women's labor history. Reflecting the internationalist spirit of collaboration across borders are two major archival collections that were deliberately digitized to provide free access to all. The *Regeneración* digital website includes issues of the well-known publication *Regeneración*, the principal medium through with which *magonistas* and supporters and adherents of the PLM and Junta communicated with one another and helped to spread the message of worker autonomy and social justice. At a conference on the legacy of anarchist thought in Austin, Texas, in 2014, the grandnephew of Ricardo Flores Magón spoke of the intent behind the digitization of material. He proudly announced, echoing the words of Flores Magón, that information should be shared and not hidden from the public. He opposed housing material in traditional archival repositories such as university libraries and called for free access to knowledge and information. The underutilized Archivo de Esteban Méndez Guerra in Ciudad

Victoria houses records of meeting minutes of the Comité Internacional Pro Presos Sociales, leaflets and pamphlets, personal correspondence, and anarchist newspaper clippings published in the Villa Cecilia-Tampico region, also housed in the International Institute of Social History in Amsterdam. These materials evidence the sharing of newspapers with labor groups in states including Nuevo León, Coahuila, San Luis Potosí, Veracruz, Sinaola, Baja California, the Federal District, and across in Texas, California, Ohio, and New York. Some of the newspapers have been digitized by the historian Mónica Alcayaga Sasso, whose work on the anarcho-syndicalist Librado Rivera and the group Hermanos Rojos was crucial to recovering the history of radical activism in this corner of the world; the digital collection on Librado Rivera is one of the best organized and user-friendly collections I have consulted.

My dear colleagues and friends from our public history project, Refusing to Forget, Monica Muñoz Martinez, Trini Gonzales, John Morán González, Benjamin Johnson, and Christopher Carmona, provided an intellectual environment for discussions of transnational state violence as well as US-Mexican borderlands history that helped me better understand the particular challenges faced by so many labor activists deemed a threat to the security of both the United States and Mexico. Special thanks to Ben Johnson for reading an earlier draft of the manuscript and for his insightful comments. Many of the presentations and discussions at the Global Labor Migration conference held in beautiful and historic Amsterdam with its long tradition of labor activism led by Leon Fink and colleagues allowed me to critically reflect on the process and challenges of transnational and global labor alliances as well as important themes to keep in mind while engaging these histories. The constructive feedback I received from the editors of *Frontiers: A Journal of Women Studies* as well as the anonymous readers of my article on Caritina Piña, which appears in abbreviated form in chapter 3, was crucial and allowed me think critically about the meaning of transnationalism from a gendered, feminist perspective. Moreover, parts of chapter 4 on the language of motherhood from an anarchist perspective benefitted from the careful editing of Christopher Castañeda and Montse Feu; an earlier version appears in *Writing Revolution: Hispanic Anarchism in the United States* (University of Illinois Press, 2019). I also had the privilege of sharing my work with Kirwin Shaffer, Kenyon Zimmer, Christopher Castañeda, and Montse Feu at an Organization of American Historians (OAH) panel and received comments and suggestions that helped me further reflect on historical processes shaped by women and the larger process of anarchist labor solidarities. I owe a tremendous amount of gratitude to the two anonymous reviewers solicited by the University of Illinois Press who were gracious enough to read the manuscript during the first and second round of reviews. Their comments, combined with historian Alice Kessler Harris's insightful comments, helped me strengthen the manuscript significantly. I cannot thank them enough. My most sincere gratitude to James Engelhardt for his patience as I revised and completed this manuscript and to Alison Syring Bassford for taking on this project. I am so appreciative of Alison's thoughtful recommendations and her commitment to seeing this book come to fruition.

I thank my friends and colleagues at Texas A&M University in the History Department and in the Latino/a and Mexican American Studies program for their continuing support: Felipe Hinojosa, Carlos Blanton, Nancy Plankey Videla, Sarah McNamara, Tiffany Gonzalez, Laura Oviedo, and all of my undergraduate and graduate students. I thank my former chair in History, David Vaught, who was welcoming and supportive as I arrived in College Station and embarked on this book project. Research funding from the Department of History and the College of Liberal Arts allowed me to travel to numerous repositories in Mexico, the United States, and Spain. A publication subvention grant from the the Melbern G. Glasscock Center for Humanities Research at Texas A&M University helped defray other costs.

My daughter Camila's sweet smile, inquisitive mind, and untainted love carried me through some very difficult moments in my life. Her understanding as a young child—tolerating her mother's absence for extended periods of time since the tender age of twelve months—is priceless. I am forever indebted to her. The tears she shed every time I left broke my heart. Fortunately, she had the care and love of individuals while I was away. I thank Oscar for caring for Camila since 2011, because without his support and great nanny skills, I would not be the historian I am today. I thank my mother and my sister Zoe for the many times they cared for Camila while I was away. Many thanks to my Latinas BCS group, in particular Sabrina Barahona, Natalia Goldberg, Karla Cabriales, Paulette Suchodolski, among others, for their support and love since my transition from the south Texas border to College Station and for the many playdates with their lovely children at our beautiful local parks. Their friendship allowed me to take much-needed breaks from the rigors of academia and their friendship has proven that community can exist anywhere.

A Note on Terminology

I employ the term *Mexicana* or *Mexicano* to refer to Mexican nationals living in Mexico and the term *ethnic Mexican* to refer to people of Mexican origin living or working in the United States regardless of citizenship. *Tejana/o* refers to women and men from Texas who trace their roots to Spanish, Mexican, and or Indigenous heritage. I use *Mexican American* to describe individuals born and living in the United States, including Texas, although it is not exclusive to Texas-born individuals. I use the term *norteño* to refer to a population residing in the northern part of Mexico, which includes the border states of Tamaulipas, Nuevo Léon, Coahuila, Chihuahua, Sinaloa, Sonora, and Baja California. The terms *fronteriza* or *fronterizo* is used to describe people born in the US-Mexican borderlands, regardless of which side they reside on.

Abbreviations Used in the Text

CGT	Confederación General de Trabajadores
COM	Casa del Obrero Mundial
Comité	Comité Internacional Pro Presos Sociales
CROM	Confederación Regional Obrera Mexicana
CTM	Confederación de Trabajadores de México
FAM	Federación Anarquista Mexicana
FOT	Federación Obrera de Tampico
FUPDM	Frente Único Pro-Derechos de la Mujer
HR	Hermanos Rojos
IWW	Industrial Workers of the World
JCA	Junta de Conciliación y Arbitraje
PCM	Partido Comunista Mexicano
PLM	Partido Liberal Mexicano
PNR	Partido Nacional Revolucionario
PRI	Partido Revolucionario Institucional
PSF	Partido Socialista Fronterizo
SDRS	Sindicato de Dependientas de Restaurantes y Similares
SERCS	Sindicato de Empleadas de Restaurantes, Cafés y Similares
UERS	Unión de Empleados de Restaurantes y Similares
UMA	Unión de Mujeres Americanas

Timeline

1864	Librado Rivera born in San Luís Potosí
1895	Caritina Piña born in Ocampo, Tamaulipas
1896	Esteban Méndez Guerra born in Zacatecas
1901	Ricardo Flores Magón, Librado Rivera, and colleagues hold Congreso Liberal, San Luis Potosí, paving the road for the emergence of the Partido Liberal Mexicano (PLM)
1909	Execution of anarchist Francisco Ferrer i Guardia, Barcelona, Spain
1910	Francisco I. Madero proclaims Plan de San Luis Potosí from San Antonio, Texas
1911	Aniceto Pizaña organizes PLM affiliate in Brownsville, Texas; collaborates with Tamaulipas peon-turned revolutionary, Higinio Tanguma
1912	Founding of Casa del Obrero Mundial (COM), Mexico City
1912	Higinio Tanguma and followers engage in anarchist-inspired rebellions in northern Tamaulipas and southern Texas; Carrera Torres family, promoting similar ideals, remain active in southern Tamaulipas
ca. 1912	Luz Mendoza and colleagues found Grupo Redención, a PLM affiliate in Harlingen, Texas
1913	Venustiano Carranza becomes Jefe del Ejército Constitucionalista

1915   Grupo Racionalista, adopting Ferrer's Escuela Racionalista frame-
            work, is founded by Elisa A. Hernández, Isaura Galván, and col-
            leagues in San Antonio, Texas
1915   Reynalda González Parra, Ricardo Treviño, and colleagues orga-
            nized a COM branch in Tampico
ca. 1915   Reynalda González Parra forms or joins Centro de Estudios
            Feministas Sociales, Tampico
1915   Battle of El Ebano over control of oilfields; Carrancistas, despite
            internal divisions, emerge as victors
ca. 1916   Deportation of IWW, PLM, and Racionalista member José Angel
            Hernández, and possibly Racionalista members and partner, Elisa
            A. Hernández; José Angel Hernández and Isaura Galván proceed to
            insert themselves in the Tampico-Cecilia labor scene after activism
            in Texas
1916–1917   Venustiano Carranza's crackdown on radical labor activists
1917   Creation of Hermanos Rojos (HR)
1917   Isaura Galván and colleagues from *Germinal* newspaper arrested
1917   Segundo Congreso Obrero Regional held in Tampico, Reynalda
            González Parra attends as delegate
1917   Massive oil strike followed by arrests
1918   Creation of the Confederación Regional Obreros Mexicana (CROM)
1919   Massive oil strike, more arrests
1920–1921   Caritina Piña arrives in Tampico-Villa Cecilia via Ocampo
1921   Creation of Confederación General de Trabajadores (CGT)
1922   Founding of Liga Cultural de Mujeres Libertarias "La Idea"; death
            of Ricardo Flores Magón
1924–1931   Caritina Piña works as Secretaria de Corespondencia del Comité
            Internacional Pro-Presos Sociales, Villa Cecilia, collaborates with
            former Villista-turned-anarchist Esteban Méndez Guerra
1924   Emilio Portes Gil founds the Partido Socialista Fronterizo (PSF);
            Portes Gil asks Francisco Carrera (from Carrera-Torres family of
            agrarian activists) to join the Calles-Portes Gil alliance; Portes Gil
            secures support from massive dockworkers union
1924   Librado Rivera arrives in Villa Cecilia
1925   May Day Demonstrations in Tampico; variety of organizations
            participate including Comité Internacional Pro-Presos Sociales,
            Hermanos Rojos, and UERS
1925   Over 200 waitresses from the parent union UERS leave the union
1925   Massive oil strike

1928	Emilio Portes Gil becomes president of Mexico
1929	Caritina Piña petitions North Carolina judge and copies Herbert Hoover on behalf of detained Gastonia Mill strikers
1929	Authorities tied to PSF attempt to disperse Clubs Femeniles Vasconcelistas from a demonstration using large water hoses
1930	Villa Cecilia renamed Ciudad Madero in honor of Francisco I. Madero
1930	Felipa Velásquez deported to Islas Marías for participating in an agrarian invasion on lands claimed by US Colorado River Land Company
1930	Caritina Piña's father dies, prompting Piña's return to Ocampo
1931	Federal Labor Law stipulates labor guarantees
1934	Lázaro Cárdenas becomes president of Mexico
1935	Frente Único Pro Derechos de la Mujer (FUPDM) founded; Tampico native Esther Chapa Tijerina joins group
1937	Day of the Land Assault, expropriation of US Colorado River Land Company; Piña marries Gregorio Ortiz in Ocampo
1938	Cárdenas nationalizes the oil industry
1949	Death of Felipa Veláquez
1979	Death of Esteban Méndez Guerra
1981	Death of Caritina Piña, Reynosa, Tamaulipas

Introduction

Reenvisioning Mexican(a) Labor History across Borders

> The proletarians, on other sides of borders, only see brothers
> living in misery who, like them, have capital as their enemy.
>
> —Félix Le Dantec

On September 20, 1929, Caritina Piña Montalvo, a Mexicana living on the outskirts of Tampico, penned a letter of protest about the maltreatment of female mill workers in Gastonia, North Carolina. Two years had passed since Piña had written, too late, in support of the Italian anarchists Nicola Sacco and Bartolomeo Vanzetti, recently executed in Massachusetts. Now, even while embroiled in the campaign against former Tamaulipas governor and current Mexican president Emilio Portes Gil, she directed a protest to Judge M. V. Barnhill of Charlotte, North Carolina and copied US president Herbert Hoover. She sent the letter in her capacity as *secretaria de correspondencia* (secretary of correspondence) of a new organization for political prisoners in Villa Cecilia, the Comité Internacional Pro-Presos Sociales.

As her letter outlined, together with other workers from Gastonia, sixteen "Mexicans," including three women and four children, had been detained and their "small houses set on fire."[1] The horrific act was ordered by a local police chief. The Mexicans and other mill laborers worked for Loray Mill and were on strike demanding higher wages from "various companies" in North and South Carolina. Piña demanded justice for the workers. Above all else, she pleaded for the release of the female detainees by invoking their privileged position as mothers and framing the injustice as an attack on family. She further argued that the workers were entitled to ask for a "reasonable salary . . . to cover . . .

their meals," because, after all, it was imperative for the good of the "great human family."[2] She described the mill owners and the authorities as "anti-labor Americans" and compared them to "Indians without any civilization." Piña closed by arguing that "the strike declarated [*sic*] to the companies [was] reasonable" and demanding that the workers be released.[3]

Piña, Esteban Méndez Guerra, and other members of the Comité called a meeting of Tampico labor organizations to discuss actions the group could take on behalf of their fellow workers detained in the United States. The meeting was set for late August of 1929, one of many gatherings of labor collectives and activists dedicated to addressing labor inequities across the world.

Piña's labor activism—including her intervention in the Gastonia affair and her work alongside other activists in a greater labor network—is the subject of this book. It explains the conditions that led to the rise of anarcho-syndicalism as a tool to achieve labor equity and women's direct role in the struggle. Women were engaged with the labor movement as leaders and constitutive parts of it. Their lived experience in the labor movement was informed by ideas and expressions of their feminist ideals. Thus, this book is about the world that produced activists such as Caritina Piña, who built on the work of the handful of women who preceded her in opening up the conversation about labor equity to include women's issues. Women have left an indelible mark on the greater Tamaulipas-Texas borderlands region's labor history. Such historic border solidarities, while imperfect, helped to build a foundation for postrevolutionary labor alliances.

Caritina Piña's plea on behalf of fellow Mexican workers abroad, as the opening anecdote relates, was framed by her understanding of family, women's experiences, class, race and ethnicity, and ideas about human dignity. Her activism in her own country and beyond the US-Mexican border formed part of a broader labor network anchored in the Gulf of Mexico, in which Piña operated as a liaison. Casting light on her ability to connect various groups of activists across the US-Mexican border and across Mexico without ever stepping outside her native Tamaulipas, I identify Piña as a transnational labor broker. She participated in and helped to sustain the rise of anarcho-syndicalism in this corner of the world, which featured one of the most radical labor movements in the Gulf of Mexico region. It stood out as radical because it applied anarchist ideals to an organizing structure that privileged worker unity outside the bounds and control of the state but differed from other competing ideologies like communism and state-sponsored socialism. Amid the rise of oil production and labor unionism in revolutionary Mexico, Piña formed part of a greater network of men and women who placed their hope in anarcho-syndicalism as the solution to labor and gender inequities.

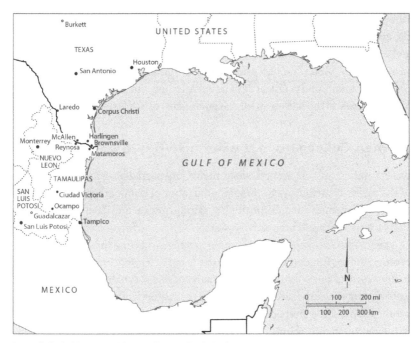

Figure 1. Gulf of Mexico and Greater Mexican Borderlands

Mexicanas in the Gulf of Mexico region such as Caritina Piña and others who take center stage in this book fought to promote labor rights locally and abroad. They did so by promoting anarchist ideals and envisioning a community of workers regardless of geopolitical borders. That is, Piña and colleagues fought on behalf of workers in Mexico and fellow workers abroad, remaining true to the anarchist ideal of a nationless world. While mainstream media outlets and state reports often labeled women like Piña "women of ill-repute," revealing how entrenched ideas of gender and sexuality shaped perceptions about women's engagement in radical labor activism, their ideas about the labor struggle reflected some of the most progressive expressions of gender equity in labor at that time. They promoted labor rights and remained loyal to the anarchist principle of direct action.[4]

In great part, anarchism and its more structured incarnation, anarcho-syndicalism, which privileged unions and collectives, flourished due to geography. Ports of entry including Tampico had historically functioned as conduits or midpoints between Mexico, the Caribbean and greater Latin America, and communities across the Atlantic. Residents, transients, and workers from these points of entry shared ideas about culture, politics, and certainly concerns over labor inequities, inadequate living conditions, and gender inequality. While the exchange of ideas among people from the Tampico–Villa Cecilia region and other ports of entry had deep roots, the Mexican Revolution—manifested as early as the 1880s and unleashed by 1910—paved the road for more robust social, economic, and political demands, including women's labor rights. This history serves as the backdrop for the emergence of activists such as Piña.[5]

Women Colleagues in the Tampico-Based Group

Based on the available archival documentation, partial biographical sketches of the major contributors to this regional labor network emerge, helping us understand women's social upbringing, family origins, and developments that shaped and informed their activist years.

The public careers of three women in particular during the early twentieth century, before Piña entered the region's labor activist scene, are important to underscore. Luz Mendoza, Isaura Galván, and Reynalda González Parra were among the earliest female voices in the region who promoted anarcho-syndicalism. They helped to promote direct action as well as women's participation in these circles between 1910 and 1918.

Luz Mendoza resided in the Rio Grande Valley along the border. It was in Harlingen, Texas, that she founded Grupo Redención, affiliated with Ricardo Flores Magón's Partido Liberal Mexicano (PLM). She was either related to or was the partner of PLM member Bernardino Mendoza, according to *magonista* literature. At least one source indicates Mendoza's participation as the lone woman among *magonista* revolutionaries plotting an armed assault on northern Mexico from Texas in the fall of 1913. She remained active after the Revolution and corresponded with staff from the various anarchist newspapers operating in the 1920s in Tampico and Villa Cecilia.[6]

Her contemporary, a Mexican or possibly Mexican American, Isaura Galván, arrived in Tampico in 1915 via San Antonio, Texas. She brought organizing experience, as she had cofounded Grupo Racionalista in San Antonio, which adhered to Francisco Ferrer's Escuela Racionalista and PLM anarcho-syndicalist ideals.[7] She worked as the *directora general* of the anarchist newspaper *Germinal* and, while she does not appear in the formal roster of the Grupo Germinal, an anarchist collective that sponsored the newspaper, she remained an active colleague of its predominantly male members.

Among the few women contributing to the newspaper *Germinal* was Reynalda González Parra. She was a cofounder of the Tampico branch of the Casa del Obrero Mundial (COM), organized in the fall of 1915, and was a member and possibly a cofounder of one of the earliest all-female anarcho-syndicalist collectives in Tampico, the Centro de Estudios Feministas Sociales. González Parra moved to Tampico from Mexico City sometime during 1915 and was among the few female anarchist representatives in the Second Worker's Congress (Segundo Congreso Obrero), which was held in Tampico in 1917. In Mexico City, she had formed part of a group of crucial educators adhering to Spanish anarchist Francisco Ferrer's Rationalist school of thought offering instruction to young boys and girls. She became part of Tampico's labor circles, as waves of Mexicans from the countryside descended upon the port in search of employment in the oilfields in the midst of the Revolution.

As Mendoza, Galván, and González Parra emerged as pioneers in the region's early anarchist scene moving forward a collective, direct-action agenda, Caritina Piña was coming into young adulthood. Caritina Piña emerged as a labor activist during the 1920s and the 1930s in Villa Cecilia, several miles north of the port of Tampico. (Cecilia was renamed Ciudad Madero in honor of Francisco I. Madero in 1930.) By the early 1920s it emerged as a bustling working-class enclave, housing many of the first oil workers of Mexico. The workers from the Tampico-Cecilia region formed part of the burgeoning industrial labor force so crucial to the formation of unions.

Piña's parents were Felicitas Montalvo, from Rancho El Manchón on the outskirts of Ocampo in southern Tamaulipas, and former revolutionary general Nicanor Piña Hernández from Ocampo. Ocampo was founded in 1749 as Villa de Santa Bárbara. In 1869, it was renamed Ocampo in honor of liberal thinker Melchor Ocampo, and by 1898 was deemed a town. Surrounded by incredible vegetation and soaring mountains, the town is still known as the "Orchard (*vergel*) of Tamaulipas." Local chroniclers from Ocampo claim Piña was born in that town between 1899 and 1902. But Piña was most likely born sometime in 1895, as the 1930 census reports that she was a thirty-five-year-old resident of Villa Cecilia. Piña's parents were not married to each other. Nicanor nonetheless recognized Caritina as his "natural" child, surname and all. Possibly by 1902, Piña's mother married Federico de León. It appears that her stepfather accepted her, but tragically, within six years of that marriage, Piña's mother died. Orphaned and perhaps unwilling to remain with her stepfather as a vulnerable thirteen-year-old, she joined her biological father and his other children, and by the end of the Mexican Revolution, the family moved to Tampico.[8]

It was during her time in the Tampico-Cecilia region that she met the former Pancho Villa soldier Esteban Méndez Guerra and Librado Rivera, long-time friend and collaborator of Ricardo Flores Magón. A member of the Hermanos

Rojos (Red Brothers), a leading anarcho-syndicalist organization based in Villa Cecilia dating to 1917, Méndez Guerra was an early anarcho-syndicalist and among the principal organizers of the Comité Internacional Pro-Presos Sociales, for which Caritina Piña served as secretary in the 1920s.[9] Méndez Guerra was born on August 3, 1896, in Zacatecas. After fighting the 1915 Battle of El Ebano in the Tampico oilfields, he moved to Villa Cecilia.[10]

The older Librado Rivera was born on August 17, 1864, in Rayón, San Luis Potosí. After Flores Magón's death, Rivera, at the suggestion of anarchist allies in Mexico City, moved to Tampico-Cecilia, arriving in 1924, only a couple of years after Piña's own journey to the region. His Mexico City colleagues who remained in contact with Hermanos Rojos convinced Rivera to relocate to Tampico-Cecilia because "the various anarchist organizations' activities were having an impact on the interests of Wall Street."[11] While it is unclear whether Piña maintained a close relationship with Rivera, she played a crucial role in his release from prison on several occasions.

Equally important to the network was Felipa Velásquez. She was born in 1882 in western Mexico, in the state of Sinaloa. Velásquez taught herself to read and received formal training as a schoolteacher. Shortly after beginning her tenure as a teacher, however, local authorities removed her from her *plaza* (post), citing her activism in the agrarian reform movement in the border state of Baja California. Both Piña and Velásquez became members of the Confederación General de Trabajadores (CGT), the principal national anarchist organization to which the smaller local and regional organizations like Hermanos Rojos were adhered after its founding in 1921.

Other women involved in the network via their written commentaries and poems appearing in the local anarchist press included María and Esther Mendoza. While not explicitly stated in their writings, Esther and María Mendoza appear to be related, possibly sisters or cousins. They belonged to Tampico's Liga Cultural de Mujeres Libertarias, founded in 1924. Jesús de Mendoza, a contemporary and colleague of Méndez Guerra and a member of Hermanos Rojos, was possibly a relative of the Mendoza women. By the late 1930s, Esther and María Mendoza appear to have moved to Mazatlán, Sinaloa, where they continued to contribute to both the Mazatlán and Tampico-Cecilia press.[12]

Hermanos Rojos sponsored at least one theater in which anarchist-inspired plays could be seen and heard. The organization brought together like-minded individuals including Spanish anarchists Román Delgado and Jorge Borrán and Mexicans Pedro Gudiño, Pedro Alfaro, Luz Gudiño Marín (the only female in the group, possibly a relative or partner of Pedro Gudiño), José H. Hernández, and Rafael Altamira among others. Hermanos Rojos, the Tampico COM, and

Grupo Germinal emerged as three of the major anarcho-syndicalist organizations in the region's early labor history.[13]

While not all of these women knew each other personally, their shared experiences expressed through correspondence, commentaries, and other writings helped create a sense of community. Equally important, the environment in which these women lived and interacted with others shaped their radical labor activism. Villa Cecilia emerged as a working-class town servicing the growing cosmopolitan port of Tampico as the petroleum industry expanded in the early twentieth century. It was home to one of the top three oilfields of the time, British-owned El Águila, and, by 1915, became the site of major military encounters between opposing revolutionary factions.[14] The Tampico region and surrounding areas including oil labor camps near *pozos petroleros* (oil wells) also witnessed some of the early massive strikes, supported in great part by anarchist groups. By the late nineteenth century, mutual aid societies and other labor-based collectives appeared as the population of oil workers and associated industrial workers grew. By 1917, a range of labor unions based on specific trades espousing anarchist ideas emerged. The region quickly became a leading site for radical labor activism, via anarcho-syndicalism, privileging organizing through labor unions and collectives committed to direct-action strategies.

Expressing support for labor rights, women employed a gendered rhetoric that, while rooted in the language of anarcho-syndicalism, privileged motherhood and maternalism during a period in which the Mexican state used the same rhetoric to craft a more unified national narrative.[15] This gendered rhetoric complemented, clashed with, competed with, or reinforced ideas of a larger women's rights movement that had developed in the early twentieth century in great part to push for women's suffrage. In anarcho-syndicalist fashion, Piña and her colleagues believed in direct action in the form of strikes, protests, and spreading knowledge via the sharing of labor news across communities. They rejected participation in any political party or state entity and neither promoted nor engaged with the women's suffrage movement.

Transnationalizing Women's Experiences

During the 1920s and 1930s, Piña's ambit consisted of women and men from the Tampico-Cecilia region not only concerned with local and national labor developments but also attuned to the precarious situation of workers abroad. Their local activism reached workers from other parts of the country, across the border into Texas and other US states, and across the Atlantic. Equally important, external labor matters shaped developments in this local network.

The group engaged labor organizations outside its community, which helped them make sense of their own conditions and struggles. It also raised funds locally to send across state lines and across the border into Texas, among other places, while also asking for outside donations to fund local initiatives. Thus, the network assumed a Mexican and regional character but operated in transnational ways.

Recent methodological and theoretical frameworks that underscore transnationalism are quite useful to better analyze how this network functioned. I employ such an approach to further excavate and complicate the "distinctiveness [of] local spaces" that, while it acknowledges external reach, seeks to not obscure this important local history.[16] The regional network built on multiple histories and multiple experiences and was grounded and continuously shaped by local and extralocal conditions, at times informed by competing gendered ideas and political ideologies, class, and race-based and ethnicity-based nationalisms. Transnationalism, here, is defined as a process, a practice *made*/occurring during the moment of exchange between people and their ideas from different regional, cultural (gendered, racial, ethnic, language), class, and historical positionalities. Examining this labor network from a transnational perspective helps to reveal complexities of solidarities and activism not simply to show the successes and limitations of such solidarities but to show instead the promise, to borrow from historian Isabel Hofmeyr, of "transnational historical practice centered around [the] circulation of ideas and shared experiences to potentially offer a route for making visible a wider range of political possibilities."[17] It is this wider range of alternative narratives that I believe can expand the field and open a space for new insights that force us to reinterpret national histories and consider new historical actors, like Piña. This is particularly important as the history of female activists in anarcho-syndicalist and other radical movements in this corner of the globe has been almost nonexistent.

The ideas put forth by the theorist Gloria Anzaldúa—grounded on an intersectionality framework that interrogates race and ethnicity, class, sexuality, and gender—critically reflect on such transnational processes.[18] Anzaldúa's work serves as a model for historians to engage the ideas of in-betweenness of borderlands spaces to create nuanced, inclusive narratives of all its residents—past and present. Although Tampico and Villa Cecilia are not on the US-Mexican border, the early *magonista* activism that took place along the border influenced labor developments in this working-class corner of the country and helped to shape an early anarcho-feminist agenda. Many activists engaged in labor collectives in the port had some connection to the border region, carried those ideas with them, and shared them with others. This also included women activists.

For women activists, engaging in transnational feminism, to build on the ideas of Clara Roman-Odio and Marta Sierra, involved a "re-conceptualiz[ation] of location, not as a fixed category that reifie[d] identity politics, but as the product of intersections of class, race, ethnicity, sexuality, age, religion and gender." I would add geography.[19] These ideas reflect an Anzaldúan lens of a feminism that was expressed and practiced in transnational ways. And, as this book shows, many of the activists preceding Piña, those who collaborated with her, and Piña herself, engaged residents and workers on the Texas-Tamaulipas border quite frequently, sharing ideas about labor justice and solidarities. In this way, southern Tamaulipas became part of the larger US-Mexican border ambit, historically a crossroads of political, economic, and social ideological exchange. Her colleagues, including Librado Rivera and Felipa Velásquez, were specifically interested in reaching out to workers across the border into places like Texas and California and were equally concerned with critiquing and chipping away at American capitalist power. Such a transnational approach to labor matters complemented Piña's own ideas about social and political change. While these were informed by anarchism, they also were rooted in this geographical space with its own history of class, racial, and gendered hierarchies. Piña's ideas thus were a product of her own lived experience in a border state, "refracted through the interpretative terms available during specific time[s] and place[s]."[20]

Frequent correspondence between labor organizations and activists, the re-printing of commentaries in locally run anarchist newspapers, conversations in labor union meetings, and the sharing of this information throughout Tamaulipas and the Mexican republic as well as across the United States formed part of women's daily activities, which helped to sustain the labor activist network. In this cyclical process, despite news traveling much more slowly than it does in today's world, the extent to which activists from far-flung places shared news about labor developments in their communities with others was remarkable. This exporting and importing of news facilitated a rich dialogue between and among labor activists in different social and geographical contexts. Thus, labor activism was informed by the region's history, compounded by an export-oriented economy (which attracted workers from all over the world). It was also informed by ideas of race, community ideas of reciprocity, gendered ideas and expectations, and political ideology and equally shaped by external news. All of these factors figured prominently in the formation of a unique gender politics that further fed a labor rights discourse.[21]

Though Piña and her colleagues emerged during an era of social transformation typically characterized as the early phase of a feminist Mexican women's suffrage movement, Piña and the majority of her *compañeras* hardly ever referred to themselves as feminists and did not promote universal suffrage. Nonetheless, their activism embodied a type of feminism that promoted women as equals and women's involvement in anarcho-syndicalist activism elsewhere. As historian Susie Porter has explained, women who identified or expressed middle-class desires critiqued societal restraints on women based on prevailing gender norms. That critique helped to create and sustain a social movement aimed at improving women's conditions whether or not the designation was embraced. Porter argued that the same applied to working-class women.[22] In fact, as Piña's case reveals, her politics of labor activism indeed helped to promote women's rights, further sustaining a broader social movement.

Nineteenth-century ideas of domesticity and femininity guided much of the debate about women's place in society and particularly in discussions about labor matters. These ideas about the presumed proper roles of women and men reflected deeply entrenched social values, as Porter and other historians examining Mexican women's labor, including María Teresa Fernández Aceves and Heather Fowler-Salamini, have shown for women in urban centers as well as in the countryside.[23] As this book shows, Piña often advocated labor rights by invoking the unique position of female workers as mothers (or future mothers). While this strategy challenged normative gender ideas via broader ideas about equality, it also had the potential to reinforce existing gender inequalities. The idea and practice of domesticity and maternalism still figured prominently in shaping women's work identities as well as their activism, even in radical anarchist circles and for both working-class and middle-class female workers.[24] Piña and her colleagues employed maternalism as a way to "extol the private virtues of domesticity," to legit[imize] women's public relationship to politics and the state, to community, workplace, and the marketplace," as scholars Seth Koven and Sonya Michel have explained for women in other parts of the world.[25] Yet, further informed by anarchist beliefs, Piña's deployment of a maternalistic politics exemplified what could be called an anarcho-maternalism that directly challenged the state as the primary guarantor of women's rights. In this way, Piña's motherhood discourse was more a grassroots language, an anarchist expression that took women's reproductive capacity and made it their own, not the state's.

Just as Piña avoided subscribing to state dictates or feminist labels, she too avoided subscribing to the idea of states' geopolitical boundaries. She engaged communities as if they were borderless. She and some of her colleagues did not desire to create a nationless or borderless world, they simply functioned as if it were the case. Indeed, as historians Geoffroy de Laforcade and Kirwin Shaffer have written, anarchism's "local, national, transnational, and transregional [nature]" was a defining characteristic. Because of the fluidity with which anarchist ideas circulated across regional contexts and geopolitical borders, ideas about women's rights based on both local context and feminist ideas abroad found a welcoming place in such anarchist circles and outlined a vision of a world free from political boundaries and free from state control.[26]

Anarchism's "transregional" nature in the Gulf of Mexico area was greatly facilitated by the creativity of the local anarchist press, which reinforced older practices of community autonomy while embracing new and imported ideas from abroad. Among the most effective tools residents employed was the direct *petición*, popular since preindustrial times. The *petición* usually took the form of a letter to community representatives as well as to other residents or heads of state. This tradition continued well into the twentieth century, as I have argued elsewhere, and became a useful tool to address widespread socioeconomic changes ushered in by modern industrialization.[27] These petitions in the form of public calls for change were printed in the local press or shared through personal correspondence. Letters and commentaries about specific labor activists or appeals to labor justice were featured in anarchist newspapers published locally. Poems, creative writing, manifestos, and commentaries circulated beyond the communities the newspapers served. As was the case in other parts of Latin America, anarchist writings were frequently reprinted and shared among labor organizations elsewhere with similar goals. Featured news and information in these newspapers served a specific purpose as newspapers "were not neutral conduits of information"; these news outlets were "gatekeepers and filterers of ideas."[28] It was through the sharing of ideas in print—as well as close interactions in communities and worksites, among Mexicans from the countryside and other growing urban centers and recent arrivals from Europe, Latin America, and the United States—that ideas about labor rights became widespread. While many of these newspapers were free, staff usually received small donations in exchange for the mailing of several newspaper issues.[29] The local anarchist press also benefited tremendously and was able to grow its reputation via newspapers in larger urban centers. *¡Luz!*, published by the Casa del Obrero Mundial in Mexico City and with access to a wider public, for example, informed its readers about which newspapers it had received and reprinted selected stories from them. In one 1917 issue, it notified its readers that *¡Luz!* editors had received "25 copies of *Cultura Obrera* from New York, 5 from *Germinal* in Tampico, 50 copies of *El Rebelde* from Los Angeles, and 5 copies of each issue (4) from *Pro Vida* from Havana, Cuba." *¡Luz!* editors pledged they would do the same exchange with its newspaper. For smaller publications like *Germinal* in Tampico, this type of advertising was crucial in getting its localized concerns and ideas disseminated more widely.[30]

Germinal and *Tribuna Roja* were among the early twentieth-century anarchist newspapers operating before Piña entered the scene. By the 1920s, the anarchist press grew and *Sagitario* and *Avante* became the principal media outlets for anarchist groups operating in the Tampico and Cecilia region. These newspapers were endorsed by the CGT as local groups became affiliated with it by 1921. *Sagitario*, published by PLM cofounder Librado Rivera, focused on promoting the anarchist ideas of Ricardo Flores Magón, strategically differentiating the positions of the CGT and the Confederación Regional de Obrera Mexicana (CROM) and featuring editorials, commentaries, and other writings by well-known as well as lesser-known female activists and female organizations.[31] Other CGT newspapers included *Vía Libre, Nuestra Palabra, La Humanidad, El Niño Libre, El Preso Social,* and *El Galeote,* although not all of the issues I consulted are complete. *Verbo Rojo,* also an affiliate newspaper, was published by CGT members belonging to the Centro Sindicalista Libertario. It was among the core groups that sought to promote anarcho-syndicalist ideas, further strengthening the CGT's overall mission of direct action via unionism outside of political parties.[32] As the CGT developed, as explained in the following chapters, anarcho-syndicalism became the preferred approach to effecting change via labor unions, associations, and collectives. Anarcho-syndicalism emerged as the more structured platform with which to promote anarchist ideas privileging unions.

Engaging Latin American Anarcho-Feminist Historiography

Studies in the field of Latin American anarcho-feminism are crucial to understanding the complexities of labor activism in the Gulf of Mexico region. Similar movements emerged in other parts of Mexico, Chile, Argentina, and the Caribbean. These case studies provide a wider historical context with which to comparatively engage and examine the lived experiences of female labor activists in Tampico-Cecilia more specifically. Before turning to Tampico, it is important to examine Latin American anarcho-feminism in order to chart the growth and importance of this topic.

For the case of Mexico, the important recovery work on the history of the Casa del Obrero Mundial (COM), the anarcho-syndicalist movement in Veracruz, and the early Partido Liberal Mexicano (PLM) network conducted by historians Anna Ribera Carbó, Heather Fowler-Salamini and Andrew Grant Wood, and Devra Weber, respectively, have helped us re-create the world of Mexican radical labor. Ribera Carbó's numerous publications on the formation, dynamics, and relationships within the COM are key to understanding

Mexican labor's early ideas about "unionism without borders," reflecting the larger intent to build a global base of workers, hence a house (*casa*) of global (*mundial*) workers. This was a direct expression of anarchism and attracted both men and women early on, as it provided an alternative response to growing socioeconomic disparities that came with industrial capitalist development and its attendant urbanization. Ribera Carbó provides partial yet crucial biographical data on some of the female pioneers of the COM, including the important leader Reynalda González Parra, cofounder of the Tampico COM. González Parra's activism exemplifies the gradual inclusion of women in the larger conversation about labor. The early COM anarcho-feminists embraced Barcelona native Francisco Ferrer's radical, rational approach to education, which proposed equal instruction for boys and girls and ardently critiqued clericalism. These ideas profoundly shaped the Tampico COM branch, which emerged as one of the leading unions in the nation and quickly garnered international support, particularly from the Industrial Workers of the World (IWW) with its similar global outlook.[33]

The Tampico COM worked collaboratively with other groups of an anarcho-syndicalist nature as well as labor collectives of diverse ideological orientation in the greater Gulf of Mexico region, particularly Veracruz. Historians Heather Fowler-Salamini and Andrew Grant Wood have examined radical labor activism in that port city and detail the gendered nature of the movement—within the *cigarrera* work sites with considerable anarcho-syndicalist support and in the renters' movement, in which women anarchists played a key role. Crucial to our own understanding of the Tampico-Cecilia experience is the way in which *obrero* and *obrera* identities emerged. Fowler-Salamini and Wood re-create the history of labor activism to include a substantial segment of the female population. In Veracruz, large numbers of women employed in the coffee export sector presented demands that were often met, given the urgency with which coffee growers needed to export their goods. Thus, similar to the export-driven sector of the Tampico-Cecilia region, which was tied to the ebbs and flows of oil demand, a large workforce could develop a strong collective voice. This improved their chances at collective bargaining compared to smaller workforces that depended on a more regional market. Anarcho-syndicalism thrived, much as in Tampico-Cecilia. Yet, as the CROM and other organizations including the Peasant League gained strength through their alliance with the state, which moved to implement pro-labor reforms, the anarcho-syndicalist push declined. The Veracruz female coffee sorters' and renters' movements stand as examples of women's effective use of unionism to negotiate issues they considered top priorities including rent, food prices, and fair wages.[34]

Both Tampico-Cecilia and Veracruz, with a long history of maritime importance, maintained strong links across communities in the Gulf of Mexico including Cuba and Puerto Rico. Building upon such historic connections, not surprisingly, workers and residents engaged in a multidirectional exchange of ideas that extended to other parts of Latin America and farther across the Atlantic. The dynamism and crucial role of the Caribbean in the promotion of anarcho-feminist and working-class ideas is evident in the work of Kirwin Shaffer, Eileen J. Suárez Findlay, and Nancy A. Hewitt.[35] By the turn of the twentieth century, women from working-class as well as more affluent backgrounds concerned with the women question participated in activist circles affiliated with anarchist reading groups and mutual aid societies. Cuba, in particular Havana, as Shaffer has amply documented, emerged as a crucial crossroads. Ideas about liberty and equality circulating in the capital—imported from Spain, Latin America, and elsewhere—grew locally and influenced developments in US states like Florida and New York; these ideas further meshed and shaped life in the island in profound ways. Cuban women as well as island immigrants formed part of this circuit of knowledge, yet, as Shaffer points out, women were also used to explain the ills of society. As with anarcho-syndicalist organizations in the Tampico-Cecilia region, Cuban anarchist newspapers employed gendered language to portray rival organizations and "bourgeois" women were cast as threats to the working class. Anarchist activists running the press encouraged and welcomed female members to their organizations. In short, despite anarchism's quest for libertarian ideals, gendered and racialized ideas often shaped ideas espoused by activists via their press and organizations.[36] This corresponds to the gendered and racialized ways in which working-class movements were structured and is evident in other analyses of Puerto Rican labor activism and individual labor leaders.

As ideas about labor equality promoted by anarchists, socialists, and communist sympathizers circulated in the greater Caribbean, the dynamic political and social context produced labor leaders like Luisa Capetillo. As Nancy Hewitt explains, Puerto Rican native Capetillo spent her childhood consuming the anarchist ideas about equality and human dignity shared by her parents. This early exposure to anarchism positioned her quite firmly, as a young adult, in the anarcho-syndicalist movement. Unlike some of her colleagues, though, Capetillo promoted universal suffrage, supporting the initiative while still remaining active in direct-action strategies via unionism. Similar to Caritina Piña and other activists from Tamaulipas, Capetillo politicized ideas of motherhood as a mother and worker herself defending the rights of *obreras*. Also resembling Piña's own limitations, Capetillo, as Suárez Findlay explains, responded to a changing cultural and political landscape that sought to reform residents and workers via deeply rooted ideas about gender and sexuality. Imperfect in some of her actions, Capetillo, nonetheless, assumed a central position in the larger social movements of the time and played a crucial role in the wider circulation of ideas in the Caribbean as well as in the United States in places like Florida.[37] Placed within the profound social and political transformations taking place in the Caribbean in the first decades of the twentieth century, Capetillo stands as a reminder of a long legacy of women's activism. Taken together, these studies by Shaffer, Suárez Findlay, and Hewitt exemplify how anarchist thought flowed from region to region through the press or via the migration of individuals like Capetillo.[38]

Other studies focused on the shared histories and struggles of workers from various parts of Latin America, including but not limited to women in anarchist movements, also shed light on the ideological links rooted in anarchist thought that brought disparate regions and their residents and workers closer.[39] Such ideas complemented and further strengthened similar working-class movements in places undergoing industrial capitalist development. The work of Maxine Molyneux and Elizabeth Quay Hutchison is of particular importance in documenting this connection with anarchist influences, specifically the role of anarcho-feminists, in places such as Argentina and Chile. The rapid growth of urban centers like Buenos Aires mirrored the path toward industrialization and urbanization that took place in Tampico and other Mexican urban centers. Molenyoux's earlier work on the emergence of "anarchist feminism" in that part of the globe corresponds to my findings about similar processes in the Tampico region. The combination of "rapid economic growth" along with "an influx of European immigrants," together with the basis of an earlier labor movement provided the necessary environment for the development of a unique anarcho-feminism.[40] Native and immigrant Argentinean women shared their critiques about social inequities and included commentaries about women's economic conditions in local newspapers such as *La Voz de la Mujer*. Molyneux's contention that unlike the "feminism as bourgeois" critique found in other parts of Latin America, in Buenos Aires, the idea of feminism emerged as a radical idea tied to revolutionary ideals based on working-class experience.[41] This origin seems to correspond to at least some of the organizations that emerged in Tampico, principally the Liga Cultural, which unlike Piña's Comité, espoused a feminist framework tied to the proletarian class that specifically spoke to *obreras*. The writings of Argentinean anarchist women such as Florinda Mondini were frequently reprinted in Villa Cecilia's radical *Avante*. References to the excesses of industrial capitalism in urban sites such as Buenos Aires and critiques of women factory workers' deplorable health conditions resonated with labor conditions found in Tampico and other Mexican centers confronting similar challenges. Around the same time as *La Voz de la Mujer* appeared in Buenos Aires, similar newspapers aimed at and by women appeared in other major Latin American cities.

In similar ways, Chilean women, attracted by anarchism's seemingly progressive stance on women's issues, became active in the nascent Chilean labor movement. While socialism and communism appealed to segments of the Chilean workforce and residents, anarchism played a role early on in the formation of a specific socioeconomic and political critique. As Hutchison explains, women did participate in the anarchist movement and early struggles to effect change. However, by the 1920s, anarchists' portrayals of women became more critical and unsupportive. Yet, because most of the writings were produced by men, Hutchison cautions that the prescriptive literature on women's education and emancipation via radical mobilizations was just that, an ideal to which anarchists subscribed. This did not "take the form of a women's movement."[42] Instead, similar to Shaffer's findings for Cuba about activists from the island employing the image of the downtrodden *obrera*, Hutchison explains that the inclusion of women's issues in anarchist publications had more to do with "the history of the ideological and activist evolution of Chilean anarchism, and not . . . the history of women's consciousness or mobilization in Chile."[43] This deployment of the female image in the anarchist press analyzed by both Hutchison and Shaffer reflects the early phase of anarchism in the Tampico-Cecilia region. Yet, by the mid-1920s, in great part due to the strength of the oil industry (despite moments of declining oil production), women from all economic sectors in Tampico-Cecilia were quite active in labor movements—anarcho-syndicalist and otherwise—from waitresses and oil camp workers to paid domestic workers. It is likely that their participation grew as female activists played a greater role in decisions about how women were portrayed in the anarchist press.

This larger Latin American anarcho-feminist historiography forms a foundation from which to further build the specific historiography of Tampico-Cecilia. The pioneering work of historian Leif Adelson on Tampico oil worker culture built upon the archival discoveries of Carlos González Salas; Aurora Mónica Alcayaga Sasso's work on Librado Rivera, Kevin Aguilar's recent work on the IWW in Tampico, and Mary Goldsmith Connelly and Myrna Santiago's groundbreaking research on women workers from various ideological backgrounds have all contributed to the creation of a rich Tampico labor historiography. Such work helps re-create an inclusive picture of the region's working class that acknowledges the participation of female workers and female activists.[44]

Repositories including the Esteban Méndez Guerra collection were organized thanks to the early work of Tampico chronicler Carlos González Salas. Further, the indexing of important working-class newspapers that documented the rich history of oil workers helped scholars such as Leif Adelson make use of this key material to re-create the social and cultural history of thousands of oil workers from the Mexican countryside, emerging urban centers, and abroad. While describing a mostly male labor force, Adelson opened up a window into the complexities of life and work in the oil camps and labor collective of the port and its working-class neighborhoods. Providing an in-depth look into the oil work culture so aptly described by Adelson, historian Alcayaga Sasso zeroed in on the circulation of anarchist thought promoted by Librado Rivera and the Tampico anarcho-syndicalist movement via Hermanos Rojos, which was consumed by oil and other workers. Her dissertation is a bibliographic treasure, as it documents the circulation of early anarchist newspapers supported, run, or promoted by Rivera.[45] Notwithstanding its detailed description of the larger efforts of Rivera and colleagues that placed Tampico and its surrounding area at the forefront of a global labor movement, Alcayaga Sasso's work, like Adelson's, did not examine the movement's gendered nature.

Few studies have incorporated a gendered analysis of Tampico's working class. Mary Goldsmith's work on female paid domestic workers during the 1930s and 1940s is a significant intervention in this area. Her analysis of labor grievances submitted by female domestic workers to the federal and state labor boards not only reveals the gendered nature of the domestic service sector, which included work in hotels and similar establishments as well as in private homes, but also testifies to the labor activism of women even in sectors that have proven challenging to organize.[46] This is significant given that women dominated the domestic service sector. They created their union and made use of the labor reforms enacted in the postrevolutionary period despite the challenges of working in disparate sites (particularly tough for those who labored in people's homes). Myrna Santiago, like Goldsmith, broadened this historical interpretation by centering on the experiences of women workers in the oil camps, continuing the labor of recuperating women's history in the Tampico-Cecilia region. Santiago's work takes a geographically broader approach, analyzing Tamaulipas and northern Veracruz. She accounts for women's labor of all classes, including that of the wives of foreign entrepreneurs, whose often invisible labor helped position the region in a larger global economy. From providing sex work to cleaning services to working in the executive offices of the petroleum corporations, women's labor in Tampico emerges as more inclusive and complex thanks to Santiago's and Goldsmith's work.[47]

Similarly, Kevin Antonio Aguilar's recent work builds upon this rich and complex research by examining the IWW and its links to the Tampico COM and the PLM, shedding important light on the international dimensions of the port's working class.[48] While the focus is documenting the transnational nature of the IWW and its appeal to PLM and COM adherents, there is some discussion of women's participation in early efforts to promote labor rights, particularly as it relates to Tampico's Centro de Estudios Sociales Feministas, in which Reynalda González Parra took part. Aguilar's work complements other studies that, while they do not focus on Tampico, are critical to recovering the history of Mexican workers and of the Indigenous workers' support for the PLM as examined by historian Devra Weber.[49]

Taken together, four major conclusions can be drawn from this scholarly tradition that sheds light on the specific Tampico-Cecilia case with respect to women's involvement in radical labor activism. First, anarchism in the greater Gulf of Mexico as well as in most places in Latin America opened up a space in which women's issues—both working class and otherwise—could be included, which helped to make sense of a growing labor unrest tied to industrial capitalism. Second, *obrera* concerns and conditions featured in the anarchist press were recruiting tools employed by anarchist groups. Yet any obstacle to the ideas and practices of anarchism was gendered in such a way that monikers such as "bourgeois" or "prostitute" were used to speak of society's ills. Third, women's participation in the more structured anarcho-syndicalist movement was crucial in sustaining a wider movement that, while it concerned itself with issues affecting women, was broader and emphasized worker unity along class lines. Finally, the region's historic ties to the Texas border region helped to create a transregional, transnational framework within which female activists spoke about rights and collaborated with women and men engaged in similar struggles; ultimately, this helped to forge a feminism that was doubly regional and transnational.

Book Structure

This book builds upon the aforementioned literary and theoretical historiographical tradition. It traces labor activism across geopolitical borders through several chapters based on multinational archival research. The circulation of ideas that shaped life and society on both sides of the border between the United States and Mexico in the late nineteenth and early twentieth centuries formed the basis of future exchange. These ideas reflected the various strands of anarchist thought and later anarcho-syndicalism, which aligned quite nicely with localized ideas about community autonomy, political rights, and access to arable land that had begun to circulate during the years leading up to and during the Porfirio Díaz regime in Mexico. Thus, my opening chapter explains how, as a burgeoning cosmopolitan port, Tampico attracted foreigners that had been exposed to unconventional ideas about access to safe and well-paying jobs abroad. Tampico was home to some of the largest petroleum corporations that dominated the world's oil industry in the first half of the twentieth century. Lured by higher wages and steady employment, Mexican men—single or accompanied by their families, from the countryside as well as nearby *poblados* or villages (including Caritina Piña's neighborhood in Villa Cecilia)—found work in the oilfields, docks, and associated service sectors. Ideas about labor rights articulated in the writings of key philosophers from Spain, Greece, and France circulated widely in the port and appealed to both Mexicans and foreigners. At the same time, Mexican women and men's ideas about labor conditions were shaped by their local experiences during the Porfirian regime, and these ideas were further exported to other places by travelers and migrants and via newspapers, letters, commentaries, poems, and manifestos.

As this exchange of ideas emerged, in great part facilitated via news sharing through correspondence and via migration flows from the Mexican countryside, so did a discourse about labor rights that began to incorporate women as *obreras* and residents with legitimate concerns. Crucial to this early women's rights agenda was a *magonista* movement that incorporated women's issues and helped to pave a broader road for the crafting of a women's rights agenda that included a push for labor equity.

As chapter 1 shows, Tampico-Cecilia became a hotbed of labor activism in a relatively short time, as its diverse population encouraged labor organizing and opened its doors to women. In the process, it became the ideological hub of the Mexican northeastern borderlands as these radical labor ideas filtered farther inland and northward along Texas's Rio Grande Valley. Along Tamaulipas's northern border with Texas, these ideas about labor rights appealed to residents and workers, given both the increased presence of recent Mexican immigrants and the long history of Mexican-origin communities in Texas. By the turn of the twentieth century, such discourse on labor rights resonated strongly as revolutionary rhetoric became widespread. The decline in socioeconomic and political power experienced by the bulk of the Mexican-origin population in Texas (among other states) exacerbated growing wage disparities. Organizations along the border with affiliations to the greater Gulf of Mexico region and northern Mexico formed part of the early foundation and the base of support of a larger labor network. This further encouraged more women to participate in activism.

Given the region's dynamic labor activism, state authorities—often in conjunction with federal authorities—worked to limit immigration to the port. They detained migrants deemed "radical" and set the boundaries of labor activism. An influx of men and women from various corners of the world arrived in search of employment in the oil sector and associated industries including shipping, fishing, hunting, hotel work, and restaurant and bar work. The number of foreign workers correlated with a surge in migrants from the Mexican countryside, like Piña, making for a diverse environment conducive, according to Mexican officials, to producing "dangerous radicals" or, in the case of female activists, "women of ill-repute." Immigrants-turned-workers imported radical ideas perceived as damaging to the stability of the region and were perceived as threats to the greater project of reconstructing Mexico in the aftermath of the Mexican Revolution. Taking this socioeconomic and political context, chapter 2 examines the gendered complexities of such developments as well as of anarcho-syndicalism itself, as it incorporated many of these newly arrived immigrants, locals, and Mexicans from the countryside. The chapter argues two major points. On the one hand, early groups such as Hermanos Rojos and the national CGT were among those organizations that embraced women's participation and promoted women as "*compañeras en la lucha*" (companions/comrades in the fight), shaping an early discourse of working women as central to revolutionary struggle. But these organizations were nonetheless highly gendered and often employed, similar to what Shaffer and Hutchison described for other parts of Latin America, references to gendered norms and sexuality. These developments took place as the revolutionary state castigated certain types of labor activism. State officials, particularly those who endorsed Venustiano Carranza's revolutionary government, as well as media outlets deemed nonanarchist or mainstream, described women engaged in anarchist or communist activism as "women of ill-repute." By the 1920s, a safer, nonthreatening state-sanctioned socialist activism became the standard by which to measure and censure all other activism. Women involved in radical activism suffered attacks on their morality and sexuality. As Mexico promoted a discourse that privileged the strengthening of families to reconstruct the nation and promote Mexican unity, women's societal roles were expanded so as to emphasize the state's renewed commitment to their equality, yet they were defined predominantly as crucial reproducers of community as mothers, wives, and caregivers. State authorities seeking to control the flow of radical ideas and regulate labor activism placed women's morality under a magnifying glass. Gendered expectations and norms rooted in nineteenth-century conceptions of morality and sexuality worked to categorize women who transgressed such boundaries as immoral. Yet women involved in the labor movement of all stripes—anarcho-syndicalist, communist, socialist, and those claiming no ideological or political affiliation—continued to promote women's rights to improve their material conditions.

Despite a thorough discussion as well as a descriptive index of the Esteban Méndez Guerra Archive published in the 1980s and housed in the state capital of Tamaulipas, there is no mention of labor activist Caritina Piña. As my examination of those holdings indicates, Piña was present in the records and present in Tampico's labor movement. Chapter 3 centers on Piña and her network and addresses this major oversight in the historiography. I trace Piña's role as secretary of correspondence in the Comité Internacional Pro-Presos Sociales, which directly positioned her at the center of the anarcho-syndicalist movement and greater labor movement. She was accountable for exporting ideas about labor and the movement itself in Tampico, as she was responsible for documenting the receipt of letters, newspapers, and other propaganda from labor organizations and labor activists across the US-Mexico border and in other parts of the globe. She oversaw material coming from places such as New York and Barcelona and shared news about local Mexican labor conditions with labor collectives in those places. Piña directly helped to produce and reproduce knowledge about labor issues not only in her native Mexico. She did the same with conditions concerning workers living and working in North Carolina, New York, Barcelona, and Buenos Aires. Nonetheless, as the opening anecdote on Piña's intervention in the North Carolina labor strike reveals, her ideas about labor justice were frequently colored by deeply rooted prejudices and personal biases concerning race and ethnicity as well as her own ideas about gender. Despite the high ideals to which anarchists like Piña adhered, they were human and had their own faults. Her limitations as an imperfect activist, revealed via some of her petitions on behalf of political prisoners, show her emerging nationalist bias stemming from the way she understood race and ethnicity.

Efforts to forge alliances and show solidarity between women and men from Mexico and other parts of the globe nonetheless continued. Piña's own engagement with others abroad and in Mexico via print media and correspondence reveals a feminism that emerged in tandem with the rise of the labor movement yet was anchored in anarchist beliefs and practiced through anarcho-syndicalism, as she believed in collective union and direct action. Anarcho-syndicalism privileged the labor organization or union as the entity by which to express, practice, and promote anarchist ideas. The Mexican scholar Guillermina Baena Paz, who compiled a foundational anthology on the origins of the CGT, defined it in the following way: "anarcho-syndicalism was a variant of anarchism, which envisioned an economic structure based on the union, which sought to reorganize society through its affiliated groups and ultimately, through its main general confederation."[50] The main activities of anarcho-syndicalists consisted of "direct everyday revolutionary action that culminated in the strike, which would bring about a real revolution."[51] Anarcho-syndicalism became the platform and foundation by which to put anarchist ideas to practice.[52]

While considered part of the radical labor wing, women and fellow union members who petitioned on behalf of political prisoners, unions, agrarian cooperatives, and similar entities often employed the language of motherhood, which underscored the importance of women as caregivers and reproducers of community. Such language was employed by the revolutionary government and used to incorporate women into politics—in limited ways, as women were still barred from voting (in Mexico) among other things. Anarchist women further politicized the idea, underscoring the premise that all were equal and rejecting any argument that privileged the state as the ultimate arbiter. Chapter 4 examines these developments and discusses women's use of the language of motherhood to advance larger, radical ideas about women's equality, particularly as it related to working-class women.

Throughout Piña's tenure as secretary of correspondence of the Comité during the mid-1920s and early 1930s, labor unionism was on the rise in Mexico in the wake of the legalization of unions in 1917. Yet, while the number of labor unions increased in Tampico-Cecilia (in the 1920s throughout the 1970s, the region was among the most organized in the country), there were women who chose not to join unions or abandoned them altogether. In chapter 5, I examine this discrepancy in what became known as the "free waitress movement," which included over two hundred women who chose to leave their union, claiming that unions were "better off left to the men." These waitresses organized, but they did so emphasizing mutualism. Scholarship on labor has explained the rise of labor unions as building upon nineteenth-century mutual aid societies. In a city such as Tampico, with well over one hundred different labor unions—from organizations comprised of carpenters, and even a domestic workers' union—the waitresses' decision to form their own "free" organization contradicted the port's crucial role in labor unionism.

As the chapter will show, ideas about morality and sexuality coupled with the state's expansion of a prostitution tolerance zone (a direct consequence of the rise of the oil industry) had a profound effect on the way in which waitresses were perceived and controlled by the local mixed-sex restaurant workers labor union. The free waitress movement thus serves as an instance of labor activism outside the confines of formal unions and reveals much about how women perceived the practice of organizing. Ultimately, I describe it as an anarchist expression. It also sheds light on how state discourse on labor rights, ideas about gender and sexuality, and questions about women's place on a more global scale could sharply differ from women's own localized ideas about their own place in labor.

Further, chapter 6 reveals the limits of transnational feminisms in the wake of the Emilio Portes Gil administration's use of women's political engagement as a tool with which to modernize gender inequality. This was at the core of Portes Gil's state-sanctioned, controlled labor activism. Beginning in the mid-1920s and through the end of the 1940s, state-initiated reforms and their accompanying discourse politicized the role of women as loyal *compañeras*. They suggested the ideal modern woman was strong and independent yet supportive of her husband or her fellow citizens, her *compañeros*, and fought for the family's well-being. The chapter will address the use of such rhetoric and its place in the broader labor movement as Portes Gil's Partido Socialista Fronterizo (PSF) sought to promote socialism to reconstruct the state and promote nationalism by further marginalizing and criminalizing anarchism and communism. Radical labor activism, outside of the confines of the state, was deemed unacceptable and thus repressed.

Taken together these chapters provide a window into women's early participation in radical labor activism, which led to the world that produced Caritina Piña. Never having stepped outside of Mexico, at least per the historical record, Piña embodied the characteristics of a transnational cultural [labor] broker, to borrow a concept from historian Samuel Truett.[53] Through the sharing of knowledge about labor rights, Piña helped to give public voice to a women's agenda that built on the ideas of early feminist voices. Piña and her network of women and men practiced a transnational feminism that, while framed in the language and context of labor, paved the way for women's inclusion, albeit uneven, in a new, postrevolutionary world. Retracing the crucial and often risky activities in which Piña and her colleagues engaged, pieced together from various repositories in Mexico and the United States, I heed historian Julie Greene's call for a transnational history that "list[ens] and learn[s] about discrete national histories, even as we examine global processes that connect them" and builds from "multiarchival research in diverse nations and serious engagement with the historiographies of those nations," in order to create a more inclusive history of labor activism in the greater Mexican borderlands.[54]

Through a journey into Piña and her colleagues' activism, this book suggests a different narrative, a different "political possibility/ies," for the study of women and labor. It seeks to underscore a *continuous* presence of women, key in shaping their respective communities via labor activism and reflects on "feminisms . . . [as] multiple and variegated not only *over* time and place, but *in* the same time and place," as articulated by historian Eileen Boris.[55] These varied experiences further exemplify what Yaël Simpson Fletcher has alluded to as constituting the concept and term *women's* in *women's activism* (just like other terms including "global" and "movement"), "to emphasize that women do not have to be self-conscious feminists to come together to better their own condition; to open the possibility of multiple feminisms."[56] The transnational feminisms Piña and colleagues practiced helped to create a "better world for all workers."[57] While it had its limits, particularly as anarcho-syndicalism declined by the early to mid-1930s corresponding to the Mexican state's co-opting of organized labor, it nonetheless left a long legacy still felt in the region today.

The Circulation of Radical Ideologies, Early Transnational Collaboration, and Crafting a Women's Agenda

[To members of] la Casa del Obrero Mundial, . . . [the Casa is
a] mother—simple and loving. . . . [I]t is time to realize that
men are unnecessary, it is time to realize that the opinion
of one is not always the opinion of the entire collective.

—Reynalda González Parra, 1915

Hailing from Mexico City and among thousands of migrants moving to the port of Tampico in 1915, Reynalda González Parra was one of the early female contributors to the anarchist press at least five years before Caritina Piña arrived. González Parra took to the pen, as thinkers before her did, expressing her frustration with the status quo through the small but influential anarchist press. The opening up of anarchist collectives and their accompanying newspapers to op-eds on women's status, poems, and thought pieces by women like González Parra, as well as editorials by male colleagues about the need to embrace women as "*compañeras en la lucha*," paved the road for the increased participation and visibility of women such as Caritina Piña in postrevolutionary Mexico. What conditions gradually increased the visibility of women's issues in the anarchist press during this early period? Why did a segment of the female population become attracted to anarchist principles? And how did they seek to put those ideas to practice, especially concerning a specific women's rights agenda in the context of labor? The gradual opening of prolabor organizations and collectives such as the Partido Liberal Mexicano and the Casa del Obrero Mundial to include women's issues in their periodicals and encourage women's participation in their ranks sparked a more robust presence of women in labor matters. The founding of such organizations, however, did not happen in a vacuum.

Anarchism's Influence in the Mexican Borderlands

Since its founding in 1823, Tampico emerged as a bustling port in the Gulf of Mexico with socioeconomic and political ties to Bagdad and Matamoros in Tamaulipas, Veracruz, Galveston, New Orleans, Havana, San Juan, and other ports across the Atlantic. Ideas about worker autonomy and livable wages found a welcoming environment in Tampico and its vicinity and circulated widely, transforming the port into one of the leading labor radical sites of the world by the early twentieth century. Tampico became the ideological hub and gateway to the Mexican Northeastern borderlands. It served as the main port for shipping and commerce for inland cities such as Ciudad Victoria, Monterrey, and towns in between, extending north toward the old Villas del Norte, which by 1848 comprised part of the border between the United States and Mexico.

The circulation of such ideas thrived in working-class enclaves including the small town of Villa Cecilia, which served as the home for hundreds, then thousands who descended upon the region. From the southern sector of Tamaulipas and toward its border with Texas, men and women, workers and nonworkers alike, participated in some of the more extreme radical activity of their time, promoting big ideas that had the potential to effect material and political change.[1]

The roots of anarchist thought date back to at least the French Revolution of the late eighteenth century. These ideas soon reached the Americas.[2] The Gulf of Mexico, in particular, shared a long history of transatlantic commerce. Veracruz and Tampico had ties to ports including Barcelona and Liverpool as well as urban centers like Madrid and Paris. Barcelona in particular had a long, rich labor history, and Catalan workers shared manifestos and other writings with their European community, Latin America, and other parts of the world. Barcelona's emergent working class shared its lived experiences in print editorials and news stories via Tampico and Veracruz. These ideas were diffused in the countryside and further inland, reaching other cities. As various ports and nascent industrial centers witnessed growth, ideas about labor justice and autonomy became increasingly represented in writings by anarchists, further influencing the growing workforce.

Gradually, different strands of anarchist thought emerged. These ranged from the nonviolent anarchism to the branch associated with assassination plots, bombs, and other more destructive forms of expression. During the nineteenth

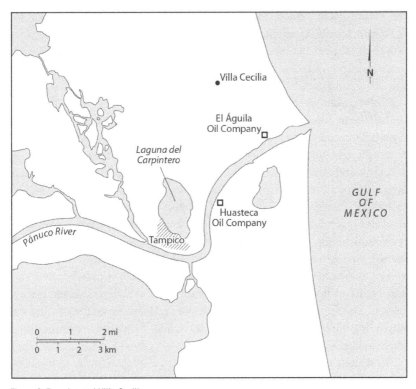

Figure 2. Tampico and Villa Cecilia

century, anarchism and other radical forms of thought began to make headway in North America. Soon thereafter, it served as the intellectual framework guiding reading clubs, secret societies, and mutual aid groups whose members sought to effect change in their local communities by acting upon such ideology.

As the French Intervention came to a close in Mexico in the 1860s, Mexican artisans, workers, and political thinkers forged what would become a more structured labor movement. Labor-focused congresses were organized throughout the country as well as in the capital. Textile, tobacco, and mine workers organized collectives and engaged in some of the earliest strikes in the country. These developments were further strengthened as anarchists fleeing political repression sought refuge in Mexico and shared their own social and political ideas. Greek socialist and anarchist (and, briefly, a Mormon convert) Plotino Rhodakanaty was among the thinkers who migrated to Mexico City. In the capital, Rhodakanaty helped to establish an anarchist organization, La Social, which emphasized "liberty, equality, and fraternity" and sought to create a pan-nationalist movement. He recruited both men and women to the organization. Some Mexican women, including Soledad Sosa, later served as delegates to the first Mexican National Labor Congress as early as 1876.[3] The passionate Greek immigrant espoused women's rights and was among the most progressive of his European anarchist contemporaries regarding women's issues.[4]

Other thinkers, such as the Frenchman Pierre-Joseph Proudhon and Russian Mikhail Bakunin, helped to spread anarchist thought in its varied forms. By the 1870s Bakunin advocated the abolition of hereditary property, the distribution of land for agricultural communities, and equality for women.[5] At the heart of Bakunin's and other anarchists' beliefs was the rejection of government and advocacy for collective and individual autonomy. In similar fashion, the ideas of the Italian Giuseppe Fanelli introduced anarcho-syndicalism as a more structured idea that privileged worker unity and autonomy through labor collectives or unions. In Spain, Madrid and Barcelona became hotspots of labor unrest, and Spanish anarchists soon collaborated with Mexican anarchists. Over 300,000 workers sympathetic to anarcho-syndicalism founded the Confederación Nacional del Trabajo in 1910 and joined forces with the Federación Anarquista Ibérica.[6] The founding of such collectives was possible given the continuous outpouring of ideas from anarchist and anarchist-sympathetic communities and individuals that shook the status quo.[7]

Conditions for women workers in Barcelona resembled those in increasingly industrialized and urban centers in Mexico. All-female labor associations emerged in the Spanish port to address growing economic inequalities and provide mutual assistance. These included the Sociedad Progresiva Femenina, the Federación Sindical de Obreras, and the Secció Mútua Feminal del Centre Autonomista de Dependents del Comerçi de la Industria.[8] Spanish anarchists, like other European contemporaries, helped to spread the ideas of Barcelona native Francisco Ferrer i Guardia, whose influence profoundly shaped the Mexican labor movement.[9]

By the turn of the twentieth century, mining centers, smelters, railroad worksites, and other industrial establishments expanded, particularly in the Mexican North, with a corresponding increase in free wage labor that shaped the contours of the Porfirian politico-economic system. While the "existence of wage workers alone did not imply the existence of a proletariat," the combination of such changes in labor systems with sharp divisions based on wage inequality and—for export-driven sectors like Tampico—the presence of foreigners and attendant industrial workers gave rise to a "collective group identity."[10] This shared experience became further radicalized as workers were exposed to anarchist ideas that had the potential to radically change people's outlook and effect material change. Such potential to alter the status quo made anarchy an attractive ideology in Mexico, best represented in *magonismo* by the first years of the century.

As Mexican historiography has shown, much of the discontent in the country grew from years of subjection to a dictatorship that limited people's political and labor rights. Porfirio Díaz cracked down on early labor organizing, much of it tied to anarchist and other socialist activity. Despite his shutting down presses and imprisoning opposition thinkers and activists, the critique continued underground. Mexicans' discontent with Díaz received support from labor organizations abroad. For example, *Páginas Libres*, a Barcelona proworker newspaper, reprinted correspondence from Mexican organizations, and editorials reflected its solidarity with Mexican workers, showcasing their support for a global working class. *Páginas Libres'* editorial team took pride in publishing commentaries on the abuses committed by Díaz. As one story put it, "Porfirio Díaz is simply a jackal . . . a monster, thirsty for blood, always seeking greatness."[11] Newspapers such as *Páginas Libres* as well as the local anarchist press played a critical role in the early spread of ideas about political and labor rights. They provided an outlet for the ideas of Flores Magón and his supporters, who became known as *magonistas*. *Páginas Libres* and *Rebelde* from Barcelona as well as scores of other proanarchist, proworker periodicals circulated throughout Europe and the Americas. Their news and commentaries were reprinted in the main *magonista* outlet, *Regeneración*, as well as Tampico and Villa Cecilia–based newspapers. These periodicals—either full issues or specific news clippings—made their way across the Atlantic, shared among activists and between organizations, carried via ship by workers and others as well as through regular mail.

Villa Cecilia and Tampico: A Home for Anarcho-Syndicalists

Villa Cecilia and Tampico became a hub of anarcho-syndicalist activity by the early twentieth century. Villa Cecilia, about four miles from the port of Tampico, was named for wealthy widow Cecilia Villarreal. After her husband Manuel Casados died, Villarreal donated land for the townsite and soon the small *ranchería* quickly expanded, reaching *villa* status. The town maintained close ties to *poblados* such as Árbol Grande that expanded as oil explorations intensified by the late nineteenth and early twentieth centuries.

In 1885, the governor of Tamaulipas, Rómulo Cuellar, authorized California investor Edward Doheny to install a *planta perfeccionadora*, the first oil processing site in the Mexican republic. Tampico had both a geological and geographic advantage. It was part of the *faja de oro*, or gold belt, along the Gulf of Mexico with rich oil

Figure 3. Warehouse of the Huasteca Petroleum Company, Villa Cecilia. Courtesy, Dolph Briscoe Center for American History, University of Texas at Austin.

Figure 4. Oil tank cars on the loading docks, Tampico, ca. 1910–1920. Courtesy, Dolph Briscoe Center for American History, University of Texas at Austin.

deposits. The port also offered petroleum corporations a reliable transportation system via its waterways. It was the perfect investment venture. A newsletter for oil investors in the United States described the region's transport advantages: "Tampico is very well located as regards inland waterways. The Panuco and Tamesi Rivers that flow through Tampico are navigable for boats drawing 10 feet for a distance of over 50 miles and for canoes drawing 1 ½ feet for a distance of 200 miles. Great quantities of coffee, hides, skins, honey, and miscellaneous other articles are brought from distant interior points to Tampico in canoes."[12]

Besides waterways, the arrival of the railroad connected Tampico to interior points in the region, including Monterrey via Ciudad Victoria, and farther north to the border towns of Laredo, Reynosa, and Matamoros with access to Texas and beyond. The same newsletter boasted of future rail projects consisting of rail bridges over waterways. Tampico's proximity to the United States, compared to Mexico City, led investors to favor it over the port of Veracruz as "it [would] be a shorter haul," once the rail line "constructed by the National Lines is well under way."[13]

Besides its historic cultural and commercial maritime ties to ports and cities across the Atlantic, Tampico's reach extended toward the Huastecan Mountains to the southwest, the *ixtle*-growing region to the west toward Monterrey, and the fertile Río Grande delta to the north toward Texas. Its strategic location as a port of entry facilitated news sharing. Tampico became, as historian Manuel Ceballos Ramírez has argued, a sort of "*bisagra*," or hinge, of the southern Gulf Coast region, which included Veracruz and other states with long histories of peasant resistance.[14]

By the dawn of the new century, foreign petroleum corporations flocked to Tampico as more petroleum deposits were discovered. Oil flowed as if endlessly, at times completely flooding old Huastecan indigenous *pueblos*. In addition to

Figure 5. Railroad yards from the bluff, Tampico, ca. 1880–1900. Library of Congress, Prints and Photographs Division, LC-D4-4166.

the American Edward Doheny's Huasteca Oil Company, the British ran major petroleum companies such as El Águila and Pierce.[15] Although other oil companies set up shop in the region, the big three—Huasteca, Águila, and Pierce—dominated oil production and recruited the largest labor force. Thousands of workers were employed at the height of oil production as Revolution descended upon the Gulf of Mexico and across the republic. The greater Gulf of Mexico region, by the first decades of the twentieth century, was dominated by oil worker culture.

An export-driven economy, combined with the increasing presence of foreign capital and an influx of working-class foreigners from diverse backgrounds in search of economic opportunities, contributed to the making of radical labor culture. Newcomers from all over the world brought with them cultural practices, food, music, and ideas about worker autonomy and labor rights. These arrivals interacted with yet another wave of newcomers recruited for oil work and general labor in associated industries. Mexicans from the countryside or from urban areas including Mexico City and Guadalajara moved to the area and joined the growing labor force in what would soon be one of the largest cities in the state of Tamaulipas.[16] (See tables 1 and 2.)

The population of Tampico and outlying areas was nearly 5,000 in 1876. It surged to 25,000 by 1915, and by 1921, Tampico alone counted at least 100,000 people.[17] By 1930, the population of Villa Cecilia was recorded at 25,704.[18] Between 1890 and 1915 the community of Villa Cecilia and Tampico grew significantly as dock and railroad work expanded corresponding to the proliferation of the oilfields: Tampico had the oil wells while Villa Cecilia emerged as the site for refineries and warehouses.[19] Villa Cecilia became a bustling working-class enclave, home to workers employed in over seven refineries and their families.[20]

The region catapulted Mexico into becoming a "net exporter of oil."[21] Frantic production for national and international consumption led to an increase in laborers. Families of the oil workers lived near the plaza Hermenegildo Galeana, "considered the center of the community," in Villa Cecilia.[22] Villa Cecilia was

Table 1. Population of Tamaulipas as reflected in urban and rural zones, 1910–1930

	1910		1921		1930	
	Rural	Urban	Rural	Urban	Rural	Urban
Tamaulipas	198,771	50,871	160,574	126,330	196,672	147,367
	(80%)	(20%)	(56%)	(44%)	(57%)	(42%)
Mexico			9,869,276	4,465,504	11,012,901	5,540,631
			(69%)	(31%)	(67%)	(34%)

Source: Adapted from Alvarado Mendoza, *El portesgilismo en Tamaulipas*, 28. Percentages have been rounded.

Table 2. Population of Tampico,
Tamaulipas, by sex, 1900–1921

	1900	1921
Men	173,647	271,955
Women	195,251	343,412
Total	368,898	615,367

Source: Periódico Oficial del Estado de Tamaulipas, June 27, 1922. AHT, Fondo: Justicia, caja
1902–1937, expediente, "Periódico Oficial del
Estado."

also within distance of the Huastecan mountainous region. There, people lived communally and held frequent gatherings involving women and men, called *círculos*. In existence since the pre-Columbian period, such practices continued well into the twentieth century.[23] Villa Cecilia and Tampico fed off one another and emerged as a crucial crossroad where ideas about community and labor rights became prominent in print media, in local theaters, and in the gatherings and meetings of a rapidly increasing number of labor unions.

Since the mid-nineteenth century mutual aid and craft-based organizations informed by communal ideas carried over from the precolonial era existed in the region. Ideas about mutual reciprocity, community support, and worker unity shaped the contours of these early organizations and continued to form the basis of collective organizing. Port workers soon created *talleres-escuelas* (educational workshops), debate centers or *círculos literarios*, and libraries. They opened up small shops to print anarchist newspapers and newsletters. The combination of these cultural practices and modern ideas about equality offered hope to a growing body of urban workers in the region who sought ways to improve their material conditions. The ideas about self-worth, fair wages, and safe working conditions enshrined in anarchist discourse were put into practice by organized labor and came to define the early anarcho-syndicalist tradition in the Tampico-Cecilia region during the revolutionary period. Anarcho-syndicalism emerged as the antidote to the increasingly hazardous working conditions, unequal wages vis-à-vis foreigners who assumed most high-level and administrative positions, and a rapid ghettoization of their neighborhoods away from the estates of oil magnates and their families.

From this small corner of the world, residents and workers shared ideas about labor rights rooted in their localized experiences and drawing from living and working conditions abroad. The region still claims a strong revolutionary historical memory, as it produced some of the most radical revolutionary Mexicans. Given this context, a whole range of labor-based associations emerged; anarchist and anarcho-syndicalists organizations were in no short supply.

The Revolution before the Revolution

Residents and transients alike who knew the borderland terrain and had family and friends on both sides of the Tamaulipas-Texas border had a collective memory of past revolts emanating from a long liberal tradition and a desire for political freedom. In 1886, as early oil exploration took off in Tampico, border native Catarino Garza launched a revolution against General Porfirio Díaz; while unsuccessful, it signaled the critical role of transnational support, as Garza received aid from both sides of the border and drew from political ideologies circulating in both countries in his attempt to topple the regime and democratize Mexico.

Like Garza's movement, by the turn of the twentieth century the socialist movement led by the Oaxacan native Ricardo Flores Magón and carried on by supporters after his death had a consequential impact on borderlands communities as well as farther inland along the Gulf of Mexico. Influenced by anarchist ideas, the Mexican intellectual unleashed a sharp critique of Díaz's repressive policies, ranging from privileging foreign interests, to exploitative child labor in hazardous mines, to women's equality. Flores Magón, at an early age, read radical texts by the Russian philosopher Peter Kropotkin and others, which deeply influenced his vision for a democratic Mexico. He influenced law school students at the Universidad Nacional Autónoma de México, the country's national university, as well as writers and artists promoting progressive, liberal ideas. Mexican authorities arrested him for leading an antigovernment student demonstration in 1892 in Mexico City.[24] He and his brothers Enrique and Jesús, as well as other activists including Camilo Arriaga and Praxedis Guerrero, by 1901 led a strong anti-Díaz resistance.

Porfirian officials had kept a close watch on Flores Magón and collaborators. As early as 1903, feeling the pressure and prohibited from publishing in Mexico, Flores Magón left the country for the United States via Nuevo Laredo. Within a short time, the PLM entered a new phase reflecting the more direct-action approach embodied in the new identity of the Junta Organizadora del Partido Liberal Mexicano. With a renewed mission, Junta members sought to "redistribute land, introduce the eight-hour work day, end the prohibition of strikes, and [implement] so many other benefits for workers."[25] The Junta's direct-action tactics reflected larger anarchist principles, while PLM affiliates continued to encourage collective organizing via unions or other means. Despite the adoption of the Junta name as a separate entity reflecting a new agenda, some of the branches did not change their name and kept, in correspondence and propaganda, the PLM name intact.[26]

Throughout the state, workers in the countryside affiliated with the PLM invaded large cattle-grazing and commercial agriculture haciendas that employed women and men as well as their children as laborers. In nearby Las Rusias near Matamoros across the border from Brownsville, Texas, "agrarian invaders" who had supported Lucio Blanco, a former *magonista* and later *Carrancista* supporter-turned-general, squatted on land claimed by Las Rusias Hacienda. These actions inspired by *magonismo* became enshrined in a deep historical memory of activism that lingered years after the Revolution.[27]

Such calls for outright revolution resonated throughout the Tamaulipas-Texas border and extended to other parts of the greater borderlands. Calls for revolution were heard as far west as the mining centers along the Coahuila-Texas border and also were shared among workers via smuggled newsletters like *Regeneración* or word of mouth in nearby Nuevo León and farther into New Mexico and Arizona. Miners were particularly influenced by calls for worker autonomy, as they were among the laborers most vulnerable to accidents and respiratory infections. *Magonista* literature frequently detailed the exploitative conditions in the mines—information deeply relatable to miners—and soon PLM branches emerged in mining sites. PLM supporter Lázaro Gutiérrez de Lara, who maintained ties with anarchists and socialists in Texas and other parts of the United States, helped to further spread the message of worker solidarity and worker autonomy in the Sonora-Arizona border. A *norteño* from Nuevo León, Gutiérrez de Lara, organized a PLM branch in the mining region of Cananea, Sonora, that led to the first major strike in Mexico in 1906.[28] He also collaborated with other activists, including John Murray and Elizabeth Trowbridge.

Other Junta adherents collaborated with Gutiérrez de Lara and supporters, including Manuel Sarabia who had helped found the Casa del Obrero Mundial (COM) in Mexico City. Sarabia and Gutiérrez de Lara teamed up with others to further expand the network of anarchists and other radical labor activists supporting the Junta, the PLM, and the COM. These organizations found support among workers across northern Mexico and in the United States including New Mexico, Arizona, and California.[29] By late 1906, Sarabia had also, as historian Thomas Alter writes, "formed a political relationship with left-wing Socialists" from Texas and elsewhere during an organizing trip to Chicago.[30] And so the network of the PLM grew.

The PLM agenda stipulated that the "work of the [PLM]" would be assisted by three main branches, spread out geographically. Tamaulipas was identified as one of those sites. Early on, the countryside and urban centers in the state played a role in bringing about a revolution to democratize Mexico, even when the PLM headquarters moved to the United States due to political repression.[31]

The PLM appealed to men and women from both sides of the Tamaulipas-Texas border, given the similarities in socioeconomic and political conditions. Texas border native and Brownsville rancher Aniceto Pizaña, Texas native Amado G. Hernández, and Higinio Tanguma from Tamaulipas acted upon the ideas espoused by the PLM. Pizaña collaborated with Hernández, who at different times lived and worked in Creedmore, Austin, and Uvalde, Texas. He regularly corresponded with the PLM staff running *Regeneración*, by this time based in California. Pizaña proceeded to form a PLM branch by 1911 in Brownsville after meeting Flores Magón in Laredo sometime in 1904.[32] Possibly with the support of Pizaña, Hernández participated in the armed attack on Las Vacas, Coahuila, and helped secure ammunition for subsequent attacks by PLM members. He also founded the Club Regeneración Tierra y Libertad in Austin in 1911.[33]

Inspired by *magonismo*, Higinio Tanguma participated in one of the earliest agrarian movements that, unlike those in other regions of the country, garnered cross-class support. Tanguma was originally from China, Nuevo León, according to several features in *Regeneración*. He had worked as a miner and in salt deposits in Altamira in Tamaulipas. By 1906 he had joined the PLM. As Catarino Garza had done previously, Tanguma along with Pizaña built a small cross-class, cross-border coalition to promote the PLM cause in Tamaulipas and Texas, framed in agrarian terms. Tanguma had also worked as a peon in northern Tamaulipas haciendas and represented an early voice of the agrarian movement to gain arable land, specifically citing the PLM platform. True to these ideals of direct action, Tanguma launched several attacks on Tamaulipas haciendas and ranchos in Soto la Marina and in Aldama. However, by 1907, Tamaulipas authorities detained him. He soon escaped jail and headed to the *sierra* in central Tamaulipas and continued a guerilla-style campaign.

Along with at least forty men, Tanguma had managed to destroy labor records detailing years of peons' debts housed in haciendas.[34] During their assaults, Tanguma and followers carried red banners reading "Land and Liberty."[35] Tanguma's agrarian activism was short-lived, as local and state authorities quelled the rebellion and detained Tanguma. After his release he fought on behalf of Francisco Madero but lost his life in a battle near Tampico in 1912.[36]

The ideas espoused by the PLM as well as references to *magonismo* in periodicals inspired entire families in Tamaulipas to take up arms. One of several examples is the Carrera-Torres family, led by Juana Torres de Carrera and her husband Candelario Carrera Muñoz, who owned a small country store. After declaring support for Madero and remaining sympathetic to *magonismo*, Juana soon became a widow after Candelario lost his life in 1915 in battle. She and her sons Alberto and Eutiquio Carrera-Torres continued the fight. In particular, Alberto Carrera-Torres, a rural schoolteacher, called for an agrarian redistribution law and direct action.[37] Earlier interaction with Manuel Villasana Ortiz, the editor of *El Tulteco* who risked losing his press after printing a PLM manifesto, likely had an impact on Carrera-Torres.[38]

Riding this agrarian wave inspired by anarchist ideas, Caritina Piña's half-brother Zenaido Piña joined revolutionaries in the Ocampo and Morelos area while Caritina was a teenager. Zenaido supported the early uprising for the PLM cause even before Francisco Madero called for open revolution in November 1910. Zenaido soon opposed Victoriano Huerta, who ordered Francisco Madero's assassination in early 1913, after Madero's ascent to the presidency in 1911. Piña was eighteen or nineteen years of age and living in Ocampo when Zenaido joined other revolutionaries, including Leopoldo Lárraga Orta and Fulgencio and Francisco Santos, during the 1913–1914 period.[39] It is unclear whether Caritina maintained a close enough relationship with Zenaido to be deeply influenced. But the fact that he had become an *alzado*, or rebel, and her father had shifted loyalties to former Coahuila governor Venustiano Carranza as he became the leading opponent of Huerta,[40] is one indication that the Piña household in Ocampo was one in which revolution was not an uncommon idea. Her father, Nicanor Piña Hernández, became a revolutionary commander loyal to Carranza's Constitutionalist forces by 1914.[41] While not a self-proclaimed *magonista*, Piña's father nonetheless shifted his loyalties from Porfirian forces to the revolutionary elites Madero, and later, Carranza. His brother, Victor Piña Hernández, however, remained a loyal Huertista.[42]

In contrast to Madero and Carranza, Flores Magón called for armed revolution at least a decade prior, not to implement yet another government, but to create a world led by the workers themselves. While revolutionary governments beginning with Madero were all but anarchist, those who pledged support for the revolution built upon the ideas of the PLM. PLM members were not all anarchists, as John Mason Hart has written, and some opted for Madero when he proclaimed revolution.[43] Yet the ideas about labor equity, anti–child labor policies, worker autonomy, and women's equality put forth by Flores Magón and other delegates in the 1901 Liberal Congress in San Luís Potosí resonated among the predominantly agrarian populace in southern Tamaulipas as well as similar communities farther north toward Texas, and remained part of the larger agenda calling for change.

Figure 6. Nicanor Piña Hernández,
Caritina Piña's father, ca. 1910.
Courtesy, personal collection of
Marvin Osiris Huerta Márquez.

Throughout the country, a growing number of industrial workers took notice of Flores Magón's message. For many, this was their first introduction to anarchist principles and other prolabor ideas. Of particular importance were liberal ideas about worker collectivism via unions and other labor organizations that publicly called for women's participation. Heeding anarchism's belief in gender equity, Flores Magón and the PLM publicly endorsed women's rights. Among the PLM principles was the adoption of a liberal platform that prioritized workers and "counter[ed] the influence of the clergy on the home, an influence which only serves to corrupt the female heart. . . . which leads to an education full of hypocrisy and false for our children."[44] These ideas, as explained via periodicals, became tools with which to fight the Díaz regime and push for the legalization of unions. Anarchist female sympathizers embraced such anticlericalism and, in some cases, adopted atheism and found in the PLM a welcoming, albeit imperfect, space.

An anarchist framework lent itself to the articulation of resistance to working women's subordinate position in all aspects of society vis-à-vis men, other women, and institutions, including the state. Anarchist rhetoric had the potential to radically transform women's thinking with respect to their relationship to

Figure 7. Zenaido Piña, Caritina
Piña's half-brother, ca. 1911.
Courtesy, personal collection of
Marvin Osiris Huerta Márquez.

religion and unequal labor practices as well. As a border native from Coahuila,
León Díaz Cárdenas, put it in the 1930s, anarchism, "originally the primitive protest, [was] naïve but powerful."[45] Critiquing its rejection of the state and any political party affiliation, hence his use of "naïve," Díaz Cárdenas noted nonetheless
anarchism's potential to effect material change as its practitioners further molded
and shaped these ideas based on their experiences and world view.

Magonismo and Ferrer's Rational School of Thought's Role in Crafting a Women's Rights Agenda

The open call for women to "join the struggle" beyond suffrage, visible in early
manifestos of the 1901 Liberal Congress and soon the PLM, the Junta, and the
COM, while riddled with gendered assumptions and expectations for both
women and men, created a viable opening for women's increased involvement
in labor matters. There are numerous examples of women engaged in promoting
a wide range of issues during the early and mid-nineteenth century—including

Figure 8. *Magonista* Lázaro Gutiérrez de Lara with female soldiers, 1911 (Cd. Juárez). Courtesy, Library of Congress, Prints and Photographs Division, PR 13 CN 2012:147, no. 44.

education, welfare, health, and sanitation. Numerous women's organizations were dedicated to charitable or religious causes, and as early as 1891, suffrage. But it was not until the turn of the twentieth century that a more structured, cohesive agenda centered on women's labor issues emerged.

The anarchist-based agenda for women's rights before and during the Revolution differed in three basic ways from a mainstream women's rights agenda. First, it was not preoccupied with suffrage as its main goal. Secondly, resembling communist-based women's organizing, it opted for direct action, although it differed in that it rejected any affiliation with a political party in general. And thirdly, while it resonated with the privileging of maternalism/motherhood similar to that emerging in socialist spheres, it distinguished itself through its rejection of religious ideas, clericalism, and affiliation with a religious institution. Anarchism attracted women early on precisely because of its ability to critique, in relatable terms, the plight of workers while at the same time critiquing institutions that, despite claims about women's societal value, set a double standard. That critique extended to one of the most dominant institutions in Mexico, the Catholic Church.

Such ideas framed *magonista* ideals and resonated with the small but radical wing of women's early organizing efforts in the predominantly rural Rio Grande Valley along the border. While separated by a geopolitical boundary, the region emerged as a close-knit community sharing not only cultural and social ways, but also an expanding economy. Attendant growth in basic infrastructure and new rail service connected rural towns and emergent urban centers. A corresponding growth in the number of Spanish- and English-language newspapers followed. Border residents who became US citizens after the signing of the Treaty of Guadalupe-Hidalgo in 1848 resumed their lives under a new government but maintained cultural, familial, economic, and political ties with northern Mexican communities.

As land in Mexico became concentrated in the hands of a few during the Díaz administration, so too did land begin to slip from the hands of Mexican Americans in the US Southwest. The border region was no exception. For Mexican Americans, the loss of land often resulted from new requirements concerning the registering of land titles under the US government. Original Spanish titles needed to be translated, and these services were costly. Land was often used as payment toward such services, including legal fees. Nonetheless, those who retained land remained afloat and formed part of the small but influential rural *ranchero* class or a small but growing group of intellectuals, which included journalists and writers. Some of these influential community members played a central role in the promotion of new ideas embodied in *magonista* rhetoric about worker autonomy, land rights, gender equality, and political expression that emerged in opposition to Porfirian policies.

Local concerns were printed in the media and shared across the border, further shaping the larger discourse over land and wage disparities, lack of political expression, gender inequities, and child labor.[46] As both the US and Mexican governments consolidated their shared border by the late nineteenth century, eliminating resistant Indigenous groups, the development of the region via capital investments would forever transform border communities.[47]

Levels of capital investments, particularly US capital, were widespread in the US-Mexican borderlands. In Tamaulipas, foreign investment during Porfirio Díaz's presidency reached incredible levels. Up to 80 percent of Tamaulipas land was in the hands of foreign corporations by the eve of the Mexican Revolution. Moreover, in commercial agricultural farms, industrial firms, and factories, absentee landowners controlled properties, foreigners supervised the predominantly Mexican labor force, and the wage gap between foreign and native workers widened. In terms of acreage, nearly 150 million acres of land, out of a total of 485 million acres, were in foreign hands.[48]

In this socioeconomic context, women too saw the decline of their communities with respect to political power. For working-class women such as Emilia Rodríguez, who labored as a seamstress, ideas featured in *Regeneración* about worker autonomy and women's contributions to society resonated with her experiences along the border. Alongside Rodríguez, María Salazar, Carmen de la Rosa, Luz Mendoza, and Elisa Alemán Hernández represented early anarchist female voices.

Emilia Rodríguez arrived in the Rio Grande Valley from Mexico in 1900. She and her husband had at least one child, a girl named Consuelo. During the formative years of the Junta, she became a widow and found work as a seamstress. It appears that she saved enough to purchase or rent a home in Brownsville. By 1906, she was among the list of supporters of the PLM and *Regeneración*. It was through a neighbor, Manuel Cueto, who both lived and worked in his small store in Brownsville, that Rodríguez received copies of *Regeneración*. She founded and led a women's discussion group in Brownsville and possibly became intimately involved with the revolutionary Basilio Ramos. It appears that Rodríguez had already been exposed to PLM ideas before she met Ramos and before she possibly befriended Ancieto Pizaña. What is clear is that by 1906, Rodríguez's reading group was aligned with other PLM-affiliated branches in the region.[49]

While printed in California, *Regeneración* made its way to a variety of collectives throughout the country. Commentaries on the topic of women's role in ushering a real social revolution appeared. Often, supporters clipped specific headlines and further shared them with community members. Among the commentaries read by Rodríguez and her group was "La Voz de la mujer," which appeared in 1907 in *Revolución*, the periodical for the PLM after *Regeneración* was shut down for a time.[50] "La Voz" urged women to "be combatants like men" and assured women that "the PLM from the beginning, has counted with women's support, that is why women are strong and they will succeed." The commentary honored a new pro-*magonista* newspaper bearing the same name founded by Isidra T. de Cárdenas, María Sánchez, and María P. García farther west in El Paso, Texas. Through this news sharing about women's value, about new collectives as well as their own periodicals, the PLM both secured new members and spread its message across states. Thus, even in regions long considered remote, such as South Texas, women like Emilia Rodríguez helped her community to remain abreast of external developments.

María Salazar and Carmen de la Rosa both subscribed and donated modest sums to *Regeneración* and helped promote the PLM cause. There is a possibility that de la Rosa was related to or was the partner of Luis de la Rosa, who became involved in an uprising in South Texas with possible ties to the Plan of San Diego. Luis de la Rosa was a close associate of Pizaña. Salazar and Carmen de la Rosa most likely knew of Rodríguez's group via Pizaña and Ramos. Directly or indirectly, the women formed part of a growing network of individuals who, even if not self-declared anarchists, had radical sympathies and appear as donors to *Regeneración*.[51] All three women—Rodríguez, Salazar, and de la Rosa—supported the cause by donating, receiving, and most importantly, recirculating copies of *Regeneración* or its other incarnations like *Revolución*. All three founded PLM-affiliated branches.[52]

Another South Texas supporter, Luz Mendoza, organized the PLM-affiliated Grupo Redención in Harlingen, Texas, about twenty-five miles from Brownsville. Although it is unclear if it was an all-female collective like Rodríguez's reading group, Redención also received and recirculated news stories printed in *Regeneración* and similar periodicals.[53] It appears that Mendoza's group continued into the 1920s as reflected in correspondence between Mendoza and Caritina Piña's Comité. Mendoza also contributed commentaries for *Sagitario* and other anarchist newspapers circulated in Tampico and Villa Cecilia.[54]

Mendoza possibly took part in armed operations together with other self-proclaimed *magonistas*. In early September of 1913, Mendoza and fourteen others—including Charles Cline, Pedro Perales, and Abraham Cisneros, led by Jesús María Rangel—participated in a planned guerrilla-style attack on Mexico using Texas as their operating base. The group attempted to cross through Carrizo Springs in West Texas in the hopes of weakening the Huertista federal forces on the Mexican side of the border. Agents patrolling the border, including Texas Rangers from Dimmit County aided by a Mexican spy, Candelario Ortiz, intercepted them. The result was a bloody encounter between the *magonistas* and the agents; two *magonistas* died and "the rest were jailed and sentenced to 99 years in prison in Texas."[55] It had not been too long since Flores Magón and his brother Enrique, as well as Anselmo Figueroa and Librado Rivera, had been detained and sentenced to twenty-three months in prison in the United States for violating US neutrality laws.[56] *Magonistas* from both Mexico and the United States launched their own media campaign, raising funds for what would be numerous legal appeals for their detained colleagues and, at the same time, helped with furthering the cause and recruitment of more members.

Via Grupo Germinal and Grupo Praxedis Guerrero, Elisa A. Hernández also formed part of the early group of women engaged in PLM activities. Hernández

Figure 9. Librado Rivera and Enrique Flores Magón, ca. 1910–1915. Courtesy, Bain News Service, Library of Congress, Prints and Photographs Division, LC-B@-2206-7, 2014689261.

became a representative of both groups farther north in San Antonio. She encouraged other women to join the fight. Early on she called on women to "liberate themselves from the stranglehold of their inept husbands," reflecting the anarchist rejection of marriage.[57] While critiquing the inequities of the institution of marriage, Hernández, like others writing during this period, did not reject love or any type of intimate relationship. She supported free unions based not only on love but on love for the larger struggle to achieve freedom and liberty. Hernández maintained an intimate relationship with José Angel Hernández, a long-time activist in both Texas and Tamaulipas among other places.

While we lack a definite count of anarcho-feminist organizations, the available data reveals the extent of collaboration and awareness among and between these groups. The Waco-based group, for example, likely received support from nearby Dallas, Texas, sympathizers, as they too had organized a Grupo Avante with an anarcho-syndicalist outlook.[58] The Gurley branch joined those of the all-female Prismas Anarquistas in Burkett, Texas, and collaborated with numerous PLM or "floresmagonista clubs . . . in Cameron and Hidalgo counties" including Mendoza's *Redención*.[59]

Forming an early collective voice along the borderlands, Alida Martínez and other women from Burkett, Texas, founded Prismas Anarquistas in 1913 using anarchist language that underscored their ideas about motherhood within the context of labor justice. Born in Texas, Martínez performed farm labor alongside her family in Coleman County.[60] Prismas Anarquistas called "for [their] demands to be heard" and became one of several Texas-based organizations with support from Tampico workers as documented in the sharing of labor newsletters and other labor-related information.[61] While motherhood would become further politicized in the postrevolutionary period and co-opted by the state to promote nationalism and women's inclusion, for anarcho-feminists during the revolutionary period, such ideas reflected their own labor experiences outside the confines of the state.

Because the PLM, via its media campaigns, mainly *Regeneración*, regularly alerted its readers to the creation of new organizations or new PLM affiliates, it helped to garner support and maintain the momentum. Prismas Anarquistas news and events were featured in *Regeneración* and such news sharing had a domino effect, sparking interest in founding similar collectives. This was crucial for early women's organizing not only because it led to more organizations with female membership, but also because it provided a wider, more regional and transnational platform by which to promote local concerns.

These all-female groups formed part of a growing community of female activists. Worker autonomy, cooperation based on older practices of mutual aid, and political equality resonated with Mexican-origin women in Texas. Tejanas and more recent Mexican immigrant women had to contend with a new socioeconomic and political reality, which was among the legacies of the Mexican American War. Loss of land, loss of political power, and deeply held Anglo views of an inferior Mexican culture had sharpened existing socioeconomic inequalities that intensified as commercial agriculture took root along the border in the Rio Grande Valley and in the fertile lands south of the Rio Grande into northern Tamaulipas.[62]

Coupled with the PLM's public call for women to join the fight, ideas about gender equity stemming from the Ferrer i Guardia's Escuela Racionalists embodied in the COM helped pave the way for a women's agenda. Founded in 1912 by the Grupo Luz in Mexico City, the COM quickly became a space that created a sense of community and solidarity among workers from various trades; in its first year of existence in Mexico City "its members participated in over 70 strikes," which was quite a remarkable feat.[63] Many of those strikers, sadly, lost their lives. Shortly thereafter, as COM branches emerged in urban centers in various Mexican states, Tampico and Villa Cecilia workers moved to found their local branch, which soon gained a solid reputation among organized labor as one of the strongest and most active in the entire country. The ideas of the

COM, based on Francisco Ferrer i Guardia's ideas, also influenced groups in Texas.[64]

Two years after Prismas was founded, a PLM- and COM-affiliated group with substantial participation of women was organized in San Antonio. Responding in good part to the increase in the number of wealthy exiles tied to the Porfirian regime who had made their home in San Antonio in the midst of Revolution, this new opposition group emerged. The Grupo Racionalista was founded on anarchist principles, mainly in the tradition of Ferrer's Rational School of Thought. It critiqued how San Antonio had become "a nest of the Mexican plutocracy" and sought to "enter the struggle for existence . . . making the fight of other anarchist centers our own and those to come throughout the continent."[65] Embracing "other anarchist centers' [concerns]," the Mexican or possibly Mexican American Isaura Galván and thirty-eight other individuals formed Grupo Racionalista in the spring of 1915. The women cofounders, besides Galván and Elisa A. Hernández, included Herminia Peña, Melchora López, Amparo Lopez Galván, Isabel González, Francisca Lozano, Susana Sanchez, Teresa Granados, Concepción B. Galván, Elvira Alaniz, Francisca Flores, Rosa García, and Severa C. Valadez. Their twenty-five male colleagues included Ricardo Treviño and José Angel Hernández, Elisa's partner. The group adhered to "the widening of the ideals of freedom."[66]

The group put forth eight resolutions with "the formation of a . . . Center for Rational Studies that embraces both sexes" standing as its first point. The founders emphasized their intent to honor rational philosophy, adopting the progressive ideas of the late Barcelona native Francisco Ferrer. Ferrer emphasized a libertarian and anticlerical philosophy, the equal education of women and men, and promoted the idea of worker autonomy via anarcho-syndicalism.[67] Grupo Racionalista also sought to include the collection of "Spanish-language anarchist newspapers" and vowed to "fight racial hatred promoted by secular and religious schools." It also committed itself to an "open and frank libertarian campaign via newspapers and all mediums possible" and sought to "dedicate itself to the promotion and its participation of any matters involving the education of the proletariat masses adhering to the most sincere and pure fraternity."[68] Grupo Racionalista's activities in San Antonio lasted until late 1916 and possibly 1917. It had built upon earlier efforts dating back to the eve of the Revolution such as San Antonio collectives like Grupo Germinal and Praxedis Guerrero. Racionalista members also had membership in like-minded organizations. Elisa A. Hernández represented Germinal and Praxedis Guerrero, Ricardo Treviño the IWW and the PLM, and José Angel Hernández had involved himself with the IWW and socialist groups from Texas. These organizations and their members would soon leave their mark on Tampico-Cecilia.

Isaura Galván, Ricardo Treviño, José Angel Hernández, and possibly Elisa A. Hernández brought the leadership experience gained in their Grupo Racionalista from San Antonio to the Tampico-Cecilia region by late 1916 and 1917. Their activism meshed with the anarchist activities under way in that region. The San Antonio exiles soon supported the new Tampico COM, which represented an "anarcho-syndicalist ideology that translated to workers' control of the means of production through unions" and nicely complemented *magonista* ideals.

Reynalda González Parra was among the cofounders of the new Tampico COM branch. González Parra collaborated with Treviño as he became closely tied to the COM and served as its secretary general in 1917 after leaving San Antonio. Support for the COM increased, particularly as the PLM moved toward a more defined "anarcho-syndicalist platform," when it adopted its Junta name.[69] In the face of a full-fledged Revolution raging in the countryside and urban centers, the COM continued its appeals to workers from different trades as well as those that "had been affiliated to or supported both the IWW and the PLM."[70] It recruited workers from artisan trades including "printers, tailors, bakers, chauffeurs, stonemasons, and carpenters," and soon attracted oil workers.[71]

The COM had grown in strength since its founding and, shortly after unions became legally recognized in 1917, it consisted of over twenty-six affiliated labor unions and numerous cooperative societies.[72] The COM supported direct action in the form of strikes and the creation of more labor collectives and promoted its ideas in *Ariete*, a COM newspaper based in Mexico City. The Tampico COM, founded in October 1915, emerged as a strong collective of labor activists, many of whom continued to promote the rationalist ideas of Ferrer. Members set up reading circles to discuss Ferrer's writings, analyze recent news stories featured in the anarchist press, or share citations with one another.[73] It also endorsed direct-action strategies via *Germinal*, which became one of the Tampico COM's media outlets, and other newspapers. COM members felt, as the historian Anna Ribera Carbó has written, that the current revolution was not the "real" revolution; theirs was yet to come and thus the propaganda was crucial to bringing about a *true* revolution that would alter the status quo in profound ways.[74]

The overlap between organizations such as the COM, PLM, and the IWW, which stemmed from their prolabor, global, and antistate agendas, helped to keep the labor movement alive. Because workers often had double or triple memberships, when one organization declined, was financially strapped, or was targeted by authorities, others remained afloat. When *magonista* leaders from the Junta entered a period of decline in 1914 and 1915, as many of its members were serving repeated prison sentences, some of the members relied on and continued promoting their cause via the COM or the IWW. As Claudio Lomnitz has written, the "junta had lost its Socialist allies, [particularly those in the

United States] who were themselves also weakened," and by "1914 and 1915" the PLM "[found itself] in poverty."[75] While the PLM had declined, the idea of anarcho-syndicalism did not, and *magonismo* continued to play a central role in labor organizations as an overwhelming number of periodicals reprinted PLM news and commentaries, all invoking *magonismo*. In the Tampico COM and other organizations, *magonismo* became synonymous with anarchism and labor rights, even after many of the original PLM founders had died.

Labor Activists as Revolutionary Bandits

State authorities promoted a discourse on the dangers of a revolutionary spillover during the early *magonista* years that led to a "bandit" frenzy. Such fear-mongering continued well into the final years of the Revolution. US intelligence reports noted how Mexican residents in Mexico and Texas "have little respect for any government and are good material from which revolutionary leaders can recruit a force of bandit outlaws."[76] Yet, according to the same report, these radicals were also a "lazy-set of people who work when they have to and loaf as much as they can."[77] Officers of the US Military Intelligence Division categorized all Mexican "peons from the border" to "the type found in Texas . . . [as] . . . vastly inferior as laborers and citizens." It further characterized the border Mexicans in the following way: "[They] are experienced in running contraband, a good shot as Mexicans go, and altogether considers himself superior to the people farther south."[78] If lines had been blurred between generation-old Tejanos and Mexican immigrants, these became more difficult to discern as the "number of Mexican immigrants living in Texas doubled."[79] Mexican-origin residents were lumped as one large group, and anyone who looked Mexican ran the risk of being labeled a "bandit" or a sympathizer if engaged in labor activism. The racialization of labor radicalism along the border had profound consequences for the Tampico-Cecilia region.

Mexicans suspected of taking part in labor activism were particularly vulnerable at the hands of the state's elite force, the Texas Rangers, whose behavior had repercussions on both sides of the border. The state force notoriously targeted labor activists (and did so up until the 1970s). Rangers and other state agents saw Mexican anarchists and bandits as one. The case of Jesús María Rangel, a *magonista* and anarcho-syndicalist who led the attack on Mexico, is a case in point. Rangel had traveled between Mexico and Texas plotting an attack on Carrancistas in the border state of Coahuila. Rangel was an old colleague of Ricardo Flores Magón and well-known throughout labor circles, as he had collaborated with IWW organizer Charles Cline and other activists. Authorities from both sides of the border sought the apprehension of Rangel, Cline, and Flores Magón. When the Texas Rangers intercepted plans for an attack organized by the group, Cline and Rangel were subsequently detained and sentenced to prison. Calls for a hanging followed immediately.[80] As Texas Rangers and other state agents intercepted revolutionaries suspected of launching assaults on Mexican authorities during the late Díaz years and into the Revolution, fears about Mexican radicals became widespread and also "hardened the racial lines between Mexicans and Anglos."[81] Just several years prior, four Mexican women were detained in San Antonio and "examined by the Immigration Commissioner" and subsequently sent to Laredo for possible deportation. After hearing about "the evidence against the women," he ordered their deportation to Mexico.[82]

The Texas-Tamaulipas border region had a long history as a site of rebellion and resistance and thus figured prominently in surveillance reports. Since the days of the Juan Cortina uprising in the years after the Mexican American War, up through the Tuxtepec Revolution led by none other than Porfirio Díaz and the Catarino Garza revolt in the 1880s to oust Díaz, the region had exemplified resistance to the state (both Mexico and the United States) and the weight of the state. This region historically had been a "site of added scrutiny."[83] This translated into frequent violations of human rights ranging from invasive health examinations to horrific lynchings to the use of rural police like the Rangers and the Rurales to suppress any threats to state progress, including radical labor activism. Labor activists—particularly those rejecting any type of collaboration with the state, as was the case of most anarchists—frequently noted the brutality with which state authorities "handled" fellow labor activist colleagues. Long-time anarchist and supporter of the PLM Jaime Vidal believed such brutality stemmed from the racial animosity toward Mexicans, Mexican Americans, and African Americans, particularly along the Texas border. In 1913, at an IWW-sponsored meeting, Vidal spoke about "the unhappy notoriety Texas ha[d] achieved in the matter of racial prejudice, especially against negroes and Mexicans; together with her record in the matter of lynchings."[84]

Vidal knew well the maltreatment of activists. His colleague and Grupo Racionalista member José Angel Hernández experienced it firsthand as he was labeled both a bandit and anarchist. Hernández had lived in Mexico and joined the Texas Socialist Party while working in Texas and living with Elisa Hernández, and before cofounding Grupo Racionalista, he organized a PLM branch in Houston. He soon faced deportation due to his collaboration with the IWW and *magonistas*. Both Elisa and José Angel Hernández, taking advantage of a community dance in San Marcos, Texas, began fundraising among the workers for the defense of Rangel and Cline. After Hernández's detention, local women and men offered support after hearing about the injustice against him committed by the Rangers and other authorities. The group, numbering "128 men and women," proceeded to "sen[d] a telegram to Texas Governor Oscar Colquitt." The San Marcos residents threatened Colquitt; their telegram warned that "if any of the Rangel-Cline group were hung, 'your state will answer before the whole Mexican community.'"[85]

Colquitt's response was to "unleash the Texas Rangers" on the labor activists as well as "the San Marcos telegram signers."[86] By late 1913, all of the 127 signers were investigated. Colquitt, "in consultation with the state general's office[,] decided that Mexican radicals could be prosecuted under vagrancy laws long used in the South to control labor and remove undesirables." The San Marcos residents were spared and eventually released, but Hernández, "the organizer of the San Marcos Defense Committee," was deported. Upon his return to Mexico, he headed toward Tampico; despite his misfortune in Texas, he found himself in the midst of a growing labor movement across the border and easily found a welcoming home.[87]

In Tampico, organized workers learned about the fate of activists like Hernández and others and continued to receive news about labor developments related to activists' arrests and deportations from the border as well as from different parts of the world. In 1918, US and other foreign observers visiting Mexico wrote about the "dangers of socialism" and how it "intruded itself upon the horizon of the Mexican peon ... preached ... by peripatetic agitators."[88] As reports of crackdowns on labor activists circulated, it became clear that Tampico was closely policed, too.

The Emergence of Grupo Germinal and Hermanos Rojos

Despite the transnational crackdown on labor activists, the ideas of intellectuals and thinkers that set off the Revolution resonated with workers and locals who sought to combat a range of inequities in order to improve their material conditions. Influenced by the founding of the Tampico COM, two new anarcho-syndicalist organizations emerged, Grupo Germinal and Hermanos Rojos.

By late 1916 and early 1917, Isaura Galván, Ricardo Treviño, and José Angel Hernández had arrived in Tampico via Texas; all had been founding members of Grupo Racionalista. Román Delgado, tied to the IWW and other labor activists, arrived from New York. Together, this cohort of thinkers brought their leadership experiences gained abroad to the formation of Germinal in June 1917. Their main outlet was a "free newspaper" bearing the same name "financed by the Tampico and Guadalajara branches of the COM, Union of Armory Workers, Communist

Society of Monterrey Trades, the Workers' Confederation of Veracruz and Río Blanco, [and] the Union of Stevedores from Salina Cruz."[89] By the end of its first year, *Germinal* published a lengthy manifesto declaring why it encouraged all to reject government and any political party, thereby promoting the basic tenets of anarchism. Its members rationalized that "government was not productive, as its main goal was to ensure the privileged role of capitalists who exploit those who produce; it is for this reason that the anarchists are enemies of the state."[90] It further critiqued the state's ongoing efforts to promote Mexican nationalism: "the nation is the creation of state agents. The division of land into nationalities does not respond to any practical end and it creates a morality that is wholly immoral." The manifesto continued, "the division of the world into nations is the cause of racism, hate, conflicts, and the capitalistic wars. The current war [World War I] is the fruit of an official school of thought promoted by capitalist societies, because since childhood it has planted in *pueblos*, racism, militarism, and the false nationalism and false love for the nation."[91] What was the solution to such entrenched ideology? *Germinal* believed it was "anarchism" as this ideology was "the only ideal that [could] combat those rivalries and the ambitions underlying those capitalistic nations."[92]

When Germinal cofounder Ricardo Treviño arrived in the port city, he joined the COM (and served as its secretary general in February and May of 1917 after resigning from the IWW Maritime Workers Union); he quickly helped these organizations spread anarchist ideas among port workers (many of them former revolutionaries). His connections helped him obtain a job as a carpenter for El Águila Petroleum Corporation. In the early 1900s, Treviño left his native northern Mexican neighborhood in Nuevo León. He crossed into Texas and remained in San Antonio where he worked for some time and joined Grupo Racionalista where he met Isaura Galván and other members.[93] Treviño, as the late historian Carlos González Salas has written, was a voracious reader and consumed the ideas of Kropotkin and Proudhon before migrating to Tampico.[94]

By 1917, Treviño was active in the anarchist circles as the administrator for *Germinal*, for which Isaura Galván was general director.[95] The experiences of activists, as Devra Weber has written, "as they understood it" in their respective organizations, whether the PLM or the IWW, "traveled back . . . with them to villages, settlements, and work sites in Mexico."[96] Galván, Treviño, and Hernández brought such experience with them. Germinal had a strong base of supporters who contributed from modest sums to more generous amounts of cash. Locals such as Severiano Pueto contributed one peso while the Carpenters' Union donated a little over thirty pesos, demonstrating the power of collective fundraising.[97]

At the same time Germinal members discussed their founding principles in late 1916, José H. Hernández, Pedro Gudiño, and Spanish anarchists Román Delgado and Jorge D. Borrán gathered to discuss the formation of an anarchist group. In January 1917, Hermanos Rojos was founded and quickly adopted the "libertarian principles of the Junta."[98] Some of its members had other affiliations including the COM, Germinal, and the IWW. These activists had plenty of experience as labor organizers and were skilled at promoting their cause and recruiting members.[99]

Hermanos Rojos outlined its agenda to not only "promot[e] the ideals of liberty" but also "fight to free all workers, without distinguishing neither nationality nor sex" and opened its doors to women.[100] It quickly opted to support the Junta's mission of direct action and grew its membership thanks to the old IWW branch's role in promoting Hermanos Rojos' agenda. Given the emergence of IWW branches between 1917 and 1918, mainly the Unión Industrial de Trabajadores del Transporte Marítimo and the Sindicato de Trabajadores del Petróleo y de la Construcción, Hermanos Rojos drew membership from the mass of workers in the shipping industry and related petroleum sector. In 1919, these units created a central IWW branch, the Administración Mexicana de la IWW, and continued collaborating with Hermanos Rojos and Germinal in launching massive strikes against the major petroleum corporations.[101]

Thus, the period between 1901 and 1917 witnessed the expansion of an anarcho-feminist agenda in PLM, Junta, and COM news outlets as well as in periodicals promoted by affiliated groups like Racionalista and Germinal.[102] The writings of well-known anarchist women appeared in such outlets, helping to broaden the conversation about labor rights to include *obrera* conditions and the ideas and activities of female thinkers engaged in labor activism. Emma Goldman's writings, for example, appeared in the PLM's *Regeneración*, and Goldman corresponded with Flores Magón quite regularly. An ardent supporter of women's rights, Russian immigrant Goldman was among the female pioneers advocating for both workers' and women's rights. Goldman founded the anarchist journal *Mother Earth* in 1906, which served as the main outlet for her ideas. Her proposals for change in *Mother Earth* were frequently reprinted in the anarchist press in Mexico among other places.[103]

Other periodicals that helped to promote women's issues early on included San Antonio's *Vesper*, run by Juana Belén Gutiérrez de Mendoza (a *norteña* originally from Durango), Elisa Acuña (Rosetti), and PLM supporter Sara Estela Ramírez (from Coahuila, living in Laredo).[104] Ramírez contributed her writings to several newspapers including *El Demócrata Fronterizo* and *La Crónica*. She published *La Corregidora*, named after the Mexican Independence heroine Josefa Ortíz de Domínguez, while a PLM member. It influenced audiences from both

Texas and Mexico.[105] From Lampazos, Nuevo León, but writing from San Antonio and other places, Teresa and her sister Andrea Villarreal (siblings of Antonio Villarreal), all PLM supporters, published *Mujer Moderna* and *El Obrero*.[106]

Many of these commentaries on women's issues by women themselves were reprinted in Tampico and Villa Cecilia newspapers. *Sagitario* and *Avante*, for example, between 1910 and the late 1920s reprinted these articles and reproduced manifestos. Gradually, these issues became regularly featured items, which helped usher in a more robust conversation about revolutionary rights for all.

Such periodicals also reprinted commentaries and poems from female anarchists from afar. Like Goldman's writing, that of US-born Voltairine de Cleyre and the Frenchwoman Luisa Michel (representing early anarcho-feminist "freethought") were reprinted and featured in the Tampico and Villa Cecilia press. Cleyre condemned the institution of marriage, the state, capitalism, and the overwhelming control of religion over women's bodies and lives. Like some of her contemporaries and those who emerged on the scene after her, Cleyre embraced various strands of anarchism from an individualistic anarchism to a communist-anarchism, "which was an idea strong among foreign-born anarchists," as historian Margaret Marsh has explained.[107] Michel, a French anarchist, by the mid-to-late nineteenth century articulated a feminist agenda couched in the language of anarchism.[108] Her "Why I Am an Anarchist," originally written in 1895, reappeared in *Sagitario* in Villa Cecilia by the early 1920s. In her commentary, Michel argued that anarchism was the ideology "closest to freedom."[109] True freedom meant self-determination, which took place only after one's freedom from all forms of subjugation.

Writings on the topics of anarchism and women's autonomy and broader civil rights, by prominent female thinkers such as Michel as well as by lesser-known female thinkers, circulated in the Gulf of Mexico region. The language of worker autonomy, self-governance, and other radical thought tied to anarchism as well as the idea of *sindicalismo* or unionism opened a space for women to voice concerns tied to local conditions that resonated in other parts of the globe. Newspapers such as *Sagitario*, with origins in the late Porfiriato (1876–1910), were among the early venues that featured such anarchist expressions. They circulated in the region and were shared between labor organizations in Tamaulipas and throughout other Mexican states as well as across international borders.[110]

Writing about such ideas as well as sharing them and acting upon them was risky business. As ideas about worker rights circulated in the region in newspapers, leaflets, and correspondence between activists (which could be intercepted), state authorites labeled those promoting and carrying such messages as radicals, agitators, or, if referring to female activists, "women of ill-repute."[111]

* * *

What had been the context that drove Galván and González Parra to participate in the early labor movement before Piña's arrival on the scene? Several factors contributed to the increased presence and inclusion of women and their labor concerns in the regional labor movement. Not only did the importation and circulation of anarchist ideas in the Gulf of Mexico region open up a public space that embraced the idea of women as equals, but also this ideological current maintained its vibrancy in great part due to an expanding export-oriented regional economy tied to a larger international economy driven primarily by oil production. Given the economic opportunities of this sector, waves of workers continued to pour in, bringing ideas along or joining the ranks of established labor organizations. This early aperture was crucial, as it forced society to consider the ideas and presence of women like Galván and González Parra, thereby making female activists more visible in labor circles and in the media. It also encouraged wider public thinking about women's status in general, as women appeared, at times quite prominently, as supporters and fighters in the struggle for labor rights in the region's anarchist press.

What had this flourishing of collectives and organizations with an anarchist outlook and early aperture for women's issues meant during this period as Mexico became engulfed in a full-fledged Revolution? While anarchist ideas in general and *magonismo* more specifically provided a public platform with which to engage women's issues via the Junta, the PLM, or the COM, the number of female members remained small compared to male membership, and the anarcho-syndicalist movement was far from reaching internal gender equity.

Even the sincerest efforts to recruit women were deeply rooted in gendered norms and expectations. For female labor activists who promoted workers' rights, activism also took on a gendered dimension that intersected with their class identity. They were not simply what authorities described as "radical" or "dangerous" in mainstream newspapers. Their activism was framed, perceived, explained, and understood in gendered, classed, and racialized terms. Rooted in nineteenth-century conceptions of morality and sexuality, the mainstream media cast women engaged in radical labor activism as immoral. If women were perceived and accused of transgressing the boundaries of decorum, particularly if the supposed moral violation had transpired in public, they could be marked as unfit and immoral, with attendant consequences for them in their communities. Numerous petitions submitted to local and state judicial authorities abound in the Tamaulipas state and Tampico municipal archives related to women defending their honor in the courts after being accused by other women or men for "putting their reputation at risk . . . discrediting their honor," particularly those engaged in labor strikes or public rallies. This could lead to their labeling as "women of ill-repute." This label was commonly applied to female labor activists engaged in more radical forms of politics—anarchism and communism—as opposed to political ideologies considered less threatening such as state-sanctioned socialism.[112]

Within and outside labor organizations, female activist leaders, collaborators, and supporters were cast in gendered terms. The ways that gender shaped labor activism and that ideas of morality and sexuality framed progressive organizations, as well as state agents' perceptions of female labor activists, take center stage in the next chapter. For their male colleagues, female anarcho-syndicalists were deemed *compañeras*, yet in the mainstream media and according to state agents, they were "women of ill-repute." Defying categories and labels, women nonetheless pursued their interests and engaged in labor activism, forging ahead as they politicized issues long considered the domain of the private sphere and the home. Women's issues typically had been considered trivial and peripheral to the labor movement. Nonetheless, women's direct participation in anarchist organizations as adherents, and as thinkers and writers featured in media outlets endorsed by progressive organizations, signaled a continuous opening for more women to craft their own future via organized labor.

CHAPTER TWO

Gendering Anarchism and Anarcho-Syndicalist Organizations

"Compañeras en la Lucha" and "Women of Ill-Repute"

> It is in the workshops, in the social gatherings, in the streets,
> that a woman becomes a bad woman, but not in her own home.
> —*El Porvenir de Tampico*, March 1, 1907

> Women should not be confined to the home . . . she should
> learn beyond what is permitted in quantity and quality in the
> same way afforded to men. . . . The formation of the girl [as she
> becomes woman] not of men, but . . . as a *compañera* of men.
> —Francisco Ferrer i Guardia, n.d.

As the Revolution in Mexico raged on, in a pattern of reverse migration a young Isaura Galván left San Antonio and headed to the port of Tampico. Galván had worked with like-minded individuals in Grupo Racionalista in the old Alamo city. Before the close of the Revolution, she managed a safe arrival in Mexico. By 1917, Galván was the *directora principal* of an anarcho-syndicalist newspaper, *Germinal: Periódico Libertario*, a key media outlet for the ideas promoted by a local anarchist group bearing the same name, as well as affiliated organizations. Whereas the bulk of Mexican immigrants moved south-to-north, Galván chose to cross the border in the opposite direction into northern Mexico. She may have been aware of espionage activities that placed her at greater risk if she remained in the United States, as she likely faced deportation if implicated.[1] Her contemporary and COM Tampico cofounder Reynalda González Parra had arrived in Tampico from Mexico City and quickly immersed herself in the anarchist scene. She had promoted and put into practice Francisco Ferrer's ideas via educational centers in Mexico City and had worked diligently spreading anarchist propaganda to other workers there. Both Galván and González Parra represented the small but growing number of women engaged in the anarchist movement in the Tampico-Cecilia region. Identified as *compañeras en la lucha* in radical labor circles yet cast as "women of ill-repute" in the mainstream media, their trajectories provide an opportunity to examine the ways in which anarchist organizations attempted to recruit more women in the "greater march toward freedom" while exposing how such collectives remained highly gendered.

This chapter examines the dynamics that shaped both anarcho-syndicalist organizations and state perceptions about female labor activists. The early organizations introduced previously, including Hermanos Rojos, for example, were shaped by members' own understandings of gender and sexuality. At times they radically challenged embedded ideas about women's supposed limited roles but at other times could seek to restrain women's behavior. Further, a gendered discussion of the Confederación General de Trabajadores (CGT) is particularly important, as the CGT emerged as the national umbrella organization for anarcho-syndicalist groups in the country, with a particularly vibrant role in the Gulf of Mexico region by 1921. Compared to other large labor associations, the CGT claimed to be the most radical of labor collectives during the period under examination.

Throughout 1917 Galván and González Parra figured prominently in the tight-knit circle of anarchists operating from their Tampico base. Relationships with like-minded individuals in San Antonio and Mexico City, respectively, likely helped Galván and González Parra connect with other supporters who followed

Table 3. Selected Confederación General de Trabajadores (CGT) affiliates, Tamaulipas, 1921

Organization	Town or City
Federación Local	Villa Cecilia
Grupo Afinidad	Tampico
Grupo Hermanos Rojos	Villa Cecilia
Sindicato de Constructores de Tanques	Villa Cecilia
Sindicato de Dragas	Villa Cecilia
Sindicato de la Continental	Tampico
Sindicato de O. del Petróleo	Villa Cecilia
Sindicato de Soderos	Tampico
Sindicato El Porvenir de Campesinos	Villa Cecilia

Sources: Adapted from *Sagitario*, various issues; *Avante*, various issues; Baena Paz, *La Confederación General de Trabajadores, 1921–1931*; and Alcayaga Sasso, "Librado Rivera y Los Hermanos Rojos."

labor news. Their activism informed early ideas about women's place in society during the revolutionary period. Women's ideas "about their own place in society," at least as echoed in the anarchist press, reflect larger concerns about the urgent need to increase women's participation in the labor struggle, ideas about maternalism as the vehicle by which women could claim equality with men, and maternalism's role in shaping anarcho-feminism, and the larger feminist movement that often took on a transnational character along the Mexican borderlands.

The increase in women's participation in this region coincided with the growth of anarcho-syndicalism as the more structured expression of abstract anarchist thought. In Tampico, anarcho-syndicalism was not a fringe movement. It thrived in great part because it built upon the earlier vibrant mutual aid organizations and *sociedades de beneficiencia* as well as craft guilds dating back to the mid-nineteenth century, which drew upon Indigenous forms of communal life.

As anarcho-syndicalism grew, drawing its membership from industries such as oil, shipping, and hospitality including restaurants and bars, it too, became shaped by societal conventions regarding normative behavior and expectations for women and men. Despite claiming to belong to the most progressive and untainted of movements, mainly because it rejected any state affiliation, anarchist organizations nonetheless employed gendered language. Such language could both challenge prevailing gender ideas and expectations for women and replicate those same ideas about gender normativity, principally regarding women's reproductive capacities. Women's characterization by their labor activist male colleagues stood in stark contrast to that of mainstream media and in state and government documents. As male anarchist colleagues described fellow female activists and *obreras* as "*compañeras en la lucha*," mainstream newspapers described female radical activists as lacking morality, reflecting broader societal norms about women's sexuality.

In Tampico, as in other Latin American cities, a "gender[ed] ideology of domesticity" served as both ideological framework and practice by which to control the labor force.[2] Such ideas intimately shaped the lives of women, including those involved in progressive labor organizations. Women's place in society—at home and at work—was framed in progressive, modern, and revolutionary terms. Modern, progressive, and revolutionary monikers cast women as crucial to state development regardless of their half-citizen status, as they were not yet allowed to vote. Conservative newspapers from Tampico, such as *El Porvenir*, featured commentaries on the role of women in the new "modern" society as early as 1907. In an article titled "El Conde Tolstoi y el feminismo" in *El Porvenir*, women were described as beings that "surpassed men."[3] The editors emphasized women's superior position, noting that "they bring children to this world," had a role as "children's first teachers," and above all else, "because they can love, sacrificing it all."[4] These, the editors claimed, were the qualities of "good women." Most editorials and print literature of the period cast women in this binary as either good or bad.[5] Labor activism frequently complicated such gendered labeling. As campaigns to control and limit "immoral behavior" took hold, the category of "foreign" contributed to a heightened sense of fear, which further castigated women perceived as transgressing societal norms. They were defined as dangerous to the political and sexual well-being of the nation and as impeding progress.

As the Mexican Revolution heightened fears of strikers and "radicals," intensifying border controls as the war encouraged out-migration, it opened doors for women for political engagement while also scrutinizing their morality. If "women stood as pillars of sexual piety and purity," as described in writings of the period, women's political labor—particularly as activists in organizations promoting radical ideas *in public* and outside of women's supposed domestic roles—was framed in gendered and sexualized terms.[6]

Women who transgressed the boundaries of normative behavior paid a high price. The "arrival" of "radicalized workers from Tampico" in other places in northern Mexico was cause for alarm and led to the detention of female labor activists such as Galván. Editorials and commentaries castigated "unruly" behavior. Reports on local strikes by "unruly workers" stoked fear that extended across the region. Mainstream newspapers detailed the strong response to labor activism, citing authorities' stern condemnation. The citizens of Monterrey, for example, were alerted to the potential "arrival of Tampico radical workers" and warned by "Governor Zambrano . . . [who]," as one popular newspaper reported, "[was] resolved to work against any responsible element that is tied to the *huelguista* [strike] movement."[7] Zambrano and other heads of state ordered the apprehension of "worker delegates arriving in Monterrey especially from Torreón, Saltillo, and Tampico." The governor had good reason to worry, as labor activists migrated to urban centers such as Monterrey and also collaborated from afar. In large print, the editorial underscored Zambrano's intentions to "arrest even the women."[8] Local and state authorities defined women and men engaged in radical activism as "threatening to society," perceived to obstruct state progress based on a culture of morality. Regardless of the stern warning for men and "even . . . women," what was clear was that a larger labor movement had been unleashed and hopes for its containment were unrealistic.[9] Women participated in and supported the *huelguista* movement as workers and members of labor unions or associations or in sympathy for workers in their families.

As economic opportunities expanded for women, so did their participation in wage labor and their labor activism. In Mexico's capital, women made up 35 percent of the paid workforce in 1910 compared to the national 12 percent. The sectors employing women included domestic work, textiles, cigarmaking, food preparation, and dressmaking. In Tamaulipas, women worked in textiles, cigar factories, *ixtle* processing, food preparation, and related industries that had expanded, particularly in urban centers including Tampico, as a response to the growing transient and resident population employed in the higher-paying oilfields. Approximately one third of the women employed outside the home, about 30 percent, were domestic workers and laundry workers in a variety of establishments including oil camps and private homes. Women's labor in sectors such as food preparation in oil camps, hotels, and the restaurant and bar industry addressed the needs of a growing predominantly male labor force concentrated in petroleum as well as dockwork, mining, and steel. Given the historic problem of labor scarcity in the Mexican North, women's labor played a crucial role in the growth of a mature wage labor force.[10]

While government statistics on female workers remain underreported, combined with other archival material, a fair estimate of the number of female workers in the state of Tamaulipas by 1930 was one third of the labor force.[11] In Tampico and Villa Cecilia alone, nearly 1,400 women labored as paid domestic workers, while other women sold food in the public plazas, worked in laundry service in the oil camps and other places, or were employed in bars, restaurants, and other eateries.[12]

As members of this growing workforce, women engaged with the state in a variety of ways to demand labor rights that included safe working conditions, equitable wages, child care, and paid vacation. Women petitioned authorities to protest unfavorable labor conditions and established networks of support through cooperatives and mutual aid societies. This engagement revealed community-based strategies to negotiate the effects of socioeconomic change, which complemented the activity promoted by the anarcho-syndicalist movement and other labor movements.

Given anarchism's direct-action approach, women supporters in solidarity with their male counterparts participated in public rallies and demonstrations as well as strikes. But these acts of public defiance were reason to question women's morality. If women could be degraded by the mere act of being shouted at in a local *vecindad* or neighborhood, then women who engaged in public protest as workers demanding rights could potentially be subjected to graver attacks. As women took to the main plazas of their communities to protest high food prices, unjustified or dramatic rent increases, labor inequities, or poor schools, their morality came under attack. Tampico workers Ramona García, Francisca Orta, Florencia Moctezuma, and others gathered at the Plaza de la Libertad (site of many future protests and demonstrations) in November 1915, attracting the support of other women. Ramona García appeared to be the leader of the group and denounced the "100% increase in rents for the *jacales*" she and her *compañeras* called home. She proceeded to denounce the "threats and offensiveness of the *casatenientes* or landlords . . . if we don't pay the rent increase, they will throw us out." She closed her petition, which was expressed in the public square at Libertad and then published in the Tampico COM newspaper, *Tribuna Roja*, exclaiming that "we hope to receive support . . . every act in the name of justice is a battle that is won in the minds of the proletariat."[13] In a collective letter, the Tampico group emphasized its position as "*obreros*," and their willingness to petition the COM not out of some personal interest or "guided sentiment," but as workers. They felt obligated to "speak on behalf of the working poor." They reminded the COM that those who would likely suffer if the injustice continued would be "our young children."[14]

The protest foreshadowed similar grassroots movements tied to basic issues such as rent, which intimately affected both workers and their families. In nearby Veracruz, for example, a strike to protest the rent hike broke out in the early 1920s in great part led by women. Many were prostitutes required to pay rent for rooms and for the use of mattresses and other items. The bulk of the women belonged to the anarchist and CGT-affiliated Libertarian Women of Veracruz.[15] As historian Heather Fowler-Salamini argued for the case of female coffee sorters in Veracruz, food, rent, and similar issues became major demands for which women protested and organized.[16]

During the early Tampico oil worker strikes, supported by Hermanos Rojos and other anarcho-syndicalist and communist-affiliated groups, women "retrieved the confiscated anarchist red-and-black flag," after federal soldiers, following the orders of Venustiano Carranza, shut down a union hall in 1919. The women then "used [the flag] to wrap the body of a dead oil worker."[17] In the same city, "ten *campesinas*, accompanied by their twenty-five children" protested a land enclosure decree by "eating in three different local restaurants and . . . refusing to pay the bills."[18] Revolution had touched every corner of society, and women fully participated in direct-action strategies within and outside of anarcho-syndicalism.

As women protested about issues that hit close to home, their public presence provoked criticism in mainstream circles scrutinizing women's morality or perceived lack thereof. Labor organizing was largely considered a male domain.[19] While local anarchist newspapers such as *Tribuna Roja* and Mexico City's

¡Luz! were supportive of the women's protests, others were not. *¡Luz!* praised the Tampico women's efforts. It underscored the importance of supporting *compañeras* "here [Mexico City] or anywhere." In a November 1917 issue, in a section entitled "Corespondencia del buzón fraternal" (Correspondence from fraternal mail), it featured a letter by Pablo Arredondo from Monterrey. Arredondo praised the "*compañeras*" from the Sindicato de Obreros y Obreras de la Fábrica La Leona María Ortiz, Luz Montero, Josefa Ayala, Eduwiges Mireles, Juana García, Francisca López, Felipa Cortés, Emeteria Dueñas, Isabel García, and Cecilia Saucedo. These women were examples to follow, boasted Arredondo. And, he exclaimed, "let it be known to all *sindicalistas* from Mexico, that the women from Monterrey are instructing men in the art of the struggle between the proletariat and the bourgeoisie. Good for the *compañeras!*"[20] In contrast, newspapers deemed mainstream that distanced themselves from anarchist publications, such as Tampico's *El Mundo*, condemned women's public activism and labeled protests or any other activism as "public denouncements." As Tampico women rallied in the public plaza against rent increases, *El Mundo* cast them as acting too much like men or engaging in unladylike behavior.[21]

Similarly, the Tampico *Diario Periódico Pólitico de la Mañana* castigated women activists. This time, the newspaper singled out Ester López de López, who "was a *partidiaria del comunismo*," or sympathetic to communism. Her husband accused her of adultery, and the *Diario Periódico* published a brief note in 1919 on López's alleged transgression. The note provided a summary of the charges against López, concluding that "it is lamentable that stoning Christian women is no longer allowed."[22]

Such harsh commentaries and public laments about the lack of physical punishment for "radical women" were supported by experts on social issues who frequently received front-page coverage in mainstream newspapers. These newspapers featured commentaries by "character experts" such as Vernon Harris. The US-trained Harris wrote on prison populations and frequently penned commentaries about imprisoned women. He explained that women could be criminals just like men and that women "become bad in the workshops [*talleres*], in the streets, and in *convites*/meetings . . . and not at home."[23] Yet, in the same editorial, Harris noted that "women were natural loving creatures [and] even those who had been imprisoned" could "be distinguished from men due to their willingness to have everything clean and they take pride in their work." His commentary was reprinted, in Spanish, in the conservative *El Porvenir* of Tampico, further promoting the apparent "natural goodness" of women based on their sex.[24]

Women's public activism fell outside the false dichotomy described by so-called social experts. While accusations of "radical" or "immoral" behavior could damage women's reputations, they could also affect women's *actual physical mobility*. Women considered of "ill-repute," "pernicious," or who "had been corrupted by the ideas of socialism, [and] anarchism" were banned from entering Mexican ports and crossing into the United States or had a difficult time doing so.[25] For example, two women aboard the steamship *Monterrey* from New York and Havana attempted to enter Tampico in 1920. Immigration authorities immediately asked for documentation, given their port of origin, and demanded that they prove their "honest and moral" character. While there was no indication of what kind of documentation women could and should provide—as officials arbitrarily applied these measures—such proof was nonetheless required for legal admission.[26]

Women's morality was placed under a magnifying glass when they engaged in any public display of labor activism, as this behavior was perceived as damaging to other women and to their communities as well as an entire nation.[27] As a "morals purity" movement promoted by reformers in the early twentieth century took shape, state authorities stoked fear among communities about the threats of anarchism further contributing to an already tense social and political atmosphere. Women who engaged in labor activism in the public square, as did the Tampico group of women protesting higher rents, were often called *mujeres de la calle* (women of the street), which connoted clandestine prostitutes.[28] The charge of immorality helped to further strengthen the argument that radical labor activism was detrimental to women and the overall stability of the country.

Male labor activists faced similar challenges. Labor activists attempting to detail and portray the abuses of government in their newspapers were frequently blamed for featuring immoral images or including immoral news coverage. In one example of framing anarchists' messages as immoral to censor radical thought, US state authorities jailed the writers of *Regeneración* (and other newspapers), accusing them of featuring immoral images. *Magonista*-inspired *Fuerza Consciente* from San Francisco printed a story accompanied with a "photo of . . . czarist troops stripping the bodies of anarchists whom they had slain." The editors' intent to create awareness of the brutality with which anarchists were treated backfired. Authorities charged the editors for featuring the "immoral images" and proceeded to censure the newspaper and shut down its offices.[29]

Racial hierarchies too cut across ideas about gender and sexuality and further exposed the delicate and malleable nature of women's identities as *obreras* in this larger context.[30] Ideas of racial superiority and inferiority framed the already damaging perceptions about women labor activists, particularly self-proclaimed anarchists. Negative portrayals of anarchists in mainstream news outlets revealed the way in which racial ideas could potentially complicate women's position as labor activists and expose them to further critique and censure. Female anarchists had been viewed with such a lens since at least the second half of the nineteenth century.[31] African American and IWW cofounder Lucy Parsons was described in degrading terms. "Anarchy is most virulent in races of African and Oriental admixture . . . Italians, Spaniards," an editorial opined, "[Parsons] speaks with a fluent illogic, easily loses her poise, and at such times drops strongly into the negro patois that is no doubt her . . . tongue." For the "semi-American breed . . . [such as] the most notorious of them, Emma Goldman," their language was simply "crass and cheap."[32]

Yet female anarchists combatted such longstanding portrayals of themselves and their intellectual predecessors through their own writings. Tampico COM cofounder Reynalda González Parra, for example, regularly contributed commentaries in *Germinal* in which she sharply rejected the idea that women's participation in the labor movement meant they were trespassing in some sphere reserved for men. She vehemently critiqued the idea that women's main objective was simply to bear children. While she lauded women's reproductive capacity, she nonetheless couched it in an anarchist framework. This in fact distinguished anarcho-feminists from their socialist feminist counterparts, as they claimed maternalism as their own, and not maternalism to serve the interests of the state. In her "A la mujer" in *Germinal*, González Parra reminded her readers that "woman [was] evolving and [now] occupies her place . . . and sees her actions and claims her right to educate herself, to learn and then use her strength to launch that final blow that will change the course of things, create a new path." She also referenced women's unique position, politicizing their role as mothers: "emancipate yourselves, because then you will produce free children and you will have contributed to the reconstruction . . . [of] a new society."[33]

González Parra had plenty of experience promoting anarchist ideas. Before she moved to Tampico to cofound the COM branch, she had provided key instruction based on the Ferrer model to boys and girls in Mexico City. Along with at least two other women and male colleagues, she cofounded Luz y Verdad, the "Ateneo Ciencia" in Mexico City.[34] González Parra influenced other women to organize including seamstresses Elena Sánchez, Ignacia Salazar, and others who formed their own union. She also influenced women who worked in factories capping bottles as *taponeras* and *cerveceras* like Elena Partida and Cristina Camacho.[35]

This early activism and counternarratives to combat perceptions of women as morally bankrupt were key to both the anarcho-syndicalist movement and a growing nationwide women's movement. Pressing on and refuting reports on the perceived dangers of labor activists throughout the country, these women helped to strengthen organized labor and helped to influence the founding of

Figure 10. Venustiano Carranza, Carrera Torres, and other *militares*, ca. 1910–1920. Courtesy, Leonor Villegas de Magnón Papers, University of Houston.

more collectives. It also placed these women in a vulnerable position. As they became identified with radical labor activism, they too faced the wrath of the new revolutionary government. In a public display of power, the forces of Venustiano Carranza, who in the spring of 1913 became *jefe del ejército constitucionalista*, by 1916 sought to crack down on radical labor activists uninterested in a partnership between government and organized labor.

Revolutionary Crackdown on Radical Labor Activists

Whether cast as women of ill-repute or *compañeras en la lucha*, women in the movement were as vulnerable to arrests and deportations as their male colleagues under the Carranza government. Arrests and the closing of newspapers in one location affected anarchists and anarcho-syndicalists everywhere regardless of gender, and no place was safe. Mexican local and state reports as well as US reports submitted by immigration officers noted how, for some time, Tampico and other ports had witnessed a "flood" of "*gente de mal vivir* [bad people]."[36]

Tampico was a bustling cosmopolitan port with "a good many foreigners from all parts of the world," according to US intelligence reports. These included

Chinese, Belgians, Italians, Spaniards, Syrians, Arabs, Greeks, Dutch, Americans, and British nationals.[37] The US Military Intelligence Division grew concerned about political currents in the Mexican North given its relative proximity to the United States. Sounding the alarm, one intelligence report detailed the way in which "labor is organized in nearly every trade . . . tending to increase the individual's ideas of his personal importance." It concluded that "the Socialistic-Bolshevik movement is at present exerting a strong influence on social conditions."[38]

The report, however, did not distinguish between the ideological backgrounds of labor collectives. Labor activists belonging to the newly created state-endorsed Confederación Regional Obrera Mexicana (CROM), compared to those from Hermanos Rojos or Germinal, were likely to receive some protection from the state and therefore were not threatened with surprise arrests or Mexican troops descending upon their labor meetings. The CROM did include some anarcho-syndicalists, such as Galván's associate Ricardo Treviño and J. Marcos Tristan, but it quickly lost traction.[39] It was not spared from criticism, even given its willingness to work with the revolutionary government. The stubborn anarchists made an easy target, according to state agents. Unlike other labor activists, anarchists insisted upon both direct action and a rejection of any collaboration with the Mexican government, regardless of its revolutionary claims.

Despite Carranza's emergence early on as a prolabor candidate, particularly given the brief pact with the COM in 1915, activists in Mexico City and Tampico came under attack as Carranza soon turned his back on the most radical segment of the labor movement. In the spring and fall of 1917, amid revolutionary factions' struggles to secure the lucrative oilfields of Tampico and surrounding areas, port authorities loyal to Carranza descended upon the old docks, cracking down on labor activists perceived as obstacles to revolutionary state progress. Intensifying the situation, over 15,000 workers with ties to the COM, the IWW, and other organizations, including Hermanos Rojos, went on strike against oil corporations, including foreign-owned Pierce and Huasteca in the summer of 1917. Former general and current governor Alfredo Ricaut, who had overseen military operations on behalf of Carranza in that region, ordered numerous arrests.[40] In the summer of 1916 and once again in 1917, El Águila oil workers struck and were repeatedly met with military force. Carranza ordered General Emiliano Nafarrate to send "military detachments and cavalry to disperse labor meetings, and arrest principal agitators."[41] His larger intent was to politically control organized labor, yet the anarcho-syndicalist segment of the movement was unwilling to enter into any kind of labor-state pact. There was no room for negotiation.[42] Long-time activists such as Treviño faced arrest and deportation as Carranza's forces unleashed attacks on Mexico City COM activists, resulting in bloodshed and numerous arrests.[43] Tampico COM members petitioned local authorities to free "our *compañeros en la lucha* . . . confined to the penitentiary in D.F. . . . for the crime of inciting strikes."[44]

As Mexico sealed its new revolutionary constitution and the United States entered the Great War, state and local authorities acted quickly to detain activists turned in by agents who had infiltrated the anarchist movement. Among those detained was Isaura Galván.[45] With this move, Tampico authorities dealt a serious blow to the anarcho-syndicalist movement. The apprehension of activists could mean prolonged periods of media inactivity, which hurt recruiting efforts. Galván along with two of her colleagues, a Cuban and Manuel Almedo, a Portuguese laborer, were arrested during the 1917 oil worker strike in Tampico.[46] Authorities detained Galván in May 1917 based on accusations of instigating a strike among the oil workers of the various petroleum corporations. Indeed, Galván had been in the thick of it. Of the three, Almedo had been arrested previously. Almedo had brought with him ideas about worker rights from his native Portugal and soon joined local *obrero* organizations after finding work in the oilfields. Shortly after arriving in Tampico, he was detained after surveillance reports detailed his anarchist activities. After US consular agents formally discharged Almedo, he attended a "meeting of the IWW . . . and . . . got mixed up in that strike in Tampico." Almedo testified that he "went to the mass meeting . . . in Tampico . . . in sympathy with them."[47] He was released only to face subsequent arrests.

During the second arrest, the Tampico military stormed into an IWW gathering seeking to apprehend "dangerous agitators." While some workers escaped "out of the windows and back doors," Almedo was caught in the middle of it and authorities apprehended him as well as an unnamed Cuban national.[48] Soldiers took Almedo, his Cuban colleague, and several members of the IWW to the rail station and proceeded to place them on a train. From there, the prisoners were transported to Monterrey via the Tamaulipas capitol, Ciudad Victoria, and eventually taken to the border town of Nuevo Laredo for processing.[49]

Galván appears to have been released within months of the crackdown. Records do not provide her testimony, but we know from her activity with *Germinal* that upon her release she found herself amid yet another round of labor activist arrests. On November 11, 1917, some of her colleagues from *Germinal*, among them the Spaniard Jorge D. Borrán, were detained in the local jail awaiting orders to be deported. Galván managed to pay the Centro de Obreros a visit during their regular meeting to relay the news. Galván informed Centro's general secretary, Macedonio Oyervides, of the developments. Oyervides then forwarded the communication to long-time activist and cofounder of the COM, Jacinto Huitrón in Mexico City, stating that he knew about Borrán and others because "la *compañera* Isaura Galván, the director of *Germinal*, informed us of the arrests during one of our meetings in the Centro." Oyervides urged Huitrón to inform fellow activists in Tampico and Ciudad Victoria, as "these [fellow labor organizations] probably do not know" of the recent development.[50] The way these networks circulated news was remarkable, as members continued reporting on arrests and developments, risking more arrests. Indeed, *Germinal*'s offices were destroyed and its various members jailed. By February 1918 the newspaper closed and the group dissolved, although it revived itself years later under the name Vida Libre. Galván was free and, while Borrán faced orders to be deported from Mexico, he managed to reinsert himself in the movement and collaborated with Vida Libre. He also appeared in 1919 as the COM-Tampico delegate at the Second Congress of the Pan American Federation of Labor in New York City.[51]

The movement's resiliency was on full display as activists organized a nationwide workers' congress in the midst of the labor crackdown. The first Congreso Obrero Regional del Sindicalismo Revolucionario had taken place in Veracruz four years earlier. Labor activists from Veracruz and other states, as well as supporters from Mexico City, joined local labor activists for a second annual meeting planned for Tampico. In October 1917, twelve Mexican states sent representatives from at least thirty-two organizations to Tampico for the convening. Fourteen of the thirty-two organizations were locally based. Carranza, now fully recognized by the United States and with access to US arms and ammunition, attempted to shut down the congress and ordered one of his generals in Tamaulipas to pursue the main organizers. Ricardo Treviño and other *Germinal* collaborators, including the well-known Russian immigrant and anarchist Alejandro (Alexander) Berkman were subsequently jailed.[52]

Besides using military force, Carranza's government also relied on paid spies to infiltrate various branches of the larger labor movement. One spy, José Andrade, helped to track down the whereabouts of Ricardo Treviño, before Treviño publicly supported Luis Morones and the CROM. Andrade appears to have met Treviño while in Texas or had been tracking him since Treviño's activist days as a member of Grupo Racionalista in San Antonio. When he spotted Treviño in Tampico, he called the authorities, informing them that "the suspected . . . radical anarchist" had been identified.[53] Years later, Treviño remarked how he felt uneasy after Andrade, whom he had befriended in San Antonio, had not greeted him. He suspected something was wrong. When Treviño stopped by the offices of El Águila to collect his paycheck, company guards immediately apprehended him. It is possible that Andrade also surveilled other former members of the San Antonio anarchist group who now were fully integrated into Germinal and Hermanos Rojos and were active with the COM and IWW in Tampico.[54] Treviño had been a member of the IWW-sanctioned Tampico Petroleum Workers Union and the Maritime Workers Union. Other collaborators were under surveillance too, as the chief of the *policia reservada*, an elite police force, kept the municipal president abreast of labor activists' movements in the Tampico-Cecilia region. The police force kept a close watch on COM Tampico members' activities and whereabouts.[55]

Betraying the basic tenets of the Revolution by 1916, Carranza ordered labor activists arrested as efforts to consolidate the new revolutionary government began in earnest. It would be a long road toward reconstruction, and removing the most radical of activists was central to that effort. The anarchists, unlike most communists and socialists, had no intention of working with any state entity on behalf of organized labor. They emerged as roadblocks to state progress. While an alliance formed between the COM and Carranza, mainly via the COM's paramiliary Batallones Rojos, it quickly dissolved. Between 1916 and 1919, Carranza ordered activists jailed or killed. He unleashed forces to stop the more radical elements of labor from expanding and, on the eve of the second workers' convention, Carranza's men arrested COM leader José Barragan Hernández from Mexico City's Federación de Sindicatos de Obreros and assassinated him.[56] Barragan Hernández, who had been involved in the planning of a general strike in Mexico City in 1916, among other activities, had persuaded some of his colleagues to cease activity while activist colleagues awaited trial for their participation in the strike that threatened to cut off electricity to the city. Appearing sympathetic to the labor cause, Carranza's general and future president Alvaro Obregón had urged Barragan Hernández to convince his colleagues to refrain from further action. While some negotiations took place, these were not held at the COM headquarters nor the Federación de Sindicatos de Obreros, and military forces easily killed Barragan Hernández.[57]

Despite Carranza's purging of COM-affiliated groups, delegates stuck to the plan and attended the Segundo Congreso Obrero Regional on October 13, 1917, which marked the anniversary of the death of anarchist Francisco Ferrer.[58] The solemn occasion to honor Ferrer was overshadowed by the tense environment as activists remained on guard. It was no secret that Mexican authorities kept a watchful eye on the attendees; even the US consul in Tampico sent a note informing the foreign investment community, among them Texan businessmen with oil interests, to remain alert.[59]

Anxieties aside, representatives from Tampico and Villa Cecilia discussed major labor issues with their colleagues in the long-awaited conference. Among the delegates representing Tampico was Reynalda González Parra from the Centro de Estudios Sociales Feministas and the Tampico COM. González Parra was probably the only female delegate (although not the sole female attendee) to the convention. It is likely that she was the lone woman featured in a 1917 photograph of the delegates in the second workers' convention. González Parra joined colleagues from the local oil unions, the Hermanos Rojos, and other labor collectives. While the historical record is limited as to the daily operations of González Parra's Centro Feminista, we know that its members engaged the larger question of women's place in society at the congress, particularly with respect to labor and politics. The Centro represented one of the earliest all-female anarcho-syndicalist collectives in the Gulf of Mexico region.[60]

While the Segundo Congreso did not resolve all the labor disputes between those wishing to align politically in exchange for protection from the state and those wishing to remain loyal to the anarchist antistate ideal, it was an important meeting given the resolutions that eventually were agreed upon. Among the principles by which members were urged to engage in their activist practices were "an insult to one [worker] is an insult to all [workers]," echoing similar calls of solidarity throughout the world by organizations such as the IWW, and "*organización sindical*" or "organizing through unions." The latter principle was voted as the "most efficient medium" by which the proletariat could reach its goals. Thus, by the final years of the Revolution, it was anarcho-syndicalism that triumphed over a more abstract anarchism in the region.[61]

(En)gendering Anarcho-Syndicalist Organizations

Two other resolutions adopted in the Segundo Congreso Obrero stood out as remarkable for the period. These reflected the larger gendered concerns of the early female groups involved with Hermanos Rojos, the Tampico COM, the PLM, and other locals including the Centro de Estudios Sociales Feministas. One resolution gave the "right to workers to avoid an unlimited procreation when this place[d] economic threats on their livelihoods," reflecting larger concerns over reproductive rights. Another resolution, appearing as point number six of ten, "recommended all labor organizations and *grupos educativos*, etc., carry and promote an active propaganda to promote and encourage women's education and women's organizations as well as that of the peasant and all of the workers who need to be in contact with the centers of propaganda [Hermanos Rojos, COM] and collectives."[62] González Parra's Centro as a participant in the congress possibly shifted the conversation to include such provisions, although most of the organizations sending representatives had not been hostile to women's issues. González Parras appears as the lone female endorsing and signing the resolutions among thirty-four male delegates at the convention. Notwithstanding its limitations, the congress reflected the gradual inclusion of women's issues in an anarchist platform.

Just as anarchists' own gendered ideas about society in general and women's place more specifically shaped their writings and political positions, these ideas also shaped the organizations in which they belonged. The early writings featured in *Regeneración* and its other incarnations, including *Revolución*, reflected the gendered way in which activism was explained and promoted. Such gendered framing was not limited to women. PLM writers critiqued those men who failed to join the movement by invoking a sense of lost masculinity. In one editorial, men who did not participate in the coming revolution were compared to women who, for the writers, did have the courage to act upon their beliefs. "The . . . female fighters put men who fail to fight to shame." It launched a scathing critique to shake up the men failing to act: "The women are a model to emulate and set an example for the men who dishonor their masculinity as they remain inactive when it is their obligation to take up arms to destroy tyranny. . . . They [women] put to shame those who do not wish to sacrifice their money, to arm the *pueblo*, who only proclaim to be armed with weapons and ammunition so that the *lucha* can begin."[63] The message was a powerful one, as the debate over women's place in society still included claims about women's inability to engage in politics—broadly defined—and any activity outside of the home. Other organizations also took to gendered logic to castigate men who remained inactive.

Although this scolding invoking a supposed lack of masculinity could possibly draw more male members, it did not have a dramatic impact on the recruitment of women. Hermanos Rojos was among the earliest groups to espouse anarchist thought and among those with a progressive position on women's place in society, both public and private, but it only had one female member, Luz Gudiño Marín. Compared to the PLM's branches, particularly the all-female ones, Hermanos Rojos lagged behind. Gudiño Marín was the partner or possibly a relative of Pedro Gudiño, among the active members of the organization and contributor of several commentaries appearing in anarchist newspapers. While women contributed to newspapers sponsored or cosponsored by Hermanos Rojos, Gudiño remained the only female member, and her background remains obscure.

Gudiño Marín appeared in the organization's roster as early as 1917, and her few writings appear until the early 1920s in *Sagitario*, *Avante*, and *Paso*. She published a short story, "El día de Navidad," in *Sagitario* in early 1924. It was a sad account of three orphans awaiting gifts on Three Kings Day. After exchanging thoughts about the Christmas gifts and other festivities, the orphans, led by Pepín, the youngest and savviest of all, discover the real truth. He tells the others that the three kings are "bad, they are all bad." Alarmed, the eldest of the three orphans exclaimed, "Shut up! The three kings are holy, they're saints!" Pepín continued as he cried, "You see . . . they're bad, because they only bring gifts to happy children, those with mothers."[64] In the story, Pepín convinces the other orphans that Three Kings Day is a fiction and, as poor and motherless children, that reality was the one they lived. In an explicit way, through her creative writing, Gudiño Marín underscored anticlericalism, one of anarchism's tenets. While not in an uplifting way, she explained how the working class was not privy to such glories, even if they were false.[65]

Like González Parra and Gudiño Marín, Isaura Galván's presence in the anarcho-syndicalist movement was key in the opening up of organizations to include women's participation. Galván had worked closely with Ricardo Treviño and Román Delgado. She played a crucial role in overseeing the day-to-day operations of *Germinal*, including the printing and reprinting of news stories, commentaries, poems, short fiction, and other types of written expression. Appearing in some of the issues *Germinal* published early on were editorials and commentaries on the "woman question." While Galván's tenure as *directora* did not last throughout the newspaper's life, the group's selection of a woman for a leadership position sent a strong message about women's inclusion in labor organizations.

As Galván operated as the *directora*, Treviño served as *Germinal*'s administrator. Together they collaborated with Román Delgado, a Spanish anarchist who arrived in Tampico sometime in the early 1900s and later joined Hermanos Rojos. Delgado was a frequent contributor to *Germinal*. In his eloquent "Adelante compañeras," Delgado "lamented" how for some time "we have seen the female workers of this port not concerned over various problems that we are committed to resolve."[66] Delgado, as did other colleagues, openly called for women to join the fight and participate in labor activism.

Delgado and Treviño encouraged women to contribute to the movement by recruiting both men and women to join the fight. González Parra heeded the call and early on shared her thoughts in the COM's *Tribuna Roja* and *Germinal*, urging others to engage in labor activism. Among the earliest published writings by González Parra is a 1915 commentary entitled "Intransigencia" for *Tribuna Roja*.[67] González Parra was ahead of her time. Reflecting a deep distrust of religion and expressing her views on modernity within labor circles, she critiqued those who still framed their societal challenges and hopes with fictitious religious ideas.

She also scolded men for "creating drama . . . when competing personalities got in the way" of the larger struggle for labor equality. She wrote, "It is about time we understand that men are not indispensable and that the opinion of one is not the opinion of all."[68] She urged all workers to treat "fellow *compañero*[s]" with respect and urged them to collaborate instead of creating drama that only delayed the mission of organized labor.

Her writings also reflected some of the earliest commentaries about organized labor from a gendered perspective, underscoring how—despite anarchism's promotion of a classless, stateless, and godless world—the idea of the family still held a central place in anarchist discourse. González Parra compared the Casa del Obrero to a mother guiding a family, but pleaded with her colleagues to not turn it into the "type [of family] that blindly follows God." She wrote, "don't make the Casa del Obrero, our common and loving mother, into what Catholics do . . . to the family . . . they tie it to God." She continued explaining how belief in God created a dichotomy that at its core destroyed the very foundation of the family. Why frame the family within this context? She argued that the COM had to, at any cost, avoid acting like God, as "God . . . either loves his children or throws them into that so-called hell."[69] For González Parra the family who blindly followed religious doctrine was doomed. More importantly, it was the structuring of family via religion that helped to breed inequality within the home.

While there is no mention of *feminismo* in any of her writings, nor did she call herself a *feminista*, she belonged to and possibly cofounded the Centro de Estudios Feministas Sociales in Tampico; she wrote in-depth critiques of societal inequality and the institutions that structured such inequality, which usually relegated women to the bottom rung of society. Her commentaries reflect the larger COM mission of "women's emancipation" promoted by Mexico City COM colleagues such as Jacinto Huitrón. Yet emancipation was a process of liberation, of freedom, of freedom from religious restraints; emancipation was not suffrage, nor collaboration with any political entity nor the state. It was through anarchist thought and action and collective unity—a unity that leveled the playing field for all—that one could finally be free. Huitrón's writings in *Revolución Social* and other outlets legitimized González Parra as a real "*compañera en la lucha*." He underscored women's roles as "*compañeras* in the struggle . . . no longer slaves of the family, of society, of religion, of work and the home!"[70]

In other commentaries published two years after her "Intransigencia" thought piece appeared in *Germinal*, González Parra further urged women to join the proletarian uprising. She promoted the goals of the anarcho-syndicalist movement and of the COM branches including the Tampico local, publicly underscoring the issues that mattered most to women workers. Among those issues were "conferences on labor issues" and "conferences focused on labor unionism among women."[71] Thus, these opportunities for dialogue complemented her direct-action approach. In 1917, she penned "A la mujer," in which she urged women, "who had, for [years], walked with their head down[,] . . . emancipate yourself, in order to produce free children and contribute to the reconstruction and the formation of a new society . . . free and beautiful."[72] Similarly in "¡Al abordaje!" she exclaimed in her detailed prose, "don't you hear the shots from the gunfire, those outrageous screams, the groans from the *hijos del pueblo* [the children of the people] who lay on the ground, their bodies pierced with bullets, not from enemies but from brothers who have been lost since childhood? Rise up! Join the multitude who enraged have now clenched their fists!" She continued, "grab your red *rebozo* and join the fight." Underscoring her distrust in religion she asked, "If you are not yet sick from the incense and the falsity of glorious promises have not yet driven you crazy . . . if you feel like a man at least once in your lifetime, then brandish the axe of vengeance and fight with a raucous voice, all aboard!"[73] González Parras's writings reflected her training as an educator and were rooted in experience.[74]

A 1917 poetic commentary penned by González Parra after her arrival in Tampico rallied local women to join the fight. In "Para las dos" (For the both of us), she outlined the class differences among women: while some were adorned "with precious stones," others wandered in the streets, with little to eat or with no home, walking aimlessly. Other women, she wrote, fortunate enough to have found a good man with whom to share their life, quickly discover, however, that he "[is] a slave of those from above." For the ills of women, "Who was to blame?" She explained,

> Shall we blame men, that tyrant who barely concerns himself with elevating women? A human being like he, with the same privileges and rights . . . we shall blame, above all, women. Rise up! Don't you know you have so many executioners? [It] doesn't matter. Rise up! And tell society, I despise you! You with your crimes, with your violations, with your half-virgins and your beauties whom despite being covered with gold and stones, are not worth what I am worth. The suffering redeems, the suffering makes [us] stronger. I challenge you! Rebel against your love and lord and tell him that you are strong, intelligent, tell them, tell him, 'I am so strong and intelligent!' Let us dig, demolish, and rebuild. The world is ours; we are two to conquer it! Woman! Rise up . . . you are equipped with reason . . . , and that is what will give you strength.[75]

González Parra challenged her peers. Women's strength did not emanate from their position as mothers of Mexico. The strength lay in them as equals, as beings, and it was their duty to fight. After all, she argued, women possessed all the qualities and skills necessary to transform their surroundings for the good of all women and ultimately all workers. Via her writings and her participation in the anarcho-syndicalist movement, she created and pushed for an agenda that placed women's equity at the front and center. This was especially crucial as it would open up spaces for women like Caritina Piña in the following decade.

Probably the only commentary she wrote in which she did not underscore women's roles in the labor movement was a short piece she published in 1917 entitled, "¡Salud!" She called on the "[urban] worker . . . peasant, [the] intellectual . . . [the] fighter who has crossed the seas and has crisscrossed the world shedding light . . . carving new spaces . . . bringing your sorrows but your hopes, too, your faith, your love, your ideal[s], welcome!" Blurring socioeconomic lines, she encouraged people from all backgrounds to fight, and she underscored the power of fellow activists from abroad. She foresaw "the foundation of what will help us reconstruct this society," via the "fusion of all of our ideas, our great ideal."[76] The "¡Salud!" commentary was representative of writings by and for women by other anarcho-syndicalist organizations. Yet her other writings signal her lone radical voice in a mostly male-dominated labor movement.

As *Germinal* published González Parra's "¡Salud!" the third national congress of workers took place. However, this renewed intent to forge a strong national labor movement proved disastrous for anarchists. The consensus after long discussions at the May 1918 meeting in Saltillo, Coahuila, was the adoption of a structure tied to the new Mexican state. The push for collaboration with the state via a politicized national labor collective diverged from the basic tenets of anarchism. The result of the congress was not only the creation of a state-endorsed national labor organization, the CROM, but also the subsequent creation of a parallel political party, the Partido Laborista Mexicano, which further solidified the early phase of organized labor's alignment with corresponding political parties. This third congress marked a new era for Mexican organized labor. Involved in the discussions that led to the creation of the Partido Laborista was none other than the newly minted lawyer and Tamaulipas *político* Emilio Portes Gil. As Portes Gil helped to slowly build a base upon which to firmly position himself in the world of organized labor, one of Carranza's rivals, Adolfo de la Huerta, launched the Plan de Agua Prieta, which Portes Gil supported. The plan rejected Carranza as well as any pro-Carranza leadership in Tamaulipas. By May 1920, replacing pro-Carranza state leadership, Portes Gil became the state's provisional governor.[77]

While some attendees at the historic third congress supported the creation of the Partido Laborista including Ricardo Treviño, other long-time anarchists such as COM cofounder Jacinto Huitrón—disillusioned, abandoned the talks.

Huitrón, by 1921, would become a founding member of the CGT, which became, in ideology and tactics, among the main opponents of the state-controlled CROM and later, an enemy of Portes Gil's new party. From this split also came support for an organization based on communist ideology. This segment, organized as the Mexican Communist Party by 1919, supported political affiliations while emphasizing worker control of the means of production.[78] What would come to aid Huitrón and the CGT was the long relationship among various anarcho-syndicalists groups in the region since the dawn of the twentieth century. Those opposing the CROM and supporting the CGT, including women's groups, remained loyal to their ideals. Albeit with plenty of challenges, the anarcho-syndicalist movement remained afloat. It did so in great part thanks to the larger efforts of the CGT, which provided a national organizing structure for the numerous groups who remained committed to rejecting state cooperation and promoting anarchist ideals.

The CGT's Role in Encouraging Women's Activist Participation on the Eve of Caritina Piña's Arrival

The broadening of the anarcho-syndicalist movement to engage women's labor issues was further strengthened during the revolutionary period. The Revolution cost many lives, uprooted people, increased sexual assaults on women, and destroyed entire villages. It also ushered in a new era for women's rights. By the mid-1920s a mature anarcho-syndicalist movement emerged strong enough to cast a wider, more national net. Such efforts to garner support from the various local and regional affiliates took place via a newly organized national entity, the Confederación General de Trabajadores (CGT).

Long-time anarchists such as Huitrón, members of the Hermanos Rojos and the IWW Tampico branch, and anarcho-syndicalists from affinity groups as well as self-declared communists who had formed the Communist Federation of the Mexican Proletariat or the Revolutionary Bloc were among those who created the CGT in February 1921.[79] The CGT became affiliated with the International Association of Workers headquartered in Amsterdam. Amsterdam was the headquarters of the early anarchist movement, attracting Mexican workers and their counterparts in other regions of the world. Sealed in the 1906 *Carta de Amiens*, the anarchist manifesto defined anarcho-syndicalism as privileging worker autonomy through union organizing. The following year in a conference in Amsterdam the idea of *sindicalismo* became more clearly defined as an "effective tool to create and intervene in labor matters at the local and international level."[80]

Endorsing such anarcho-syndicalist principles, the CGT followed COM tradition. It welcomed women into the organization and moved to incorporate organizations such as the Union of Anarchist Women in Mexico into their sphere of influence.[81] It increasingly defined itself in opposition to the CROM, as the "true, revolutionary organization . . . adopting direct action that consist[ed] of, among other things, workers' themselves directly handling their own issues," underscoring their rejection of political action and collaboration with the state.[82] By 1924, the CGT had at least 120,000 members from a variety of affiliated organizations, including the large electrical workers' union, and continued promoting their slogan, "Comunismo Libertario." The Tampico branch of the CGT warned its members and the general public of "the false rhetoric of a united front," as it reminded readers that "any individual who governs will be the people's enemy and will condemn people's liberty." It further argued that "all government is bad, as it represents violence, thievery, and oppression."[83]

As class solidarity and worker autonomy via direct action outside government politics defined the CGT's goals and ideas, these were further shaped by gendered ideologies that pressured men to embrace women's activism as a sign of real masculinity. Despite anarchism's stated goals of gender equity, anarchists were not free from gendered biases. Notions of morality tied to normative ideas of gender and sexuality that privileged men's virility, masculinity, and honor guided much of the rhetoric framing labor activism. As historian Sonya O. Rose has argued for working-class men in Great Britain, "respectab[ility] was a requirement for working-class men wishing to gain and exercise suffrage." Such "good citizenship," even for "militant" laborers, which included virtues tied to working-class masculinity, was "necessary to preserve their 'spirit of manhood.'"[84] Among even the most militant of labor activists such as Ricardo Flores Magón and his brothers, ideas of masculinity further informed the rhetoric of social justice. In his "Los ilegales" (The illegals), Flores Magón noted that "the law castrates," and those who were subjected to the law who did not dare to transgress it, the *castrados*, "could not possibly become men."[85] Socialist and anarchist ideology advocated that man "should be rebellious and not passive . . . and should not allow himself to be exploited."[86] Esteban Hernández, a fellow Tampico "*obrero rojo*," or radical (red) worker, who was accused of murdering the long-time Tampico socialist Isauro Alfaro, was used as an example of "masculine virility." Alfaro, a long-time dockworker activist, had played a crucial role in expanding what had become a state-sanctioned socialist movement. When a news story featured Hernández as the possible culprit, he was commended for his "virility." According to the anarcho-syndicalist newspaper *Alma Obrera*, Hernández's virility allowed him to expose the supposed violations committed by Alfaro and the prosocialist Gremio Unido de Alijadores (dock-workers' union).[87] Compared to anarchists who owed nothing to the state, the state-endorsed dockworkers' union lacked real masculinity; thus, the murdering of a socialist could possibly be condoned.

Men who violated the tenets of anarcho-syndicalism lacked the capacity to be fully realized, or real men, as only real men exhibited and promoted the "right" ideas. These included the capacity to treat women, and particularly female labor activists who fought in the *lucha*, as real *compañeras*. For anarcho-syndicalists and other supporters of organized labor, women workers and women union members were "*compañeras en la lucha*" in theory and practice.

* * *

CGT affiliates and its newspapers defined fellow female activists such as Rey-nalda González Parra, Luz Gudiño Marín, and Isaura Galván as *compañeras en la lucha*. Mainstream media, however, continued portraying female radical activists as women void of any morals. The early activism of women in the region, however, slowly broadened the conversation about women's place in organized labor and in society in general, reflecting what was actually happening on the ground. As the discourse about women's place continued in the press—both anarchist and mainstream—more women engaged in paid labor, and more of them joined the ranks of organized labor.

As the Revolution came to a close, the industrialization project resumed and so did women's labor in commercial establishments, factories, and the oil camps. Coupled with the increased visibility of editorials and commentaries on the topic of women's labor, women's presence as paid laborers stood as a reminder that the labor force was diverse. It also signaled a shift in women's rhetoric about their place in the labor movement. Women's position as moth-ers, particularly those working and caring for children or *madres obreras*, as well as women's potential as future mothers, would become highly politicized in the country. As the state incorporated the language of motherhood hoping to seek a safe way to legitimize women's participation in Mexico's reconstruc-tion, radical female activists too privileged motherhood. Yet theirs was firmly placed in the context of years of anarchist thought on women's equality free from the state, religion, and marriage. The earlier network between anarchist collectives and PLM branches served as a foundation for the continuation of transnational exchange, including ideas about motherhood that transpired in the postrevolutionary period in which Caritina Piña took part.[88]

The postrevolutionary period brought with it new challenges for the next generation of female activists. Galván and González Parra's early groundwork during the nineteen teens foreshadowed the activism of Caritina Piña, Felipa Velásquez, María Mendoza, and others during the 1920s and 1930s. From freeing political prisoners who critiqued the revolutionary government that had, in their view, violated the very foundation of the Revolution, to fighting for agrarian reform and fighting against a wave of state-sanctioned socialism that soon threatened the existence of anarcho-syndicalist organizations, activists such as Caritina Piña embodied the hope of an anarchist movement that could finally bring about a real revolution. The following chapter retraces the local and transnational reach of Piña's labor network as anarcho-syndicalism entered a new phase.

CHAPTER THREE

Feminismos Transfronterizos in Caritina Piña's Labor Network

> This indescribable outrage committed by those eternal detractors of human emancipation . . . force us to . . . ask you to make the necessary propaganda and reproduce our *manifesto* . . . to make it known to all the workers of the entire world the atrocities that are committed on a daily basis against our *compañeros* and most sincere fighters.
>
> —Caritina Piña, July 6, 1929

Shortly after the last battles over the strategic oilfields took place during the Mexican Revolution, Caritina Piña emerged as a community activist in Villa Cecilia's working-class neighborhoods. Like Isaura Galván and Reynalda González Parra, Piña was a migrant who found Tampico-Cecilia to be a welcoming place for radical ideas. Her childhood was rooted in the countryside in the small town of Ocampo, about 125 miles west of Tampico. Born mostly likely in 1895 to Felicitas Montalvo and Nicanor Piña Hernández, Piña lived a good part of her childhood in the home of her stepfather, Federico de León, as Piña Hernández was married to another woman while maintaining an extramarital relationship with Montalvo. Although he could not register Piña as a legitimate child, Piña Hernández recognized her with his surname, as his "natural" child. In 1908, only six years after Montalvo had married de León, and as Piña entered her teens, Montalvo died, leaving Piña an orphan.

Piña Hernández was involved in local politics and the military in his native Ocampo, yet his active life did not prevent him from assuming his fatherly duties. Upon Monalvo's death, Nicanor took Piña to live with him and his wife, Demetria D. Gutiérrez, and their children.[1] During the late Porfiriato, Piña Hernández served as an alternate member of Congress and, on the eve of the Revolution, he was mayor of the town. When Caritina Piña was only seventeen and living with her father and her half-siblings in Ocampo, Piña Hernández oversaw a group of Mexican *rurales* in the town and vicinity and actually combatted early *magonistas*, including the agrarian rebel Higinio Tanguma and his men. Yet, following the twists and turns of the emergence and decline of various revolutionary factions, Piña Hernández soon lent support to Venustiano Carranza. By 1913 he was a colonel and, that fall in the midst of Carranza's crackdown on radical labor activists, earned the title of brigadier general overseeing the cavalry. Given his son Zenaido's rebel proclivities, it is likely that Piña Hernández felt it necessary to support the Revolution on behalf of Carranza. As a mature young woman, Piña surely was aware of her father's actions and his support for the Revolution, though the extent of his influence on her is unclear. It was not uncommon for former Porfirian federals to support a revolutionary faction, just as revolutionaries could switch sides from Villistas to Carrancistas or vice versa. In a small town such as Ocampo, and as someone with social and political capital, Nicanor could easily transform into a pro-Revolution figure. By the end of the Mexican Revolution, he moved his children, including Caritina, and his wife Demetria to the Tampico area. This migration to Tampico is unsurprising—thousands of Mexicans and foreigners, lured by expanded economic opportunities, made the journey.[2]

Figure 11. Caritina Piña Montalvo, ca. 1920. Courtesy, personal collection of Marvin Osiris Huerta Márquez.

So, by 1920 or 1921, the Piña Hernández family found itself in the Gulf of Mexico region. It is possible that upon her father's departure from Tampico, as he was reassigned to Mexico City for military duty in 1924, Piña decided to live on her own or had done so upon the family's arrival.

Piña's activism on behalf of political prisoners—in the form of outright protests and letter-writing campaigns and via alliances with men and women such as María del Jesús Alvarado, Esther and María Mendoza, and Felipa Velásquez—evidenced an expansive regional network of female anarcho-syndicalist activists, whose work continued the legacy of pioneers Isaura Galván and Reynalda González Parra.

Radical labor ideas circulated widely in Villa Cecilia via propaganda plays and newsletters and were voraciously consumed by petroleum workers, female oil camp laundry workers, and other Mexican migrants from the countryside.[3] Residents and workers alike attended community theaters featuring anarchist plays by Ricardo Flores Magón, Pietro Gori, and the Frenchman Octave Mirbeau. Members of Esteban Méndez Guerra's anarchist group Luz del Esclavo, who also actively participated in Hermanos Rojos, were among the actors in those plays. The anarchist plays featured in Villa Cecilia's theaters often ran daily and attracted the predominantly working-class community. For many, particularly those who were illiterate, this was the main vehicle by which to keep abreast of labor issues locally and abroad. Further, those who could read anarchist newspapers featuring reviews of such plays read aloud to those who gathered to listen, exchanging thoughts and beliefs with one another. This was the Villa Cecilia that welcomed Piña.[4]

By the time that Piña entered the world of labor activism, according to census records, she lived in a household separate from her stepfamily. She shared a home with Gregorio Ortiz, an *obrero* originally from Guadalcazar, San Luis Potosí, who in 1930 was thirty-two. It is unclear whether Piña met Ortiz in San Luis Potosí or in the Tampico area, but they maintained an intimate relationship living in free union. María Flores, a thirty-eight-year-old unmarried woman, also lived in the same household, as did two minor children: Gelacio and Dolores Ortiz, eleven and ten years old, respectively, and likely to be Gregorio's children. All household members indicated their ability to read and write, unlike the majority of the households interviewed in that neighborhood in Villa Cecilia. Piña was the only one in the household who hailed from Tamaulipas.[5]

While almost all of the other residents interviewed in that one block during the 1930 census reported Catholicism as their religion, Piña and Gregorio Ortiz indicated "*ninguna*" (none) to the same question.[6] The makeup of the household as well as her lack of religious affiliation seem to correspond to her adoption of anarchist ideas. Although Piña's writings did not engage the topic of free union and free love, her colleagues' writings, in newspapers she supported with donations, did. Jaime Vidal and Ricardo Treviño encouraged their *compañeros* to reject the institution of marriage and find love free from restraints. Women from the Liga Cultural and others also condemned the practice of marriage and further critiqued clericalism. Piña received newspapers featuring those commentaries and was responsible for their distribution. She was a subscriber herself and donated money on numerous occasions; she was well aware of those ideas. Further, her own mother's free union with her father probably shaped her outlook on marriage.

Villa Cecilia, as recounted by the archivist of the Madero Historical Archive and local histories, was a tight-knit community that was intricately tied to oil worker culture. Piña's exposure to community labor-based activism likely included an introduction to the history of activism of the early IWW locals, the PLM, and female pioneers like Galván and González Parra. Her deep involvement with radical labor activism positioned her well as a regional labor broker. Piña was a product of Tampico-Cecilia radical labor politics. Her new hometown had witnessed a surge in labor radicalism. Many of her worker friends had joined the CGT, as she later did, and had been engaged in anarcho-syndicalism much earlier. By 1929, her politics envisioned an equitable world for all workers. She wrote to the Grupo Libertario Sacco and Vanzetti, a Spanish-speaking activist collective in New York, about creating a "just and better world for all workers," echoing the calls for worker unity without borders spoken by those who preceded her.[7]

Piña's labor activism was a type of "political, cultural, and ideological work."[8] She became *secretaria de correspondencia* for the Comité Internacional Pro-Presos Sociales, organized by Hermanos Rojos member Esteban Méndez Guerra.[9] Her duties included receiving correspondence from and welcoming new groups, petitioning on behalf of political prisoners, distributing newspapers, fundraising, and maintaining records of donors and their monetary contributions, among other tasks.[10]

Despite her work with the Comité, the 1930 census reported Piña as an unmarried Mexicana *"dedicada a quehaceres domésticos"* (dedicated to housework).[11] Moreover, despite her presence in the archival record and her seemingly vocal position as *secretaria de correspondencia*, the late writer Carlos Gonzáles Salas, in his foundational text on the history of the labor movement in Tampico, failed to mention Piña in his overview of the Archivo Histórico de Esteban Méndez Guerra.[12]

While she may have been engaged in *quehaceres domésticos*, her daily labor in local organizations helped sustain the larger anarcho-syndicalist movement.

Figure 12. Tampico street scene. Courtesy, Library of Congress, Prints and Photographs Division, LOT 11356-29.

Given her role as head of correspondence, Piña kept abreast of daily developments locally and abroad. She welcomed Grupo Libertario from the border town of Edinburg, Texas, upon its founding. Edinburg resident Eduardo Guzman's letter to *Sagitario* in 1925 was processed by Piña and printed in the newspaper. He explained how both men and women in his Rio Grande Valley community had the "sole intention to fight for the dissemination of new ideas, those that guide us in the direction of equality, liberty, love, and justice for all." It was "this reason" that led him to form a new group in the border town.[13] Piña and others continued to communicate with Guzman's group, sending information on strikes in the area, particularly those involving oil workers.

Piña and other female members in the movement played key roles in maintaining much-needed momentum in the midst of renewed labor arrests. Self-proclaimed anarchists (and those who were perceived to be anarchists) were frequently in and out of prison. Often, imprisonment was quite lengthy. Only four years after PLM member and COM supporter Librado Rivera's release from the federal penitentiary at Leavenworth, Kansas, in 1923, he was once again detained after freely moving about Tampico's labor circles. This time he served a six-month prison sentence in the Penitenciaría Andonegui in the port city. Rivera wrote inside and outside of prison and led a remarkable activist life. In a note to President Porfirio Díaz years earlier while in St. Louis, Missouri, he wrote, "it is useless and rather ridiculous to keep hiding with a pseudonym in this country [the United States] to evade your government's persecution of the members of the Partido Liberal Mexicano. . . . Since I am one of those members which I consider a great honor and distinction, I am resolved to . . . accept all responsibilities . . . of what is to fall upon me."[14]

The work of sending communiqués, particularly to raise funds for political propaganda and legal appeals for political prisoners such as Rivera, was crucial for the movement. And while the arduous work of submitting petitions to free Rivera eventually worked, authorities once again detained the old *magonista*. In the summer of 1929, he was detained in Tampico along with Esteban Méndez Guerra and his eight-year-old son and a fellow activist, José Inés Mena. During their imprisonment, General Eulogio Ortiz tortured Méndez Guerra, Rivera, and Mena.[15]

Venustiano Carranza bestowed the rank of brigadier general on Eulogio Ortiz in 1916, after Ortiz's service to the Villista army. After a short exile in the United States he returned to Mexico and by 1919 supported the Agua Prieta Plan, like Portes Gil, and he quickly became a two-star general. Ortiz's torture tactics would soon figure prominently in the Cristero Rebellion during the mid-1920s; Ortiz encouraged and participated in the torturing of priests to "break them physically and psychologically" to curb the antirevolutionary state rebellion led by Catholic fanatics.[16] Although Ortiz ordered the torture of the labor activists, there is no evidence indicating that Méndez Guerra's son was tortured, although it is possible he witnessed the whole ordeal.

Despite the repeated prison sentences and torture in the cells endured by some of the political activists, and despite the arduous work of petitioning, raising funds, and hiding or setting up new locations from which to spread news and propaganda about the need to free the prisoners, that work continued. Piña and others in the network pushed for the release of Méndez Guerra and Rivera while working to free other prisoners who had been sitting in jail for years. The work included raising funds to distribute among the prisoners themselves as well as funds for legal counsel and appeals. One of the cases taken up by the Comité was of the imprisoned *magonistas* who had been jailed in the south Texas border region since the fall of 1913. There is no evidence indicating that Luz Mendoza, the apparent lone woman in the *magonista* group that skirmished with the Texas Rangers, remained imprisoned; yet, her colleague Jesús María Rangel was still serving his ninety-nine-year sentence for violating US neutrality laws. For the

Table 4. Selected list of labor organizations in Villa Cecilia, Árbol Grande, and Tampico, operating between 1912 and 1940

Casa del Obrero Mundial-Tampico
Gremio Unido de Alijadores
Gremio Unido de Boleros
Gremio Unido de Cargadores
Gremio Unido de Carreteros
Gremio Unido de Marineros
Gremio Unido de Tranviarios
Grupo Ácrata de Estudios Sociales, Árbol Grande, Tamps
Grupo Ácrata Femenino "Rosaura Gortari"
Grupo Ácrata "Luz al Esclavo"
Grupo Ácrata el "Sembrador"
Grupo Anarquista "Afinidad"
Grupo Germimal
Grupo Gladiadores de la Libertad
Grupo Hermanos Rojos
Grupo de Obreros de la Planta
IWW Grupo Tampico
Liga Pro-Defensa Posseedores y propietarios en pequeño del eijdo de Tampico y Villa Cecilia
Sindicato de Agricultores El Porvenir del Campo
Sindicato de Albañiles, Mecánicos y Electricistas
Sindicato de Artes Gráficas
Sindicato de Carpinteros
Sindicato de Dependientas de Restaurantes y Similares
Sindicato de Electricistas
Sindicato de Forjadores. Local No. 100 del Trasporte Marítimo
Sindicato de Jornaleros
Sindicato de Motoristas y Anexos
Sindicato de Paileros y Herreros
Sindicato de Peluqueros
Sindicato de Pintores, Navegación interior
Sindicato de Sastres
Unión de Chauffeurs y Mecánicos de Tampico
Unión de Fogoneros y Marineros de la Naveg. Int
Unión de Mecánicos del Puerto

Sources: *Germinal*, various issues, *Sagitario*, various issues; AHEMG, IIH-UAT, Fondo Presidencia, caja 1917, #1, and caja Centenario, exp. "Lista de invitados a la celebración Centenario," 1930.

magonistas, all Rangel and his colleagues had done was cross into Texas in order to launch their plan "to wrench that region from *Carrancista* control."[17]

For more than a decade, between 1913 and 1925, supporters from the various anarcho-syndicalist groups as well as other labor affiliates worked hard to release the prisoners. In 1925, as part of the larger effort, supporters worked on a fifty-two-page book detailing the story of the political prisoners, "including two photographs of the detainees: one when they were arrested in 1913 and the other one of the last six of the survivors." The book had two purposes: "to inform readers of the story of their struggle and to raise funds for the last of the detainees' legal appeals."[18] Fellow *magonista* Blas Lara along with others, including former Cananea strikers, had previously formed a political prisoner defense fund. The fundraising was crucial as "Texans ... [made] loud calls for a hanging: they wanted Rangel, Charles Cline ... and others ... dead." The funds acquired via numerous petitions allowed supporters to hire a lawyer. Attorney Harry Weinberger was able to win the release of the last of the detainees in 1926, although by that time two of the prisoners, Eugenio Alzalde and Lucio Ortiz, had died in prison.[19]

Maintaining the daily activities of news sharing directly helped the movement remain afloat as well-known leaders were jailed. Piña played a central role. She sent local newspapers to other groups in exchange for funds to help Rivera, Méndez Guerra, and Mena's case; this work, while valued in the pages of *Avante* and *Sagitario*, went unacknowledged or was condemned in the mainstream media.[20] Workers from the various petroleum companies in Tampico soon joined Piña's efforts to publicly decry the abuses and demand the prisoners' freedom; authorities eventually released the detainees. As Piña put it in one of her letters to an activist colleague, she worked hard to defend those "who have been incarcerated . . . for the fallen ones." She felt it urgent to respond to the increase in detentions for social and political involvement in Mexico and across the border in the United States.[21]

The founding of a Comité de Defensa Pro-Presos Sociales created a space for women to work collectively with men and women from different parts of Mexico and abroad. The Comité energetically protested the arrest of Rivera and the closing of the anarchist newspaper *Sagitario* in Tampico, the assassination of Ricardo Flores Magón, and the death of *norteño* supporter Lázaro Gutiérrez de Lara.[22] The creation of committees for the defense of political prisoners was a common practice among anarcho-syndicalist organizations. The COM had created a Comité General de Defensa de los Presos in 1918.[23] In Veracruz and California, for example, the Comité Pro-Presos and the Comité Pro-Presos de Texas, respectively, were created to collect funds and "make propaganda" in order to help obtain the release of detainees and pay for legal fees. In San Francisco, California, the Comité focused its energies on behalf of Jesús María Rangel.[24] The Tampico network had done its best to promote the cause of the "Texas martyrs," to quote the PLM's description of its members Rangel, Abraham Cisneros, Charles Cline, Pedro Perales, Jesús González, and Leonardo M. Vásquez. As early as 1913, Librado Rivera and colleagues from Tampico had rallied behind imprisoned *magonistas* in Texas and had called for monetary donations to aid the prisoners in *Sagitario* editorials. Even as late as 1924, *Sagitario* noted a donation of twenty dollars from the IWW Tampico local and a fifteen-dollar donation from Coahuila to help the Comité's cause, and its editors gratefully thanked supporters.[25]

The "rebellious work" of Piña, as media outlets described it, and that of members of the international solidarity movement such as the Spanish-speaking Cultura Proletaria de Nueva York, of which anarchist colleague Jaime Vidal was a founding member, eventually "led to [Librado] Rivera's release," and soon thereafter, that of the other detainees.[26] In this way, Piña operated transnationally and globally, raising awareness of Rivera's "unjust" imprisonment; she appealed to groups outside of Mexico to continue to support the cause and free Rivera and others. Major newspapers such as those published in New York covered similar arrests and helped to spread the word about events happening in various corners of the world; these often attracted more global attention, as in the case of Italian American anarchists Sacco and Vanzetti.[27] Piña and the Cecilia and Tampico-based organizations such as Hermanos Rojos and Méndez Guerra's Luz del Esclavo did not, and perhaps could not, rely on such widespread global coverage, because of their smaller size; thus, reprinting news stories from newspapers abroad was crucial to their survival. These stories became part of the larger conversation about justice among workers and organizations from different parts of the world. Piña and supporters helped to sustain and raise awareness of issues affecting the local community via outlets like *Avante*, *Sagitario*, and other local papers, distributing entire issues of periodicals or clippings tucked in the regular mail sent to new subscribers and supporters.

Sagitario had gained a solid reputation as Rivera's newspaper. By the late 1920s it "had a wide circulation . . . throughout Mexico and abroad."[28] *Sagitario* became *Avante* between 1927 and 1930, in response to authorities' shutting down *Sagitario*'s main offices, and Rivera had become the new editor of *Avante* while living in Villa Cecilia.[29] *Sagitario* and *Avante* formed part of the larger corpus of newspapers urging transnational collaboration among organized labor.

As historian Lisa McGirr has written regarding the emergence of a global network in the wake of Sacco and Vanzetti's conviction, workers envisioned a world that brought them together because they often engaged in activism collectively, despite physical distance.[30] The later execution of Sacco and Vanzetti in the summer of 1927 sparked the creation of new groups with their own newspapers or newsletters dedicated to liberating political prisoners and groups formed precisely to address the questionable execution of the Italian American anarchists. Some groups kept Sacco and Vanzetti's memory alive by naming their organization after the activists, as in the case of Grupo Libertario Sacco y Vanzetti from New York.

The rise in labor activism associated with the Sacco and Vanzetti case also helped to raise awareness of political repression in remote places. Like-minded activists shared information and strategies to prevent the arrest of fellow labor activists. Shortly after Tampico's Comité featured stories to raise awareness of the Sacco and Vanzetti case, Juana Rouco Buela, a Spanish labor activist who migrated to Buenos Aires as a young child and soon became one of the most vocal advocates of labor rights in Spain and South America, wrote on behalf of the Italian anarchists. Her support was featured in Mexico's *Tierrra y Libertad* (Land and Liberty) and also reprinted locally.[31] Since newspapers outside of Tampico featured stories on the efforts of activists such as Buela, it was one way for Piña to learn about the female activists' greater efforts, even if her path would never cross Buela's.

The same year, 1927, Buela's support was featured, Tampico anarcho-syndicalists had made inroads in other Mexican cities by collaborating with various groups. Méndez Guerra and Hermanos Rojos members Pedro Gudiño, Gonzalo Ruiz Carillo, Santiago Vega, and others promoted the anarcho-syndicalist cause in urban Monterrey. The Tampico group and the Monterrey CGT-affiliated metallurgical workers shared strategies and concerns faced by workers and peasants from the greater Mexican North. CGT-sponsored newspapers also included brief notes between editorials and commentaries urging workers and supporters to boycott certain products, as in the case of the El Fenix company employing workers producing matches. It urged all to "Boycott!; fellow workers . . . every time you visit the store to buy matches, reject the brand El Fenix!"[32] This was an important strategy, particularly as cigarette consumption among men and women across the nation increased. The sharing of information, organizing strategies, and calls to boycott products was also facilitated by the CGT's promotion of anarchist ideas via events. During the fourth CGT congress, held in the summer of 1925, just as during the previous meetings, CGT members agreed upon several resolutions, among them "to invite the Dramatic Group (Cuadro Dramático) from Hermanos Rojos to travel throughout the country" performing key anarchist plays. The CGT agreed to host conferences related to labor issues at every event where a play was being presented.[33]

The promotion of anarchist principles via newspapers, correspondence, poems, and dramatic performances locally and throughout the country helped sustain the larger anarcho-syndicalist movement, particularly as Emilio Portes Gil appealed to organized labor to further strengthen his political position. By 1928, Portes Gil had assumed the presidency, acting as interim president. Within a year, he began to order the apprehension of radical labor and political activists, just as Carranza had years prior. He was directly responsible for the apprehension and torture of Rivera and Méndez Guerra. Rivera had published several scathing articles in *Avante* attacking Portes Gil for co-opting the idea of socialism to promote "the good of the nation," for his "own benefit."[34] Rivera also exposed former heads of state Alvaro Obregón and Plutarco E. Calles, as well as Portes Gil, for covering up government violence against the Yaquis in northern Mexico. As payback, Portes Gil ordered the torture of Rivera, Méndez Guerra, and other detainees.[35]

As Piña continued to receive news from New York's Grupo Libertario Sacco y Vanzetti, she sent her new colleagues a letter that provided an overview of her *compañeros* Rivera and Méndez Guerra's torture and imprisonment without sparing the reputation of Portes Gil. She urged the organization to send funds and spread the word in their own circles about the unjust detention of her Mexican colleagues. She explained that there were others who remained imprisoned and insisted that justice had to prevail. In this way, she brought local struggles to the forefront beyond the confines of northeastern Mexico as she appealed to a global community for support. She wrote, "This indescribable outrage committed by those eternal detractors of human emancipation . . . force us to . . . only . . . ask you to make the necessary propaganda and reproduce our *manifesto* . . . so as to make it known to all the workers of the entire world the atrocities that are committed on a daily basis against our *compañeros* and most sincere fighters."[36]

Authorities soon released the physically weakened Mexican *compañeros*, and Piña resumed the daily tasks of handling the correspondence, seeking funds, and spreading relevant labor news. Her female colleagues collaborated, spreading ideas about labor rights and women's issues. Local residents María del Jesús Alvarado and Domitila Jiménez contributed to the dissemination of information via *Avante* and *Sagitario*, distributed through Hermanos Rojos and the Comité Internacional Pro-Presos Sociales. Del Jesús Alvarado joined the Comité and became Piña's colleague. She participated in meetings and, as recorded in a handful of meeting minutes, was vocal regarding issues of concern to the global community. Del Jesús Alvarado offered an "extensive report" on individuals who had been apprehended during meetings or detained while distributing "propaganda" circulars in Tampico.[37] She also was one of eighteen women alongside Esther Mendoza who organized themselves into the Liga Cultural de Mujeres Libertarias "La Idea" of Tampico.

Liga Cultural de Mujeres Libertarias "La Idea"

Liga Cultural's motto was "*comunismo libertario*," adopted by many others during the period. It appealed to women from around the globe to "wake up!" as "[the Liga] extended its fraternal invitation to fight."[38] The manifesto framed its calls using gendered language that cut through the usual class discourse shaping most organizations of the period. Its members further underscored women's double marginalization. The woman was "a slave among slaves,"

Table 5. Liga Cultural de Mujeres Libertarias, Tampico (1922–?)

Name	Newspapers Featuring Writings	Assoc. with Other Organizations
Almazán, Lorena		
Cruz, María		
De Alva, Esther	*Sagitario*	
Del Jesús Alvarado, María	*Sagitario*	Comité Internacional Pro-Presos Sociales
Figueroa, Martina		
Guillen, Concepción		
Lozano, Rita		
Luna, Francisca		
Martínez, María		
Mendoza, Esther	*Sagitario*	CGT
Mendoza, María	*Sagitario*	CGT
Morado, Josefa		
Narváes, Maura		
Rodríguez, Aurelia	*Sagitario*	Hermanos Rojos; delegate to the CGT
Ruíz, Concepción		
Solis, Francisca		
Solis, María		
Soto, María		
Vega, Julia		

Source: *Sagitario*, June 6, 1925, and González Salas, *Acercamiento*.

explained Liga members. Women were "the victim[s] among victims." The commentary appealed to women as mothers, sisters, and *compañeras* in the struggle.[39]

The Liga Cultural members promoted specific women's issues and pushed general labor rights for all. While the biographical data on its members is limited, records indicate that some of the Liga members had ties to Hermanos Rojos, the Comité Internacional Pro-Presos Sociales, and the CGT. Along with the contributions of del Jesús Alvarado and Mendoza, Aurelia Rodríguez's writings were among the most scathing featured in *Sagitario* and called upon on women from all walks of life to promote women's equality. Rodríguez urged "married, unmarried women, [and] those who have lost loved ones, mothers and sisters" to fight for freedom. She lamented how "the injustices of the despotic rulers . . ." led to "the arrest and confinement of our brother judged a criminal. . . ."[40] For Rodríguez, everyone had to speak up "about the truth . . . speaking about justice. . . ." It was a right bestowed upon all and she reminded women to contribute to a new society. The call was also directed to those working at home, not only outside it. Rodríguez continued, "in our home, celebrations . . . wherever, with brothers, with a friend, with those that don't act . . . plant in all of them the seed, the idea of freedom, the ideal of justice . . . become that link that brings together the universal family of tomorrow, that which will blur the boundaries of nations

... of religions ... do not believe in the idea that there are no oppressors and no oppressed ... become part of the vanguard of the rebel army." She closed her impassioned call by urging women to "claim land and liberty ... pick up the red flag."[41]

Rodríguez wrote about all workers in general in her other commentaries. Her erudite background was on full display in "Insurrección," published in *Sagitario* in 1925. She explained how "insurrection or rebellion has been the driving force" that "moves mankind forward and has brought forth change." It was this "insurrection" that drove "Galileo to affirm the movement of the world despite forces that [sought] to obscure it." Rodríguez continued, crediting "insurrection" to Newton, Büchner, the French Revolution, and the fall of the tsar. It was this "insurrection" that brought about "liberty, progress, the truth ... it is because of this [insurrection] we can dream today and it can become reality tomorrow." What is "today something utopian, becomes mathematics tomorrow."[42] She then referenced contemporary figures who ranked among the leadership of the movement or had recently passed: "Without insurrection, men such as [Praxedis] Guerrero, ... Flores Magón, ... Ferrer, ... Sebastián Faure ... would not be grand men ... or without Germana Bertón ... [what would become] of the exploited ones, those righteous and conscious people ... without her [Bertón], [what would become] of the downtrodden ones; insurrection should be the free men and conscious collectives' action ... the ultimate action ... of slaves, the hungry ... [the] oppressed."[43] Although Rodríguez did not mention the plight of working women specifically in this commentary, that such a powerful call to all workers was penned by a woman sent a strong message not only about *Sagitario*'s commitment but also about the anarcho-syndicalist collectives' belief in a tradition that opened spaces for women to articulate their thoughts about liberty and freedom. Thus, the call to action for *all* included women even in thought pieces that did not specifically reference women.

Rodríguez's call to action to "all women" and "*a la mujer mundial*" (to the global woman) in *Sagitario* reached audiences beyond Tampico and Villa Cecilia. Through general correspondence between Piña and other groups, entire issues of *Sagitario* or clippings of those specific commentaries circulated in the Rio Grande Valley, among other places. Manifestos calling for change, because "women suffered just like men," were urgent and sent as propaganda to encourage others to join. Women "too are awaiting liberty."[44]

It is unclear if Domitila Jiménez joined the Liga, but her commentaries appeared in *Sagitario*, and she was among those who donated funds to maintain its publication. We do know that Jiménez promoted the anarcho-syndicalist

CGT-led movement and reminded *Sagitario* readers that achieving women's equality was paramount. She explained how women also felt anger and disgust like men and assured readers that women too sought to destroy the "three main poisonous heads: government, capital, and the clergy."[45] She also wrote "The Six-Hour Shift," which appeared in *Sagitario* in 1926 calling for a shorter workday; in the end, the eight-hour workday was adopted.[46] Jiménez's *Sagitario* commentaries, via Piña's distribution work, circulated in Edinburg, Mercedes, and Harlingen, three Texas border towns with pro-CGT groups and with a historical legacy of PLM-affiliated organizing.[47]

Another activist plugged into the labor network but from afar was Felipa Velásquez. A working-class self-taught teacher, Velásquez soon joined the agrarian movement in Baja California and, like Piña, became a member of the CGT. Before moving to Mexicali, she worked as a rural elementary schoolteacher in Mazatlán but was soon fired, accused of inciting peasant uprisings.[48] She emerged as a strong supporter of Hermanos Rojos, keeping up with anarchist developments in Tampico. In *Avante*'s September 1, 1928, edition, Velásquez wrote a scathing editorial attacking the Catholic Church and its stranglehold on women. Her editorial "El credo" ridiculed the Catholic Creed and turned it on its head, pledging loyalty and belief only in the "Santa Madre Anarquía and in the frailty of the stomachs of the poor."[49] She endorsed CGT principles, among them an "exhortation to all members of organizations whose goal is to seek freedom to abandon the practice of baptizing their children and all practices that in any way represent a religious practice."[50] Baptizing children was just as bad as continuing religious instruction to young adults. She wrote to Librado Rivera, who published her note in *Avante*, in which Velásquez detailed the following exchange between a young female student and an instructor at a Sinaloa school promoting religious education.

—THE INSTRUCTOR ASKS [THE YOUNG WOMAN]: do you believe in God?
No, replied the señorita.
—Why not?
Because there isn't one.
—What, don't you see what that is in the sky?
Yes, but it's all space.
—Thanks to whom is that you eat?
Thanks to my mother who makes the food and my brother who works.
—No! you eat thanks to God!
No.
—You must ask him for forgiveness; and worship him.
No . . .

—You will be condemned!

Who cares? All poor people are [condemned] already.[51]

The anarchist press featured news on recently formed groups emerging throughout the country.[52] In September of 1928, for example, María Encarnación García submitted a request to *Avante*'s editorial committee hoping that Tampico's labor circles would take note of her new group. García reported on the newly formed group Sindicato Feminista Josefa Ortíz de Domínguez, affiliated with the CROM, from the town of Matamoros in Coahuila and complained that despite its petition to the governor of Coahuila to improve the condition of *obreros* (as she awaited a response), "justice will never be granted for those below the authorities . . . hence one must bring justice to places where it is nonexistent." Therefore, as García explained, the organization was "donat[ing] one peso and ninety cents" to Hermanos Rojos in order to claim a space in its newspaper. The Sindicato Feminista remained active and supported workers' movements well into the 1930s.[53]

Despite Hermanos Rojos' disapproval of the CROM due to its loyalty to the new revolutionary state, collaboration with the Sindicato Feminista was tolerated. The acceptance of such requests from CROM affiliates whose political ideology allowed for collaboration with the state points to at least some flexibility on the part of the anarcho-syndicalists. As Margaret Marsh has argued, activists could engage in "theoretically inconsistent" approaches while maintaining similar goals.[54] Further, it was common for anarcho-syndicalist organizations to maintain contact and collaborate with communist or other prolabor organizations. The Gremio Unido de Alijadores de Tampico, the main dockworkers' union, which would later support Portes Gil's Partido Socialista Fronterizo and opt for the socialist route, regularly informed the Comité Nacional del Partido Comunista of its elections and planned strikes and other union-related activities.[55] In this way, formal ideological and party lines were not as fixed in the everyday, on-the-ground practices of labor activists.

Similarly, gender boundaries were often negotiated. Negotiating such boundaries could take on specific language with which to frame labor struggles. Liga member Esther Mendoza—whose writings appeared in Tampico, Mexico City, and Monterrey—employed *compañera* and *compañerismo* language, yet promoted a discourse of gender equality that offered a radical alternative to the "support your *compañero*" rhetoric popular in state-endorsed newspapers. Mendoza's editorial, "A la mujer," spoke to "*compañera*[s] of my sex," and questioned women's actions, arguing that if in fact woman was "that tree branch who bears fruit for the man yet he humiliates you . . . why do you degrade yourself?" She called on all women to "learn your mission, learn about your value, come to occupy the position that you deserve."[56] In a short commentary entitled "La idea," her colleague and possible relative María Mendoza reminded "*compañeras*... [that] it was through loving and embracing life ... one could reach liberty and freedom."[57]

María Mendoza, several years prior to writing "La idea," had written a lengthy and derisive piece against the Catholic Church that appeared in *Avante* entitled, "Lo que prefiero" (What I prefer). She wrote that she "preferred the love of a dog, over the love of a perverted god . . . preferred believing in the truth and the natural even if it causes me pain, over lending my faith to something false." Her sights then moved from the church to men; while she critiqued the system of patriarchy and gender inequality, she argued that she "willingly and happily would kneel before a good man and not before a wooden figure, of clay or even marble that represents a god of the blind."[58] She equated the tyranny of capitalism to the falsehood of religion and she took solace in "the love in her heart for the profound words sketched in the pages of books written by the wise fighters [against oppression]."[59] Yet, as she advocated for "the light of anarchy," she spoke of emancipation and freedom in terms of "*hombre*[s] *libre*[s]" as a stand-in for humankind and rarely referenced the emancipation of women specifically as some of her colleagues did. But anarchy as an idea and movement in Mendoza's writings took on a gender. "She," referring to anarchy, was envisioned as a female. "¡*Viva la anarquía*, she brings the light, the truth, and love!" Mendoza exclaimed in her editorials.

Her words reached subscribers and subscriber-contributors including Luz Mendoza from the border in Harlingen, Texas, who had organized the anarchist Grupo Redención years earlier. Mailed clippings of some of these commentaries sustained the sharing of ideas specifically concerning women in the context of labor across regional and geopolitical divides. Women's ideas about freedom, equality, and love thus were grounded in local conditions but continuously shaped by the sharing of knowledge.[60] Thus, María Mendoza underscored the importance of women's awakening as a key component to the creation of a strong and prolabor family and further shared those ideas with other women and men from the regional network.

The emergence of new groups in other towns with similar goals and philosophies helped to advance the movement and served as a source of inspiration, especially in the wake of more arrests of prominent activists. Groups with a feminist orientation were particularly important to the growing interest in creating and sustaining all-female labor collectives. In the same year in which she urged *compañeras* to find "liberty and freedom," Mendoza reported to *Sagitario* about the formation of a group "ever so important" as it honored a Revolution-era anarcho-feminist by naming itself Grupo Cultural Libertario "Margarita Ortega." Ortega (who adopted the name María Valdés to evade state surveillance) fought in the Mexican Revolution. She was familiar with weaponry, had medical skills, and was considered a *magonista* "soldier" who took up arms with the PLM in 1910. After a temporary self-exile in Phoenix, Arizona, she returned to northern Mexico after the death of her daughter and rejoined PLM efforts in Sonora, only to be executed at the hands of the government in November 24, 1913.[61] The women argued that their group adopted "anarchist ideas," and the decision to honor Ortega "came from all of the membership that included both sexes."[62]

Meeting records indicate that members from the Grupo Cultural Libertario "Margarita Ortega," along with Piña and María del Jesús Alvarado, were among the women in attendance during the 1930 and 1931 meetings organized by the Comité. While there is no personal correspondence between Piña and the Ortega members beyond official communication between the organizations, it is possible the women maintained a friendship. What is clear from the historical record was their active presence in these public meetings—frequently taking the podium, directly shaping the outcome of agenda items and resolutions. Equally important was their engagement of one another through their ideas despite, in some cases, physical distance.[63]

Via María Mendoza, the Ortega groups asked "those who sympathize with our ideas, please send us anarchist propaganda such as books, pamphlets, handbills, and newspapers."[64] Despite receiving coverage only in the small anarchist press, information was shared about new groups, new members, and labor causes in even the most remote village. The multidirectional sharing of news and accompanying donations was impressive and key to the survival of anarcho-syndicalism, resembling other networks in the Caribbean and greater Latin America.[65]

* * *

Just as the Mendoza women and Jiménez invoked the language of the revolutionary family and further politicized *obreras'* roles as mothers, so did Caritina Piña, once again in 1930. This time she helped her colleague Felipa Velásquez. That summer, Piña was to deliver a report to nine labor organizations and their representatives who had congregated for a special meeting at the Pierce Oil union hall in Villa Cecilia. The meeting commenced at 10 p.m., called to order by members of the Comité. After roll call, a quick report on the finances of the committee, and a summary of its efforts to prevent Baja California political prisoners from deportation to the Islas Marías, Piña took the podium. "Haciendo uso de la palabra," speaking to the group, the *compañera* Piña told her audience that "she had complained to the governor [of Baja California, José

María Tapia] in the most energetic manner against the atrocities and crimes committed against the workers of that state and demanded the release of all political prisoners and pleaded with the governor to stop the deportation of the prisoners to the Islas Marías."⁶⁶

She underscored that among the detainees was their "comrade" Felipa Velásquez, who was apprehended along with seven of her children. This, according to Piña, was atrocious. She pleaded with her colleagues to give this matter priority among the other issues to be handled by the Comité. Taking male or female prisoners was one thing, but seizing *compañeras* with their children was simply unjust. The discussion continued until 12:45 a.m. with the nine organizations, including two oil workers' unions, a philharmonic union, and an unnamed all-female group all at hand. Piña discussed other issues concerning the labor movement and vowed to take the message back to its members and continue to spread the word.⁶⁷ Piña's activism, in collaboration with that of others, applied pressure that resulted in Velásquez's eventual release.

Anarcho-feminists made their presence well known both in the press and via direct action supporting strikes, agrarian movements, and campaigns to release political prisoners. They engaged in letter-writing campaigns, circulated antigovernment editorials, and assumed leadership positions in organizations. The voices of Piña, Jiménez, Rodríguez, and Velásquez, among others, were direct examples of women's active participation as a fundamental component of radical labor activism. Such visibility—much greater than in the nineteen teens—chipped away at the idea of a largely male *obrero* class, particularly important in the region as the predominance of male workers in the oil sector made it especially difficult to redefine the image of "the worker." Further, their increased presence in the press and on the ground undermined normative ideas about women's roles and was proof that women too could promote anarchism's direct-action agenda. Not only was women's capacity to engage in direct action clear, their participation also sent a message to organized labor and communities in general that women could negotiate gendered boundaries or outright transgress them.

The continued direct action employed by Piña and her colleagues helped to keep the idea of women as *compañeras en la lucha* as one that was real and intricately tied to labor rights, thereby honoring the very ideals of anarchism. Rejecting collaboration with the state yet not rejecting their identity as crucial reproducers of community, they reified the role of *obreras* as working women, working mothers, working daughters by further politicizing the idea of motherhood and maternalism within the context of anarcho-syndicalism. The following chapter further excavates such intersections of radical labor activism and maternalism in the quest for labor rights among anarcho-feminists.

CHAPTER FOUR

The Language of Motherhood in Radical Labor Activism

> Women, rise so that your wombs can produce great lions
> . . . not slaves, so that they can exterminate the enemy.
> —Aurelia Rodríguez, January 1, 1925

> Sleep little baby, sleep now, because here comes the friar who will
> only teach you lies. This sweet little boy, who was born in the day,
> all he wants is to be taught anarchy, the truth. That is the only
> way he can achieve happiness and no longer will he be a slave
> to the bourgeoise. *Compañera* Ana, why does the little boy cry?
> Because he has lost his liberty . . . sleep little baby, equality has
> arrived, long live the great red banner! Long live land and liberty!
> —M. C. Guerrero, "Hymn for the Birth of the People's
> Son/*Canto al nacimiento del hijo del pueblo*"

Caritina Piña's use of the rhetoric of motherhood as a tool with which to promote labor rights reveals how anarchist ideals radicalized and further politicized the role of working mothers. Piña and her colleagues' ultimate goal was the spread of anarcho-syndicalism. Such activism, frequently in the form of writings and letters of protest, often spoke to the larger concern and belief that *all* workers regardless of gender were entitled to a dignified way of life. Anarcho-syndicalist women's activism reveals how ideas about motherhood figured prominently in their political engagement. Yet compared to the use of the language of motherhood and maternalism by state-affiliated labor collectives, as well as the emergent anti-anarchist and anti-communist Partido Socialista Fronterizo (PSF), anarcho-syndicalist framing of motherhood further radicalized the idea of the working mother without bowing to the demands of the state.

The Mexican revolutionary state's agenda of "full social integration" was shaped by a state-sanctioned discourse on motherhood that defined women's status as both precarious and privileged. Women's reproductive capacity as the producers of community and the nation's future workforce was touted as crucial to the country's progress and to the formation of strong families. Yet it was precisely because women served as principal caregivers that mothers were presumed in need of special care. Working-class mothers had to prove their worthiness as good, morally sound mothers as middle class and social reformers of the period continued to cast them as socially inferior given their public presence in paid labor.

Motherhood as a radicalized concept framed Piña's activism while working in the Comité. In April 1929, a year before she became involved in the fight to free imprisoned mother Felipa Velásquez, workers from Gastonia, North Carolina, went on strike, led by the National Textile Workers Union. Among the first women to hold an elected leadership position in American unions, Ellen Dawson collaborated with activists—including communist and National Textile Workers Union leader Fred E. Beal—to organize the over 1,800 workers in the Gastonia Loray Mill owned by the Manville-Jenckes Company of Rhode Island. Workers demanded higher wages (twenty dollars per week), an end to piecework, "equal pay for women and children . . . [and] better housing at lower rents." They also demanded union recognition.[1] Piña wrote a petition on behalf of Mexican workers in the mills. While historians who have written on the Gastonia strike do not mention the presence of Mexican American textile workers at the Loray Mill, Piña wrote there were at least three Mexican women workers (among the Mexican male workers) and referred to the presence of their children in the strike. It is also possible that Piña's note regarding sixteen Mexican Americans referenced an arrest in the aftermath of the Gastonia strike. She may not have distinguished between the Gastonia affair arrests and other, subsequent arrests. We know that the textile labor force in Gastonia included a large segment of women workers and young workers (in some reports, described as children). It is possible that because Mexican Americans were categorized as white, they may not have been identified as such by historians writing about the strike. The substandard conditions for female textile workers in Loray seemed to fit a global pattern. Piña's Comité frequently received news about textile factories' working conditions and had collaborated with organizations from other countries focused on freeing political prisoners. Piña became equally committed to the Gastonia affair just as she had done with local labor injustices.

One of the sixteen workers who was charged with murder in the aftermath of the bloody strike was female leader Vera Buch. Buch had learned about the

Socialist Party in the United States during her time at a tuberculosis sanatorium. She had grown up in poverty, and the camaraderie of a fellow female patient at the sanatorium who was a member of the US Socialist Party shaped Buch's early days as a political thinker and activist. The Connecticut native later joined the Socialist Party and the IWW and, in 1919, the Communist Party USA. Since the tender age of fourteen, Buch had a remarkable résumé—she joined the Young Pioneers of America, "did organization work among children of the textile workers of Passaic" in 1926, and helped to organize child miners as part of her tenure in the Children's Miners Relief Committee of New York.[2] Buch, Amy Schechter, and Sophie Melvin traveled to Gastonia to help organize the strike. Melvin went specifically to "organize the children to help in the conduct of the strike."

Buch's task, among others, was crucial yet difficult as she worked on bridging the racial divide between Whites and African Americans in Gaston County. Earlier organizing efforts to incorporate African Americans into the labor struggle in that area of the South had gone awry when Communist leader George Pershing from the Young Communist League "had bowed to white workers' demands and strung a rope between blacks and whites. . . . the blacks did not return to future meetings."[3] Further, in one organizing meeting, a White male worker replied to Buch's call for worker solidarity in the following way: "I won't never have nothing to do with no niggers no how." As Gregory Taylor has pointed out, this worker "seemed to speak for the majority [of the White labor force]," further deteriorating the already fragile collaboration between White and African American workers.[4] Gaston County, like places across the South, had a long history of slavery, and Jim Crow was pretty much intact. The Communist Party had a history of supporting African Americans and was a staunch advocate of the Dyer Anti-Lynching Bill, but it, too, had to cater to its White worker base; it remained a difficult juggle through the final days of the Communist Party's influence in North Carolina, as late as the 1960s.

During the final days of the strike, workers suffered from hunger and physical violence at the hands of guards from the state as well as the company. Some workers lost their lives to this violence. Others were jailed. Buch, along with two other women, faced substandard conditions in the Gaston County jail. Their male colleagues, jailed like the women, awaited their fate. As Buch sat in the jail, in the wake of the violence, she wrote how she and others attempted to remain strong, "avoiding demoralization." She explained how she and the other detained women "sometimes felt like a pack of dirty, smelly, helpless and forgotten animals . . . we had completely lost track of the days."

Five months after the strike began and two months after the violence and arrests of workers, Piña penned her letter in support of the detained Gastonia strikers. Petitions from the International Labor Defense and others poured in as well.[5] Aligning herself with the female Gastonia workers and leaders, Piña's petition seemed to reflect the larger efforts of Buch to bring workers together despite their racial and ethnic backgrounds. Yet Piña's own ideas about race and ethnicity and her gendered understandings of the labor movement shaped her critique and feelings about the labor situation across the border. What made the Gastonia strike and subsequent arrests of workers particularly urgent for Piña was the arrest of both women and their children (many of whom were also workers) and the fact that Mexicans were involved, including three Mexicanas and their children. Family and motherhood were front and center in Piña's letter as she pleaded with Judge M. V. Barnhill, explaining that the workers were only asking for a "reasonable . . . salary . . . to cover the value of their meals." She added that women had been detained along with children, violating the sacred and "great human family."[6] Her letter of protest was sent to Judge Barnhill when the trial moved to Charlotte, and she sent a copy to President Herbert Hoover.

Her petition on behalf of the Gastonia Mexicans—nine men, three women, and four children—was supported by local Tampico organizations. Piña, Esteban Méndez Guerra, and other members of the Comité held a meeting in late August of 1929 to discuss actions the group could take on behalf of their fellow workers across the border. The Comité, despite political disagreements with some of the organizations, belonged to the state-level Federación Obrera de Tamaulipas and worked with "three [of its] organizations" that sent representatives to the August meeting to discuss the Gastonia workers. Attendees agreed to "initiate a campaign against the *yanquis* authorities . . . against this criminal act."[7] The Comité members urged all workers to support the cause, given that the "lives of the victims in Gastonia ran the risk and had been threatened with electrocution."[8] In joing the campaign, the Comité set aside ideological differences, including those with pro-*comunismo autoritario* Socorro Rojo, which contradicted the Comité's idea of *comunismo libertario*.[9] Another group that collaborated with the Comité was the Frente Unico Pro-Derechos de la Mujer (FUPDM), a popular nationwide women's organization that had a strong branch in Tampico and whose membership included educated, affluent women such as Esther Chapa Tijerina.

Chapa Tijerina, a Tampico native, was a communist, educator, doctor, and cofounder of the FUPDM, which became one of the largest women's rights organizations. While Piña most likely knew about the FUPDM's Tampico branch, the historical record does not provide evidence of collaboration with said branch or any sort of relationship between Piña and Chapa Tijerina. Piña's activism, while rooted in anarcho-syndicalist thought, aligned nicely with some of the issues at the forefront of the FUPDM's agenda, with the exception of women's suffrage. Support for issues dear to the FUPDM and those supported by communist groups, particularly women's economic and reproductive freedom, occurred in a kind of "contingent solidarity."[10] Comité members including Piña, María del Jesús Alvarado, and Esther Mendoza, who advocated anarcho-syndicalism in different venues, operated in the midst of two emerging camps within the larger, national women's movement: the communist members of the FUPDM and the more mainstream members of the FUPDM such as Margarita Robles de Mendoza.[11] Piña, like others in the Comité, focused her energies on freeing political prisoners (many were self-identified communists) tied to the larger labor and political movement. She played a pivotal role in aiding activists imprisoned for promoting ideas that challenged the status quo, regardless of their organizational affiliation or ideological or philosophical orientation.

Ten days after Piña submitted her Gastonia petition, a large crowd of workers affiliated with the Federación Obrera de Tamaulipas gathered in front of the American consulate in Tampico to protest "Yankee imperialism" and the "injustices in Gastonia" in anticipation of the North Carolina state authorities' threat to electrocute the detained strikers from Loray Mill.[12] As the demonstration continued, Tampico authorities, in Loray Mill guard fashion, ordered the municipal firefighters who frequently collaborated with the police to disperse the demonstrators with "bursts of water." Supporters of the march suggested that the heinous act was ordered by none other than the "*jefe nato*," the natural-born boss; demonstrators referred to Portes Gil as the *jefe nato*. Cynically, supporters joked that municipal authorities "could not use the toilet without Portes Gil's permission."[13]

Solidarity among organizations with distinct ideological outlooks was common during moments of crisis and during celebrations marking major labor milestones. As historian Elizabeth Hutchison has explained for the case of Chilean anarchists, "a rhetorical similarity between anarchist and Marxist texts on the woman question" existed, and workers frequently collaborated based on common interests and shared labor struggles.[14] Such bonds also existed in the Gulf of Mexico region. In 1925, in a show of solidarity similar to the massive 1919 oil strike, over 25,000 people from at least forty distinct organizations came together in the streets of Tampico to celebrate several labor milestones. Among the organizations joining in the celebration was the Unión de Empleadas de Restaurantes y Similares and Piña's Comité Pro-Presos Sociales, as well as several other organizations from Villa Cecilia.[15]

Figure 13a and b. Anarchist demonstration against the police in Tampico, 1925. Courtesy, International Institute of Social History, Amsterdam.

In the end, after numerous petitions from organizations from the United States as well as Mexico, the three female Loray Mill strike organizers were released on bail—two on $5,000 bail.[16] Piña's use of the phrase the "great human [Mexican] family," while it echoed the family-focused rhetoric used by the revolutionary government under the Portes Gil administration, was couched in an anarcho-syndicalist framework and became a popular tool with which to articulate issues specific to *obreras*.

Mother Activists and Their Children

The petition to the North Carolina judge as well as President Herbert Hoover emphasized this privileging of motherhood and women's central position in the new postrevolutionary period. For Piña, though, it had special meaning. She also underscored the female activists' precariousness, as these working mothers had brought their children with them. She applauded them because this was precisely the behavior mother-activists needed to model for their children. She referenced the children's presence during the arrests in Gastonia, articulating women's delicate but crucial position in the world of labor as the reproducers of community, the mothers of future workers. For Piña, the privileging of maternalism was an empowerment for *obreras* and it was one that was further politicized as a way to extend labor rights to all women.[17] Her privileging of women's reproductive capacity helped to promote worker solidarity, which followed the basic tenets of anarcho-syndicalism popular in CGT-affiliated groups like the Comité and Hermanos Rojos.

CGT endorsed Grupo Tierra y Libertad "Librado Rivera," based in Los Angeles, which frequently shared news with the Tampico group and echoed a similar message. It reported to its Tampico and Villa Cecilia affiliates on the birth of a baby boy by one of its members. The "*compañera* Anita Contreras Cayaso, who forms part of this group . . . 'Grupo Librado Rivera,' gave birth to a baby boy whose name will be Francisco . . . until the boy is old enough to choose his own name," the notice read.[18] The head of correspondence for the group and possibly a relative of the new mother, David Contreras, added that while the father of the new baby was "young, not only in age but in the formation of ideas, at least he did not come from a [religiously] fanatic family." He proceeded to share a song written by M. C. Guerrero, "Hymn for the Birth of the Son of the People." While the English translation loses the rhythm of the original Spanish version, the translation nonetheless captures its anarchist message.

> Sleep little baby, the big day has arrived when you will no longer be a slave of the three evils. Sleep little baby, sleep now, the big day of liberty has arrived. This

sweet little boy is a hero and he only wants to learn the truth. Sleep little baby, sleep now, because here comes the friar who will only teach you lies. This sweet little boy, who was born in the day, all he wants is to be taught anarchy, the truth.

That is the only way he can achieve happiness and no longer will he be a slave to the bourgeoise. *Compañera* Ana, why does the little boy cry? Because he has lost his liberty. We must rebel in order to conquer it and leave it as inheritance to this great treasure. Sleep little baby, equality has arrived, long live the great red banner! Long live land and liberty![19]

The song, inspired by anarchist thought, politicized the mother-child relationship. Having children and nurturing was not frowned upon; but nurturing had to be honest and had to include truth-telling, for that was the education to which all children should be entitled upon birth. The language of motherhood and of maternalism was prominent in these anarcho-syndicalist organizations and radicalized its very meaning.

Women's status as mothers first and foremost had been the source of public debate since the late nineteenth century. As early as 1900, newspapers featuring commentaries about women underscored their status as mothers as a privilege and as a marker of distinction—in most cases, a positive distinction. In the anarchist newspapers *Tierra y Libertad* and *El Productor* circulating in Madrid and Barcelona, for example, editorials and commentaries written by prominent anarchist and anarcho-syndicalist women promoting women's equality from the vantage point of motherhood were quite common. The writings of the Spanish anarchist and former textile worker Teresa Claramunt, for instance, underscored the unequal status of women from the Iberian Peninsula and were reprinted in newspapers published in the Gulf of Mexico region. In an essay she wrote for Barcelona's *El Productor* entitled "A la mujer," Claramunt spoke of women as worthy companions. She explained, "Women need to free themselves from their inherited errors for the good of their children and they must collaborate with men, who are her companions in the plight."[20] Women's "natural instincts," including "love, beauty, and friendship," were under attack, explained Claramunt, and women had to fight to save themselves and take pride in their "natural" attributes. Such women's virtues, as these commentaries explained, would be the tools by which women's advancement could be achieved. Women's rights, particularly labor rights, could possibly be realized employing the same tools. This language of motherhood and the rhetoric of women as strong and loyal yet fierce companions resonated with similar discourses circulating in the region, particularly *compañerismo*.

One contemporary of Piña's and contributor to *Sagitario* who also radicalized the meaning of maternalism was Dora Andrew. In her "¡Abajo charrateras criminales!" (Down with the criminal epaulettes!) she used the analogy of women's taking up arms and urged women to "throw away those cartridge belts, those rifles, and cease wearing those damn epaulettes that represent criminals, and be free like the air you breathe . . . and you will inherit the earth as your nation and your home as your religion . . . and your sacred and loving mother will sway you [in her arms] during your moments of rest, singing the hymn of liberty."[21] The association of the feeling of liberty, of freedom, with the embrace and love of a mother was a savvy one, as it was a relatable reference.

Similarly, Liga Cultural member and *Sagitario* contributor Aurelia Rodríguez invoked the image of the mother to bolster the need for women's equality. She directed her commentary at mothers specifically, urging them to rise up so that their wombs could produce "great lions . . . not slaves, so that they can exterminate the enemy."[22] Rodríguez appears as one of the few women delegates to the CGT in its numerous congresses in the mid- to late 1920s.[23] Her male colleagues remembered her as a *compañera* who did not like to be referred to as a "*señorita*, but a sister [in the struggle]" and always spoke "with a feminist tone . . . using a simple and inviting language . . . anytime she spoke about the labor movement."[24]

Her "feminist tone" resembled women's voices from elsewhere in Latin America. As in Chile and other parts of Mexico for example, early expressions of women's place in labor and society and women's status as mothers and wives found prominence in locally produced anarcho-syndicalist newsletters.[25] The term *feminismo* or *feminista* was sometimes used by anarcho-syndicalists referring to working-class women and their struggles, but in Chile, as Hutchison writes, "anarchists tended to use the term feminist exclusively to refer to (and to denigrate) bourgeois women."[26] Yet an increasingly radicalized idea of the virtuous mother as justification for labor protections for working-class women was promoted in various ideologies. In the few anarcho-syndicalist commentaries and writings where the term *feminista* appeared, it often focused not on the meaning of the term or of a bourgeois movement but on the day-to-day realities of work life that involved women's activities, as in *actividades feministas*.

More important was the call for women to share these ideas with others at home and at work. It was within this context that anarchist women radicalized the idea of motherhood—often turning the term "natural" on its head. In numerous public debates, women's "natural" qualities hinting at their distinctive biology were used to argue against women's involvement in matters considered public. Yet Rodríguez and others put a spin on "natural" and argued that women's "natural" role included advocating for labor equity for all, even *obreras* and *campesinas*. In the anarchist tradition, all members of society were not only entitled to basic civil rights but also responsible for actively working toward gaining such rights.[27]

In *Avante*, commentaries by prominent anarchists including Emma Goldman were reprinted and featured alongside equally fiery, passionate, and articulate activists such as Florinda Mondini from Argentina. Mondini argued, "Let us prepare ourselves to conquer that which is our right to possess, our liberty.... We will reach this goal if we preoccupy ourselves with our own education instead of worrying so much (and this happens frequently) about the . . . latest fashions . . . and frivolous things."[28] While Mondini recognized her male counterparts as *compañeros*, she remained critical of their struggle against the excesses of industrial capitalism and proclaimed their shortcomings in the greater labor movement, especially their neglect of women: "Men, our brothers, our *compañeros* who by some special situation were able to reach some respect and liberty, do nothing so that we may be privy to those same privileges." Yet Mondini, among the more radical writers contributing to *Avante* during the late 1920s, invoked a gendered reason to fight against the evils of capitalism as well as for her freedom and liberty as a working woman. "If as women, we wish to position ourselves in the rightful level we deserve as mothers who love their children, we have the inevitable responsibility to guide their footsteps toward liberty. We would be cruel mothers if we failed to guide our children toward that same liberty that we have yet to come to know." If this were not done in the name of combating the evils of industrial capitalism, working mothers and all mothers "would not be worthy of their children."[29]

By fighting, all women, including single working-class mothers, were worthy of their children. Facing greater challenges, single working-class mothers could be shunned by community members. As historian Nancy A. Hewitt noted regarding Luisa Capetillo, who like Velásquez engaged in labor activism on her own with no partner, single mothers too "demanded the kind of education and social services that would allow women to act effectively in public as well as private spheres."[30] While mainstream media outlets could frame single mothers as immoral women or as a hindrance to state progress, the everyday experiences of unmarried mothers or working single mothers engaged in activism reflected their actual contribution to society.

Compañeras and "Varying Beauties"

Propaganda outlining the actual contributions of women to society and the need for collaboration continued to raise awareness of the persistent wage discrepancies among men and women. El Grupo de Propaganda Anárquica, in a bulletin section entitled "A la mujer," for example, explained that "men and women suffer the effects of the same tyranny," and therefore it was urgent that "*compañeras*, make your sisters, husbands, fathers, and friends organize and help workers from the entire world."[31] The bulletin continued, "We are *obreras* and because we are women . . . and are paid less as compared to men, are made to work more." And "we suffer from the impertinence of foremen or the boss; if we grow weak, they will steal our hearts with that same cowardice as our labor is stolen." Female readers were urged to cooperate as *compañeras* were treated "inferior to men, humiliated, underappreciated" and must "fight alongside . . . working brothers . . . against the greed of capital."[32] Propaganda Anárquica called attention to the persistent gender inequities.

Underscoring women's maternal powers as well as their rightful place in organized labor and in the larger world of politics could fall on deaf ears. Societal expectations still abounded concerning women's behavior, with consequences for women of all class backgrounds engaged in activism. Mainstream organizations focused on suffrage were plagued by superficial treatment based on their sexuality and appearance. When the Comisión Inter-Americana de Mujeres, a respected organization that frequently collaborated with US suffragists on the issue of Mexican suffrage, helped organize the Sixth International American Conference, local newspaper coverage on the important convention reduced it to a gathering of "varying beauties" and printed the news story in the beauty section. Comisión delegates took issue with the sexual politics overshadowing the actual accomplishments of the convention.[33] The calls for political equity put forth by the Comisión were featured in Tampico's most popular mainstream daily, *El Mundo*, alongside several advertisements promoting women's "natural" beauty. Superficial characterizations of women's physical appearance and dress eclipsed the serious political demands of the Comisión. The Comisión-sponsored Mexico City conference, which had taken months of planning and commitment by hundreds of women, was reduced in significance in an instant. Featuring the conference on a page dedicated to beauty products and health tips, as opposed to its section on politics, for example, revealed the newspaper's superficial treatment of the convention and, by default, women's rights. Moreover, to the left of the article on the convention's agenda was an editorial, "The short skirt creates problems for the proper way of sitting."[34] Women's modern dress posed a problem in the eyes of the editors; it eroded "proper" normative behavior for women. And the feature on the skirt was lengthier than the summary of the convention's main points.[35]

*   *   *

The radical motherhood that anarcho-syndicalists promoted had the potential to shape the way working women and working mothers were perceived in the greater labor movement. Aurelia Rodríguez, Felipa Velásquez, and Caritina Piña, among other women, used radical motherhood to make sense of women's rightful place in society. Albeit always facing challenges, the idea of radical motherhood empowered women by politicizing that which had been used to disadvantage them and paint them as the weaker sex, as well as to argue for their reliance on men, marriage, or a larger benefactor such as the state. Motherhood was politicized—not to produce revolutionary mothers to serve the new revolutionary state, but revolutionary mothers capable of producing true fighters without the usual state blindfold that drove Mexicans to serve the new government.

The regional network's ideas about maternalism and women's place in society migrated across communities and were further shared, informing a continuous reconstruction of women's identities. Shaped by local and extralocal class and gendered ideas, Mexican women participated in such transnational circuits.[36] These ideas resonated strongly as the number of women workers increased nationwide. For women in the Tampico-Cecilia area, accustomed to a community that supported labor organizing, the calls were heard loud and clear. Everyday experiences in this context of labor organizing as well as what was learned or "accumulated" about other women's experiences in similar situations informed Piña's labor network. These multidirectional solidarities reflected how women's labor activism embodied a transnational process *made* in the circulation of ideas and not simply a product of local conditions.[37] Such transnational feminist identities reflected the anarchist tradition as a type of liberation, of a continuous learning and relearning of others' plight and struggle that shaped the ways in which women made sense of their embattled communities and those facing similar conditions far away.

In the midst of the strengthening of anarcho-syndicalist collectives vis-à-vis the rise of an organized state-led socialist prolabor party, there were women who considered alternative forms of labor organizing. Frustrated with unions and opting to "leave the unions to the men," but rejecting state-led socialism, nearly two hundred waitresses from the Tampico area abandoned the mixed-sex union of restaurant workers. This, however, was not a rejection of labor organizing. The waitresses chose instead to organize themselves based on "mutual respect." The waitresses from the Sindicato de Dependientas de Restaurantes y Similares, affiliated with the CGT, walked out on their union by the mid-1920s. Why would these women abandon their union at a time when unions had gained leverage and carried more weight in Mexican politics, and during a crucial moment when women such as Piña and others were achieving positions of leadership in organized labor? The emergence of the *"meseras libres"* movement in the midst of the state's increased efforts to control organized labor as well as to harness women's political power for its own interests during the formative years of Emilio Portes Gil's Partido Socialista Fronterizo takes center stage in the following chapter. The *meseras libres'* rejection and decision to leave the Sindicato de Dependientas de Restaurantes y Similares was, at its root, an anarchist expression rejecting formal unions over the choice to "mutually support one another."[38]

CHAPTER FIVE

"Leave the Unions to the Men"

Anarchist Expressions and Engendering Political Repression in the Midst of State-Sanctioned Socialism

> We should organize around ideas of mutual respect and
> understanding . . . we'll leave the unions to the men.
> —Las Meseras Libres, January 11, 1925

Venustiano Carranza's crackdown on radical labor activists during the height of the Mexican Revolution had weakened the anarcho-syndicalist movement. Yet Caritina Piña, Aurelia Rodríguez, Felipa Velásquez, Esteban Méndez Guerra, and other activists had helped to maintain its momentum, shared news about labor matters, and worked to free political prisoners. The anarcho-syndicalist movement remained on guard and kept moving forward.

As the radical segment of the labor movement gained strength locally and abroad, the labor reforms that many workers had hoped for in decades prior, including the right to organize and a minimum wage, finally had become reality, enshrined in Article 123 of the new Mexican Constitution (1917). While these were real labor concessions, to the anarchists, the state had won a major victory. Their critique stemmed from the fact that Article 123 bestowed power to the state as the main arbiter between labor and capital via the newly formed labor boards. While the bulk of the workforce made use of the newly created labor arbitration board, the Junta de Conciliación y Arbitraje (JCA), workers affiliated with the Tampico COM and affinity groups rejected it.[1] Amid an unprecedented number of petitions for union recognition submitted to the labor boards, including women workers, there were workers who instead broke with labor unions.

One of the most radical labor activist waves of the region, the case of the "movimiento de las meseras libres," or free waitress movement, is both a unique moment in the long history of labor activism in Tampico and a window into the complexities of women's involvement with organized labor. Feminist labor activism anchored in Tampico and the Gulf of Mexico emerged alongside women's activism in other parts of the globe, who were equally invested in the promotion of labor unity and gender equity.

In 1925, over two hundred waitresses decided to "leave . . . unions for the men." Such an outright rejection of unionism in a historically prolabor port begs several questions. Why would women workers serving a vital export-driven industry in a port with a history of radical labor activism among anarcho-syndicalists, communists, and socialists abandon a recognized and legal union? And why would women's public practice of alternative labor and political activism, as was the case with the waitresses and followers of José Vasconcelos, be treated trivially, with ridicule, and in some cases brutally? As the female leadership among the large group of *meseras* declared their intent to abandon the union, they were reduced to a basic dichotomy of "men-looking girls or pretty ones."[2] At the same time, the political campaign of José Vasconcelos, the education minister running against socialist Emilio Portes Gil for president, attracted scores of women who formed Clubs Femeniles Vasconcelistas. Yet, in one of their massive peaceful demonstrations in support of Vasconcelos, local authorities called on the fire department, which proceeded to disperse the crowd of "cheerleaders" with powerful gushes of water from the city's newly built modern water hose system. This chapter takes these moments as, on the one hand, for *meseras libres* an expression of anarchist feminism, and on the other, for the Vasconcelistas, evidence of how women's public political participation, even when state-sanctioned, could be brutally repressed. Both cases illustrate the way in which ideas about gender norms and expectations framed women's activism as unimportant. Yet, on the ground, their activism represented full expression of agency and solidarity.

Mexican women, like their counterparts in the United States, Latin America, Spain, and France had made considerable gains by the mid-1920s, represented in rights under the new Mexican Constitution. While limited, there had been some concessions—mostly in the form of protective legislation including policies on night shifts, hazardous work, and child labor. Workers approached the newly created labor boards to register new labor unions or submit grievances. Women workers too submitted claims to the *juntas* as early as 1918 to demand labor protections related to night shifts and the right to petition for lost wages related to unjust firings. The large strikes on behalf of the oil workers of the region had, while costing numerous lives, forced the nation and the world to acknowledge the power of organized labor.[3] In fact, although some workers participated in direct action such as the massive strikes against petroleum corporations, others submitted grievances to the *juntas*, wrote newspaper articles, or did both.[4] While by no means were labor policies always followed or easily enforced, they moved the country in the right direction, recognizing labor issues and the role of the worker in the crafting of a democratic Mexico. These gains became further solidified when Mexico implemented its Federal Labor Law in 1931.[5]

In Tampico, the growth of the port sparked by the expansion of the oil sector contributed to the larger modernization project that was well underway by the 1920s and further promoted in the 1930s. As new oilfields and refineries emerged, attendant wage labor sectors grew, fed by a continuous demographic explosion that also contributed to the port's rapid urbanization. Migrants and locals joined the ranks of the workforce, becoming part of the base from which political and labor organizations drew their membership. The outlying *poblados*, including Villa Cecilia, had also grown closer to Tampico. By mid-decade, the region, which comprised part of the the state's fourth district, led the state's economic growth.[6] As the petroleum industry expanded, this fourth district became a leader in the state and national economy and, combined with the oil sector in Veracruz, led oil production in the country and ranked in the top ten globally. Thus, migration to the region by women, men, and entire families remained steady, at least for some time. The population figures for Tampico and outlying areas reached 25,000 by 1915, and in 1921 approximately 100,000 people resided in Tampico alone.[7]

Female labor dominated the restaurant and bar industry, but that sector has been overshadowed by studies that focus solely on the larger, predominantly male, oil labor force. *Obreras* in the restaurant and bar sector contributed to the growth of the region, as this industry directly addressed the basic needs of a growing consumer demographic—the bulk tied to the oil sector. The early 1920s brought with it a temporary decline in oil production (alleviated only by the opening of new wells), resulting in layoffs and a surge in strikes as well as a reduction in the total industrial employed workforce, but support sectors such as the restaurant and bar industry nonetheless remained crucial.[8]

The *meseras libres*, comprised of both locals and recent female migrants from the countryside and other urban centers, formed part of this restaurant and bar labor force. This female labor force was diverse, ranging from servers with years of experience in eateries and bars in the Tampico-Cecilia area to those with one or two years in the industry. The women gained employment in the various cafés, restaurants, and cantinas in the Tampico-Cecilia region, including La Sevillana, El Suizo, and Cafe Louisiana, and soon obtained membership in the Unión de Empleados de Restaurantes y Similares (UERS) via affiliates including the Sindicato de Empleadas de Restaurantes, Cafés y Similares (SERCS) and the Sindicato de Dependientas de Restaurantes y Similares (SDRS). It was in this context of increased union participation in the region as well as throughout the country that the two hundred waitresses made history in the port.[9]

Not only did this movement emerge in the wake of increased union participation, it also developed in the midst of a new wave of union-led strikes that in and of themselves were major labor milestones. During 1924 and well into 1925 a wave of strikes hit the region due to massive layoffs as oil production declined.[10] Amid such activity, young waitresses affiliated with SDRS broke with the union and created a grassroots collective organization. This was a particularly crucial moment in the history of organized labor in the region. The years of crackdowns on radical labor activists and the violence from oil companies' *guardias blancas*, or company guards, had claimed many lives, but workers had gained union recognition and collective bargaining. The oil workers from the British-owned El Águila had succeeded in gaining their first collective contract with the company in 1924, with other major oil unions following suit.

Despite these major labor victories, the organized waitresses prefaced their action by explaining they opted to "leav[e] the union to the men." The case of the free waitresses, as they chose to call themselves, not only reveals the politics of gendered hierarchies but also signals a shift in labor activism in this historically radical port. This movement of a large female labor force publicly showcased a reliance on a collective effort outside the bounds of the state and demonstrated the continuing relevance of community action, as it privileged older models of activism such as mutual aid societies. While neither a rejection of labor activism nor a sign of the decline of unions, the *meseras libres* movement was a direct response to state regulations imposed on female restaurant and bar workers and an expression of anarchist ideals. It was a direct response to the ways in which both the state and the labor union sought to regulate the sexuality of its waitresses.

The Rise of the Partido Socialista Fronterizo

The rise of Portes Gil's Partido Socialista Fronterizo had, since its founding, involved repression and violence directed at anarchists and communists alike. During the municipal elections in 1924, the short-lived Partido Obrero Socialista Tamaulipeco (POST), whose main membership hailed from the Tampico local of the Sindicato Mexicano de Electricistas, the main electrical workers' union, emerged as an alternative political party to the PSF. The *electricistas* had supported the CGT over the CROM and were among the most radical of the country. Among the electrical workers' union members were communist sympathizers, including labor leader Tito Durán y Huerta, known to businessmen as "the dangerous communist agitator." Bloody encounters transpired, and as the PSF claimed victory, POST leaders were jailed. POST supporters had been blocked from voting at the polls or had encountered threatening "armed Partido Socialista members." Within a short period, the PSF had emerged victorious, placing its candidates in key political positions throughout the port.[11] The POST continued its activities and held a rally in early 1925 "to protest the flagrant violation of the public vote." The tally of the votes, handled by PSF sympathizers, was irregular, and attacks on pro-POST voting locations went uninvestigated.[12] While repression and violence kept certain voters away, the way in which the PSF recruited its own supporters and disciplined them was equally important. PSF politics were framed in gendered ways that sought to dictate how and when women, in particular, could engage in labor activism.

Portes Gil's rise to political prominence and the creation of the PSF in 1924 mirrored the rise of other conservative socialists across the US-Mexico borderlands as well as other parts of Mexico and the United States. Portes Gil, like socialists including Eugene Debs, placed social reform at the heart of the region's transformation. For Portes Gil, Tamaulipas and the rest of the country could only fulfill its full potential—including labor equity—if it were socially reformed. He believed that this could only be accomplished with a strong state. Portes Gil's policies were undergirded by an idea of "civilization through schooling." This agenda helped to shape political identities to reflect a sense of regional belonging with clear class and gender differences.[13] As historian Leif Adelson has written, "Compared to the repressive politics of previous leaders" such as César López de Lara, for example, Portes Gil emerged as sympathetic to organized labor and thus, a better option.[14]

The rise of the PSF signaled a shift to a more concrete and effective alliance (compared to earlier CROM-based efforts) between the state and workers' organizations. Efforts to control labor via a state-sanctioned labor party were not unique to Tamaulipas. Like Portes Gil, governors from the states of Tabasco and Michoacán, for example, had sought to build up support among the peasantry and urban workers to use as a political base. This model continued in Mexico well into the late twentieth century; PSF discourse, by the late 1920s and into the 1930s, shaped the Partido Nacional Revolucionario (PNR), the predecessor of today's Partido Revolucionario Institucional or PRI. This state-centered discourse was imbued with ideas about gender-normative behavior that framed women as revolutionary mothers who represented "morally sound" Mexicans while promoting the interests of the state. It merged the older nineteenth-century conceptions of domesticity with modern ideas about the role of women as citizen-mothers. While the PSF's platform boasted as its priorities "the social, economic, and political liberation of women" and it acknowledged that women "possessed the necessary faculties to promote the public good," the goal was never a comprehensive liberation of women.[15] That is, the PSF did not promote the reproductive and economic freedom of women. The new soon-to-be-state-sanctioned party came to rival the old anarcho-syndicalist organizations and, to an extent, was a political tool to tame the most radical corners of labor.

PSF supporters claimed to have women's interests at heart; however, their idea of women's emancipation was limited to promoting secular education for women and emphasizing the state's role in helping women in urban and rural environments become fully "modernized." The PSF's women's rights agenda stood in stark contrast to the ideas promoted by anarcho-syndicalists, including access to birth control; the importance of (unremunerated) domestic labor; rejection of religion, particularly Catholicism and/or clericalism; and full labor rights for women and children.[16] The PSF co-opted women in two main ways. It harnessed women's political power by incorporating them into Ligas Femeninas, female quasi-political clubs, and by encouraging their participation in Anti-alcohol Leagues, the Ligas Anti-alchólicas. PSF political clubs created a facade that legitimized women's inclusion in formal politics, and the anti-alcohol leagues placed women front and center in a statewide morals campaign. In return, Portes Gil and the ruling party allowed women to participate in party plebiscites, although they "were required to be accompanied by a male [representative]."[17]

Portes Gil had publicly castigated socialists during his young adulthood. He had served as director and written numerous editorials for the state's *El Cauterio* as a young adult and in 1912, during the *magonista*-inspired uprising of Higinio Tanguma, he had chastised "socialists" and hoped that "authorities chased [them] to bring peace to the region."[18] But upon receiving his education degree, he based his new vision on using the idea of socialism to build a cross-class coalition. Portes Gil left Tamaulipas and headed toward Mexico City to study law after earning his education degree; upon graduation he quickly became involved with politics and in May 1919 he had acted as legal counsel for the Pierce Oil Company workers, supported the 1919 general strike, and was among those jailed and transferred to Chihuahua for a brief period. Thus, Portes Gil easily earned the respect and loyalty of some of the oil workers' unions, peasant leagues, and regional elites that laid the foundation of the PSF.[19] Having earned the respect of a cross-class segment of the region, Portes Gil easily received popular support for the governorship.[20] He would use the power of the governorship to further consolidate labor organizations, regional elite networks, parent organizations, and women to implement social reforms. As a newly minted lawyer and politician, his vision for postrevolutionary Tamaulipas embraced his own version of socialism, which would have a lasting legacy on the country's political identity

As the PSF gained momentum in various corners of the region, anarcho-syndicalist adherents found support in the CGT-backed Federación Obrera de Tampico (FOT). FOT members from Tampico and Villa Cecilia had joined attendees from different corners of the republic at the organizational meeting in Mexico City in late 1924. At the convening, "fifty unions with over 36,000 members . . . reject[ing] participation in politics, advocat[ing] direct action and promot[ing] [a] decentralist organization" formed part of the more radical labor branch that emerged as one of the PSF's main opponents.[21] The following year Tampico and Villa Cecilia anarcho-syndicalists moved to found an FOT local. The local adopted the national bylaws, among them "prohibiting any worker from participating in any political party."[22]

The FOT remained strong in Tampico despite some infighting and conflicts among its members, who disagreed on the approach to combatting the growing power of the state and Portes Gil. The FOT included organizations that ranged from the Tampico-based Liga Cultural de Mujeres Libertarias, oil workers' unions, and other smaller labor associations and unions. It supported local strikes, including a protracted struggle of the local teachers' union in the fall of 1924, and continuously reported to a variety of media outlets covering Tampico labor politics. It sent bulletins to anarchist-leaning newspapers as well as those with communist affiliations, including *El Machete*, one of Mexico City's major outlets for the Mexican Communist Party.[23] The FOT also included many of the labor organizations that Caritina Piña supported and those that came to Felipa Velásquez's aid when she and her children were detained.

The FOT had supported Velásquez's cause and mirrored earlier CGT efforts to include a women's agenda in its official platform. What was this women's agenda, and how did it differ from pre- and postrevolutionary-era ideas promoted by women and men via the *escuelas racionalistas*? It claimed that women's "revindication" was hard work, and that the organization expended "energy in this region" for its eventual realization.[24] It proudly listed the organizations with a strong female membership affiliated to it, earning the reputation as a committed supporter of women's rights. More general points included "the emancipation for all workers . . . and direct action . . . to abolish capitalism."[25] Yet, as the local waitresses soon realized, even those CGT-affiliated organizations, despite their reputation as more radical vis-à-vis the PSF or the CROM, were shaped by members' ideas and perceptions about women's sexuality and gender.

Among these labor unions that were adhered to the CGT and the FOT was the Unión de Empleados de Restaurantes y Similares (UERS). The UERS's membership included many waitresses, although as historian Mary Goldsmith has pointed out, "included none [women] in its leadership unit."[26] While the FOT, similar to the PSF and in consultation with the male leadership of the UERS, denounced capitalism and patriarchy and featured commentaries by women on the question of gender equity in its publications, the majority-male leadership moved to limit and regulate women's sexuality in the mid-1920s—particularly that of the female waitresses who formed part of the union.[27] The FOT prohibited the organized workers from any *libertinaje* or licentious behavior, singling out its female members. In this way, the reformist policies of the commonly described "radical" FOT mirrored those of the "conservative" socialist PSF.

Caritina Piña, like female activists who preceded her, supported the principles of the CGT, and sources indicate that she was not in any way opposed to the FOT. The CGT, which endorsed the FOT, embodied anarcho-syndicalism in a formal, organizational way. The CGT prided itself in its staunch position against any government control. It reminded workers through its editorials in the CGT-endorsed *Sagitario* and *Vía Libre* of its "well-known independence from the government and from politically based strategies to resolve issues between capitalists and workers."[28] In its second convention in 1922, the CGT reinforced its commitment to the ideals from its inception. It vowed to "fight for the freedom of social prisoners" and reminded all that this fight had to be engaged internationally.[29] It also declared its "commitment . . . to fully support[ing] the peasantry creating a wave of 'love and fraternity' that created bonds of solidarity between craft-based workers with those who work and cultivate the land."[30]

Despite its affiliation with and support of the CGT, after a long struggle for the inclusion of *meseras* in the union, the municipality of Tampico discussed the possibility of a *reglamento* or set of rules to which all female restaurant workers had to subscribe. In the summer of 1924, Tampico officials approved legislation, with union support, to oversee *meseras*. This was explicitly framed in the context of unionized waitresses, signaling a departure on the part of the CGT. Long known for its rejection of the state, at least on this issue, it cooperated with the state to regulate its female members. The opening clause established that "waitresses could work daily in the cantinas, cafés, restaurants, and similar establishments from eight in the morning until ten in the evening" but under-scored the importance of business owners' not being allowed to force *meseras* to work beyond an eight-hour day.[31] The fourth clause referenced the expected behavior for *meseras* while at the worksite. It specifically prohibited women from "acting immorally" and threatened to levy a fine on each business owner if one of their *meseras* "committed an immoral act." A fine ranging from 100 to 500 Mexican pesos could be levied upon business owners with a fifteen-day jail sentence if they failed to pay; business owners reacted by implementing harsher labor controls. Coming just months after the founding of the FOT, the Reglamento would create waves in the FOT-adhered union of restaurant and bar workers. The Reglamento contained explicit language regarding waitresses' comportment in the workplace. *Meseras* "were not allowed to sit with their cus-tomers, drink with them or engage in such activity while within the cantinas, café, restaurant, etc."[32]

As the oil industry expanded, it attracted young women from the region and other parts of Mexico as well as from countries including France and Russia to cater to the sexual needs of a growing male oil labor force. Long practiced since the early days of the port's establishment, prostitution expanded along with demands for more oil wells, which prompted state authorities to more closely regulate the industry. Women, however, frequently bypassed municipal controls regarding prostitution, particularly by engaging clandestinely. The city, in re-turn, pushed hard to control and regulate such perceived intransigence. This fit a larger national pattern of a desire to control prostitutes, as historian Katherine Bliss has documented for other parts of Mexico.[33] Mexican authorities went to great lengths to regulate prostitution, cracking down on it and promoting a propaganda campaign against seeking such services, among other efforts.[34] But regulating the industry remained a difficult one due to the large population of single male oil workers.[35]

Meseras could not practice prostitution while at work—legally or otherwise.[36] The Reglamento de Meseras stipulated that if authorities found "*meseras* were registered prostitutes, they would proceed with the utmost speed to penalize them based on the Reglamento Sanitario and their certificate of registration would be cancelled."[37] A carefully placed moral clause followed: if *meseras* were "caught committing immoral acts" the full weight of the law could fall upon them. The case of three local women further illustrates the speed and severity with which authorities could proceed when encountering women suspected of breaking the law. Tampico authorities arrested María García, Elena García, and Carmen Ayala and sent the women directly to the Hospital Civil for practicing prostitution "clandestinely" in a local brothel. Municipal authorities registered the three women at the local hospital, so their records remained open and subject to close supervision to prevent them from practicing outside legal parameters.[38] That same year, as the Reglamento went into effect, authorities arrested local resident Rosa Castillo, despite her insistence she was not a prostitute. She was arrested in the company of a man who "committed immoral acts in late hours of the night." Authorities arrested and questioned Castillo while allowing her male partner to leave the police station.[39]

Meseras' work hours varied, and those working late shifts usually found themselves defending their "honor" when stopped by local authorities in the late evening or early morning hours. The occupation of *mesera*, for local authorities and as reflected in popular culture (to this day), implied certain gender and sexual norms. Authorities required women wishing to work as *meseras* to register with the municipal authorities, who instructed the women to undergo a medical examination. Such routine inspections guaranteed bar and *cantina* owners not only a healthy supply of female laborers but also that potential *meseras* looked a certain way, as their physical features were also routinely recorded and captured in photographs. Municipal law required prospective waitresses to present a valid certificate demonstrating a clean medical history, four photographs, and a physical home address and required *meseras* to inform authorities if and when they moved to a new household. The new Reglamento extended some guarantees and protections to *meseras* in the event of "unjust detention by city police or sanitary agents." If agents abused their power, they too would face consequences. Yet rarely were agents questioned for their abuse of power, nor were they stripped of their badges.[40]

All this developed amid a growing national women's suffrage movement during the first couple of years of the Portes Gil governorship. In 1925, the Congreso Internacional de Mujeres de la Raza, also known as the Congreso Feminista, articulated its vision of women's goals as well as strategies to meet such goals. In general terms, the group was heterogenous; there were those considered part of the "moderate" group and the "radicals"; the latter supported by the likes of Elvia Carrillo Puerto.[41] Elvia's brother, Governor Felipe Carillo Puerto, had led a radical socialist movement in Yucatán that had developed differently than Portes Gil's more conservative socialist approach. Elvia, with the support of her brother, publicly advocated for women's reproductive rights and promoted the ideas of Margaret Sanger and the use of birth control.[42] This stood in stark contrast to the more moderate positions of other women. At times clashing while at other times reaching consensus despite ideological differences and competing agendas, the larger women's movement in which Elvia Carillo Puerto took a leading part was particularly vibrant during these decades. While there is no evidence indicating the adoption of a specific birth control agenda in Piña's labor network, reproductive rights formed part of the larger goal of women's full emancipation.

Organizations such as the Consejo Feminista Mexicano, composed of "teachers, office workers, and other women who advocated for the vote," sent delegates to the Congreso Feminista.[43] At the congress, male delegates trivialized the divisions among the women. A representative from Chiapas, César Córdova, reduced the female delegates to mere appearance. He explained that the divisions were simple to understand: "what has developed is a split between the pretty ones and the ugly ones." Despite such sexist characterization, the women delegates pushed on; delegate María Sandoval took the stage and explained that those who had congregated in Queretaro to create a constitution, referencing the historic 1917 Constitution, "had left a door open so that the Congress could bestow rights upon Mexican Feminism."[44]

While perhaps not the simplistic, sexist portrayal of women's issues articulated by Córdova, CGT supporters also gendered labor matters to cast opponents in a negative light. Reducing labor matters to "a fight among *comadres*," *Sagitario* writers defending the CGT compared the infighting in the PSF to women "pulling their hair in a fight," or "*desgreñándose*."[45] Besides ridiculing PSF men and discouraging workers from joining the PSF or supporting Portes Gil, the editorial further compared politics to a female prostitute. "Distance yourself from that putrid prostitute, *la política* . . . *obrero* go to the Union, go to the centers of freedom, go to those places that lead you to freedom."[46] The sexualized and gendered way in which both conservative socialist and radical anarchist organizations portrayed labor matters was problematic and hurt overall efforts at gender equity.

Perceptions about competing class interests further complicated the gendered framing of labor issues. As an editorial in a Tampico newspaper, *La Opinión*, put it in 1924 regarding "Mexican women's feminism": "Let us not focus exclusively on women from the middle class, but the needs of the unfortunate from the lower classes."[47] The editorial continued, "the woman of the middle class is[,] among us, [described as] 'woman,' while those from the lower classes are simply '*hembra*' in the most rudimentary way." The editorial's use of the term *hembra* was telling. While *La Opinión*'s message placed working-class women at the forefront and sought to put them on par with middle-class women, it nonetheless invoked a term that was pejorative, as *hembra* commonly denoted female animals. The editorial continued, explaining that the "middle class woman only need [the tools] to be lifted, while the woman in the lower classes needs to be picked up." The male writer went on, "let us free women from two apocalyptic beasts who devour her: the *metate*, bestowed by the Indians, and the needle, brought by the Spaniards."[48]

In the midst of these developments involving international women's congresses promoting suffrage as well as a continuing discourse on working-class women's needs, *meseras* abandoned their labor union but still honored their commitment to one another, calling for "grassroots" collective action.[49] They had opted not to accept the PSF's call for "uplifting" working-class women and rejected the new Reglamento. Within a year of the Reglamento's implementation, the grassroots movement of *meseras libres* gained momentum in response to the limitations placed upon them. Carmen Aranda, known as "Pellandini" by her customers, along with other eighty other *meseras*, joined forces as *meseras libres* and soon recruited more women. In a series of interviews with reporters from Tampico's mainstream *El Mundo* in 1925, Aranda explained her motives for joining the movement and declared, "let the men stay with the union."[50] Aranda believed that women should instead "organize around ideas of mutual respect and understanding." Ignoring the concerns raised by the group of *meseras libres*, the reporter instead focused on the waitresses' appearance, much like César Córdova had done—their demeanor, way of speaking, and physical attributes, only reporting on their demands in the latter part of the story. *El Mundo*'s reporter trivialized the struggle of the newly independent *meseras*, reducing them to a news feature on "cosmetic beauty," which the report claimed was required for their profession.

Like Aranda, the *mesera* simply referred to as "Paz" explained her desire to "feel free" at work, which in her view the Reglamento clearly obstructed. Paz had worked in hotels and as the "separatist movement," as she called it, grew, Paz helped to recruit seventy women to leave the union despite her reputation "as a strong supporter of *sindicalismo*." Only a couple of *meseras* remained in the *sindicato*, mostly those serving in the *directiva* or executive committee. Paz reported to *El Mundo*, "The union is simply not doing anything for us anymore" and claimed that despite name-calling on the part of union members who called her an "*esquirla* [sic] [strike breaker]" for splintering the union, she held tight to her prerogatives. "We are the majority [women] who broke from the union . . . and we do not regret our actions." She closed the interview informing the newspaper that "frankly, I believe we, women, are just not fit for unions and that should be left to the men," echoing Aranda's message that "men should just stay with the union." Aranda, Paz, and their *compañeras* were resolved to "not be bullied by our unionized sisters," and they insisted that they were "resolved to face anything that may come our way."[51]

The *El Mundo* reporter proceeded to trivialize both Paz and Aranda's narration of the events. The reporter described Aranda as a "tall and strong looking young woman," before proceeding with Aranda's rationale for leaving. Paz was simply described as "thin and cute." The media description of the women reflected larger concerns over the question of women's modernity, as historian Anne Rubenstein has explained for women of Mexico City who bobbed their hair and whose "long limbs" and athletic image were frequently the focus of attention.[52] Almost all of the *meseras libres* sported short hair. Paz alone was able to recruit the seventy *compañeras* to join the "separatist movement," yet the media downplayed this feat. The reporter described Paz as not only a real leader but "a leader with beard and all!"[53]

Meseras such as Paz and Aranda economically contributed to their homes as wage earners through their labor in cafés, restaurants, bars, saloons, and similar establishments. They frequently catered to a predominantly male oil labor force as well as company management, many of whom were foreigners. Many of them complained that customers "took liberties with them . . . [and] they were the victims of crude jokes" and accused men of expecting sexual favors in exchange for extra pesos. A popular Mexican ballad of the time, "La mesera," referenced the liberty often taken by men with waitresses. The man in the ballad grows hungry (which in popular culture can also mean sexual appetite); he makes a stop at a local eatery and recounts: "A dark-skinned woman approached me who was to die for, she asked me: what would you like, you may order whatever you like sir; I am here to serve you sir, here, I am, the waitress." After he orders two plates, he instructs her to "sit with me so we can have some fun." As the night winds down, and after much drinking, the man suggests she follow him home. "I told her, at what time can we leave? She answered me, no baby, this is where we disagree, but if you have a couple of dollars I'll even dance a polka with you."[54] As the song winds down, the *mesera* has the upper hand and decides how far to go. She ate with the male customer, she drank with him, and if he paid, she could grant him a dance. But, according to the popular song (still heard in local radio stations today), she refused to "go home" with him.

As in the *corrido*, the *meseras* negotiated their circumstances. Resolved to address their situation and frustrated with the unresponsive nature of their male-dominated union, the large group of restive *meseras* "creat[ed] an organization of mutualism that provide[d] assistance when their misfortune required it." When asked what brought them together as "*libres,*" the *meseras* explained that "it was a strong bond of solidarity . . . that helped [us] to seek economic and moral improvement."[55] Their response echoed the late nineteenth-century mutual aid adages of many of the societies in the region. Although there is little evidence of a similar case of all-female union members turning to mutual aid organizations, there were mutual aid collectives that operated in the region since the late nineteenth century. Some of these *mutualistas* had not opted to convert their organizations into unions, including the Sociedad Mutualista "Hermanos del Trabajo," founded in 1900 and in operation during the 1920s.[56]

In the midst of "an intense movement of workers to find freedom . . . via a union," the women chose another path. In leaving a CGT-endorsed union, the women's decision to organize collectively outside the union revealed a grassroots, bottom-up choice that was, in spirit, anarchistic and antistate. Nor did they choose to join the CROM. The CGT had, early on, vociferously encouraged folks to remain distant from the CROM, charging that the organization "follows the path of political action as the tactic and strategy for all worker-related struggles against capitalists." It continued in a lengthy editorial: "Those same supporters of workers' rights [who belong to the CROM] support or end up occupying positions like lawyers, judges . . . working in positions endorsed or created by government in the labor boards, that directly depend on the government, even the president himself acts as mediator between workers and the bourgeoise."[57]

A couple of days after the large group of *meseras* had abandoned their jobs, declaring their intent to enter into individual work contracts with their employers as opposed to collective union contracts, the *meseras libres* set out to recruit other waitresses in hopes of expanding their reach. They encountered a few problems, including facing frustrated and upset bar and cantina owners. These owners perceived them as "unruly workers." The business owners' concerns stemmed from the potential damage of the movement to the economic viability of the service sector. The group congregated in the Centro Comercial de Tampico headquarters, "to which almost all business owners adhered" and discussed whether they wished to hire *meseras* who had left their jobs due to conflicts with the union. Among the issues discussed was the *meseras'* audacious petition to the mayor that detailed their complaints against the regulations set by the union, their desire to work "freely," and their intent to return to work on their own.[58] Yet the business owners could not reach a consensus. They felt pressure from the union to not hire independent waitresses but they needed those experienced workers.

Local authorities also responded. As women sought ways to negotiate and balance economic opportunity and autonomy, authorities linked the *meseras* with prostitution. Outside the regulatory world of legal prostitution, women— whether they labored as *meseras*, street vendors, or in similar sectors—felt the weight of the state as its agents sought to crack down on illegal prostitution and further regulate the practice; the city expanded the Reglamento de Prostitución in 1927.[59] City officials boasted the apprehension of over 120 women in 1931 who were clandestinely practicing prostitution. Together, the fines that were leveled on the women surpassed 1,390 pesos. This "severe fine" due to their "immoral commerce" was touted by city officials. The report claimed that 780 prostitutes were apprehended in the streets and in homes and then sent to the Hospital Civil to ensure that their health condition did not affect city residents. Of the 780 women, only 337 women were released with a bill of good health and allowed to return to the zone of tolerance.[60]

In the midst of a state crackdown on illegal prostitution, the state's and unions' efforts to control the sexuality of female workers mirrored the larger efforts concerning *obreras* in the interior of the country. Organized or not, *obreras* participated in a May Day parade in Mexico City the same year in which the Tampico *meseras libres* confronted the union and became independent. As historian Susie Porter has written, "waitresses and women from the printing industry dressed in black skirts and red shirts, attesting to their anarchist beliefs," marched in the capital demanding that they be treated with dignity. Among the banners displayed at the parade included those bearing messages underscoring women's strong moral character often attacked due to their position as workers and mothers. Many protested their exclusion from some unions.[61] As May Day protests continued, "more than one thousand waitresses met to protest low wages, long hours, and inappropriate and poor treatment by both employers and customers."[62] Waitresses complained that they were often targets of sexual harassment. Whether they were outright excluded from unions or abandoned unions themselves, working women found ways to express their discontent and advocate for their own well-being. And, similar to the popular *corrido*, at the end, it was the *mesera* who sought to negotiate her own conditions. The *meseras libres* possibly remained in contact with other organizations and kept abreast of developments via the local mainstream press. During their ordeal, however, *Sagitario*, the leading CGT newspaper, did not include a single commentary or editorial on the *meseras*' decision to leave their union.[63]

Working against the *meseras libres* was not only the popularity of unionism but the newly created labor boards and the pressure on business owners to abide by new labor regulations. One of several examples includes a labor dispute between a café owner and employees. Mr. Nixon, a US national and owner of Café Louisiana in Tampico, had been negotiating with his workers and finally had pledged to not hire "anyone who was not affiliated with the [café] union." The settlement came only after Nixon had engaged in a protracted labor struggle with the union. Workers complained that "this gringo . . . of the Louisiana [café] seems to be completely reluctant [to concede]." Eventually, Nixon agreed to the wages demanded and to "provide adequate and healthy meals" to workers. The lengthy eighteen-clause contract with the union satisfied the workers, at least momentarily. The local labor board ordered Nixon to pay 1,500 pesos to the workers who had been dismissed. Thus, those outside the registered unions could find it difficult to secure employment.[64]

Nonetheless, *meseras libres* Paz and Aranda promoted collectivism outside the unions and organized on their own terms. Leaving the CGT-endorsed union was a tough decision as it meant the loss of a large labor union's support. The women's collective organizing outside of the union revealed, however, a grassroots, mutually benefiting movement that embodied anarchistic ideals.[65] Other women continued to participate with the FOT-affiliated UERS despite its efforts to sexually regulate its workforce.[66] The UERS continued to recruit anarcho-syndicalists, promising that the union stood, "always against . . . communist ideas."[67]

Activism continued in the region with the emergence of other women-led groups voicing their concerns. This time, via political party female auxiliaries, women engaged in electoral politics endorsing a former minister of Education for the presidency. As women participated in the founding of Vasconcelista female clubs in the region, it became clear that even for women outside of the anarchist movement, their public participation was not welcomed.

A Similar Fate: Clubs Femeniles Vasconcelistas

As José Vasconcelos—an educator, writer, and the former minister of education (1921–1924) during Alvaro Obregón's presidency—launched his presidential campaign in 1929, he garnered substantial support from women in the region. Soon Vasconcelista clubs emerged. It was during Vasconcelos's final year as minister of education that Portes Gil organized the PSF, and not long after that PSF and Vasconcelos forces clashed.[68]

In the midst of the *meseras libres* movement and as their mutual aid collective had solidified, politically motivated violence had begun to intensify, corresponding with election season. On October 1929, a group of close to forty PSF armed men shouting ¡*Abajo* Vasconcelos! (Down with Vasconcelos) attacked a house that operated as a meeting place for the Vasconcelista Club "Aquiles Serdán," one of the antireelection party clubs. The men had gone out on the town after a PSF meeting and, by late evening, had consumed alcohol excessively. They threw rocks and intensified their attack by opening gunfire on the house.[69] Several of the men climbed to the top of the house and removed the antireelection party's flag. Fortunately, there were no fatalities. In their complaint submitted to the mayor of the city the following day, members of the Vasconcelista Club denounced the violence and explained that many of the men who were "part of [the] mob that instigated the attack" were in fact municipal employees adhered to the PSF. The mayor ordered the city police to investigate the incident.[70] A police investigation, however, did not end the attacks. Within a month, another antireelection club, "Club no.13 Lic. José Vasconcelos," was attacked by twelve men, all from the PSF. Worse, the men, also municipal employees, used an official city vehicle to bring down the party's flag. That representative clubs had been attacked was such a common occurrence in the city and the outlying area that the president of the antireelection party "urgently demanded guarantees and protections for our brethren" during organizational meetings and at the polls.[71] In January, Vasconcelos himself had suffered an attack at the conclusion of his border tour. When he left Nogales, as he arrived in Guadalajara to deliver his speech, local anti-Vasconcelistas blocked the entrance to the theater. He eventually delivered his speech at the Plaza de la Universidad, where over twelve thousand supporters rallied him on.[72]

The emergence of Vasconcelos as rival to Portes Gil in the presidential race became the spark for an already tense situation in Tampico. Portes Gil had built a labor-based alliance further functioning as a political foundation that had helped to catapult him to the governorship and then the presidency. Taking on Portes Gil was a monumental challenge. Just as the large group of waitresses had decided to abandon their union, over three hundred women identified as Vasconcelistas directly challenged Portes Gil. In the fall of 1929 and as the PSF gained strength, so too did a faction of the residents in support of Vasconcelos. "Thousands of women" took to the street. Marching through the streets of Tampico, the women participated in a "mute" march, holding signs with a simple but clear message for the head of state: "Garantías y Justicia Piden las Mujeres Tampiqueñas" (The Women of Tampico Demand Liberty and Justice). They raised awareness and promoted the Vasconcelista clubs as politically engaged citizens.[73]

Despite their public display of political power and initiative to take their demands to the streets, the Vasconcelista women's actions were explained in gendered terms to promote a particular understanding of political activism. Much like the media representations of the *meseras*, Vasconcelista women, as the media put it, still had to be "protected by their men." The women came from the *club femeniles* pro-Vasconcelos and called others to join them at one of the city's main plazas, La Libertad. Despite the thousands of women gathered in the plaza engaged in a peaceful protest, the city's fire department quickly arrived at the scene with several large hoses.

Quickly and with great force, the water descended upon the women. The call to open the hoses on the women had come from PSF municipal authorities to prevent them from organizing around Vasconcelos's agenda. That afternoon, the city known for its tradition of worker solidarity became a symbol of repression. Only this time, the call had come from those supporting the prolabor leader, Portes Gil. In a show of resiliency, drenched and all, the women refused to disperse. Vasconcelista women marched toward the main plaza, away from the large hoses connected to the new water supply near the docks adjacent to the Plaza Libertad. A couple of minutes elapsed as the women marched on. Soon, the firefighters' commander Manuel Cervantes ordered his men to stop; his men left the scene shortly thereafter.[74]

The Vasconcelistas, by this time "an enormous group of women," clothes drenched, had arrived at the plaza and continued their mute demonstration with residents clapping and cheering.[75] The actions taken by PSF-supported municipal authorities loyal to Portes Gil and to presidential candidate Pascual Ortiz Rubio were not surprising. As historian Alcayaga Sasso has noted, once Vasconcelos gained a considerable following in various regions of the country, the government of Portes Gil, backed by former president Plutarco Elías Calles, unleashed military force to quash any support for the former minister of education.[76] Only days before the massive demonstration of Vasconcelista women, a group of women and children had gathered to protest a demonstration for presidential candidate Ortiz Rubio. These Porristas, or "cheerleaders" as they were identified by the Ortiz Rubio campaign, were used as a "*contra-manifestación*" (counterprotest) to make the march "look bad." The report gave women little credit for their political stance and political engagement, and it emphasized the supposed manipulation of women and children, defining them as apolitical. It claimed that the Vasconcelos campaign placed them at the protest "to make *escándalo* [noise]."[77] The women and children, the same individuals defined as key members to the creation of a modern nation, were reduced to pawns in a political game directed by men from the PSF.

*   *   *

The promises for women's "emancipation" by both the state-backed PSF and the radical CGT endorsed by the FOT fell short. Despite the rhetoric of gender equity, women's importance in society, in organized labor, and as representatives of a new modern Mexico was overshadowed by the discourse that painted women as footnotes to the larger story of labor activism. These key supporters of social labor reform were described as "cheerleaders" or as *compañeras* of modern Mexican men, reduced to their physical attributes and framed in apolitical terms. The limits of labor activism even in this radical corner of Mexico were palpable. Women were the subjects of social control from both ends—the conservative PSF and radical anarcho-syndicalist organizations like the FOT. In the female political auxiliaries like the Vasconcelista *femeniles*, its members were cast as obstacles to political progress and not as key contributors to public political policies. Worse, women experienced not only rhetorical attacks but also actual *physical* attacks.

No single political faction, including Portes Gil's Ligas Femeninas, protested the unprovoked attacks on the Vasconcelista female supporters. Driven away with powerful water hoses in one of the most public places of the city and in a region with a long history of labor activism from all ideological persuasions, the women Vasconcelistas were treated horribly. When the presidential elections finally took place in November 1930, military forces stood guard at all voting places in the region and throughout the country, exemplifying the tense political situation. Pascual Ortiz Rubio, who formed part of Calles (and Portes Gil's) political sphere of influence, easily won the presidency.[78] Subsequently, several individuals attempted to assassinate Rubio Ortiz and, despite lack of evidence, the revolutionary government accused and jailed so-called pernicious foreign communists, including the famed artist Tina Modotti.[79]

Women remained either obstacles, unequal collaborators, or "cheerleaders," or were reduced to quasi-political actors whose physical attributes were valued more than their political acumen. They were perceived as mere residents who could help promote social reform or were in need of social reforming themselves. The reality, however, was that *meseras libres* and Vasconcelista women's clubs engaged in their respective labor and political activism despite challenges and the risk of physical violence. Notwithstanding such treatment, they left an imprint in the region's labor history through their various forms of *feminismos*.

Women continued to actively participate in political and social movements joining demonstrations and strikes. The *lavanderas* (laundry/washing women), for example, working in the oil camps "employed by the same company, joined the nearly 4,200 strikers from Edward Doheny's Huasteca Petroleum," as oil and other workers from the refineries and related sectors went on a strike during the summer months of 1925 sparked by massive layoffs. While *Sagitario* only mentioned "the large number" (of *lavanderas*) and did not specify how many joined the strike, it reported on "the solidarity [they demonstrated] with the comrades . . . not a single one deserted, not a single complaint was heard, despite capitalist newspapers reporting on the failure [of the strike]."[80]

Women's activist legacies with regard to state-sanctioned politics, as with Vasconcelistas or *meseras* in radical organizations tied to the CGT and FOT, reveal the way in which the modernization and reconstruction of a country was

Figure 14. Women workers in Mexican public laundry. Courtesy, Miriam and Ira D. Wallach Division of Art, Prints, and Photographs, New York Public Library.

built more on the *impression* that women could engage the state politically and less on the *actual* acceptance of women as real political actors, even in Mexico's most radical corners. Despite the various expressions of *feminismos* informed by anarchist ideas and women's direct political engagement—broadly construed— there were limits to what feminism could accomplish as state-sponsored socialism made headway.

CHAPTER SIX

A Last Stand for Anarcho-Feminists in the Post-1920 Period

I end these lines with a reflection . . . as my mind winds down, I seek a solution. . . . Why was inquisition imposed [upon me] to correct what was considered wrong?

—Felipa Velásquez, writing from the Colonia Penal de la Isla María Madre, June 12, 1930

Emilio Portes Gil's call to action in the inaugural conference of the Partido Socialista Fronterizo (PSF) foreshadowed the state's marginalization and repression of anarchists and their communist counterparts. The PSF positioned itself vis-à-vis communism and anarchism as the moral, proworker choice that would effect real change as it aligned with the revolutionary state. In explicit terms, Portes Gil couched the rise of the new Socialist Border Party in direct opposition to anarchism, explaining the urgency of a unified "political party that incorporated all of the labor organizations."[1] With respect to communism, Portes Gil claimed that "gradually, we will promote a democratic socialism, without limiting citizens' liberty, as is often the case with the communist system."[2] Portes Gil's new social pact with organized labor undergirded the revolutionary regime and its goal to reconstruct the nation.

With Portes Gil at the helm, state agents including educators from across Tamaulipas promoted women as crucial components of the larger quest for state reconstruction. The Tamaulipas native rewarded supporters and loyal unionists who helped him promote his vision of socialism as well as the PSF's goals. Among those loyal to Portes Gil were longtime dockworkers' union activists Isauro Alfaro and Nicolás González, who received protection from Portes Gil.

Given Portes Gil's close relationship with some of the El Águila union leadership since 1916 and 1917 during his days as a lawyer, it was unsurprising that Serapio Venegas, an El Águila union leader, assumed a leadership position in the Junta Central de Conciliación y Arbitraje, the state's labor board in Ciudad Victoria.[3] Political loyalty, as Alfaro's, González's, and Venegas's cases demonstrated, paid off and helped the greater socialist movement by encouraging more workers to join the party.[4]

Socially Reforming Families

The PSF's call for action sought to socially reform entire families for the "good of the nation." Portes Gil urged all to follow him in creating a new era for the state. Not "the old school that teaches within four walls in a dark room," Portes Gil argued, but "a new school of liberty, new horizons . . . that will break with the same forms of oppression originating in capitalism; a school that dissolves class-based prejudices and those prejudices that . . . destroy . . . that are the seed of discord and hate in all nations."[5] Using anticapitalist rhetoric he assured workers and residents, "we will not tire of promoting the civic duty of a nation, promoting the courage, valor, optimism and responsibility to all so they can defend themselves . . . from public servants who we demand demonstrate good behavior and morality."[6] In this way, he attempted to bring workers from various sectors together by appealing to their sensitivities and employing a labor rights discourse.

Newspapers such as *El Surco*, the principal media outlet of the state's agricultural school, promoted much of the PSF's larger social message and described Portes Gil's administration as a revolutionary government. *El Surco* encouraged the transformation of the peasantry, emphasizing the need for cooperation that encompassed the entire family. The domestic nature of women was key to creating a unified and modern country. In its bimonthly editions and *campesina* (female peasant) section, the male editors of the newspaper along with several female contributors focused on cooperation in the countryside. *El Surco* reflected the larger concerns of the Mexican state, to avoid a second revolution by fostering nationalism to secure confidence in the new revolutionary government. Editorials and news articles focused on the urgency of crop cultivation in the countryside in the newly created *ejido* (cooperative) communities and *rancherías*. The editors urged *norteños* to "intensely cultivate" the land so that the demand for foreign imports could decrease. Increased domestic production meant that families could benefit from goods they produced and further fueled the development of the local, regional, and national economy. The editorial entitled

"Cooperación en el campo" (Cooperation in the countryside) was a call to all workers and residents to collaborate in the cultivation of the land to produce surpluses that could result in exports, which would help increase the flow of capital into Mexico. This modernization vision was framed in agrarian terms espousing *agrarismo*, which unions such as the Liga de Comunidades Agrarias, Sindicato de Campesinos del Estado, and agrarian leagues from Villa Cecilia further popularized.[7]

Agrarismo was also framed in gendered terms. The official state school of agriculture, the Escuela de Agricultura, worked in concert with the state to use *agrarismo* to promote women's new revolutionary roles. Engineer Gustavo Segura, who served as school director from 1926 through 1930, argued that now that "economic liberty" had been achieved, the people had to "sustain and increase the production in their *ejidos* to justify, first, the executive solution that makes them owners of what used to be nonproductive land, and secondly, to demonstrate to society in general the veracity and justice of the Mexican agrarian reform."[8] Engineer E. Martínez de Alva, the school's previous director, had employed a similar discourse. He urged *campesinas* to assist *campesinos*: "We wish for the household to be a comfortable one so that the chores of the *campesina* can be observed and those [chores] can be executed without difficulty."[9] He stressed the need for *campesino* homes to be "more hygienic, clean, and more comfortable so when the *agricultor* arrives at home, he could wish to stay there, truly resting from fieldwork fatigue."[10] The official state rhetoric underlined the female responsibility to take "good" care of the home because it was necessary for the well-being of the *campesino*. Thus, the education espoused by Martínez was one that intertwined agricultural and home economic values. Commentaries and other thought pieces on women's equality in this context filled the pages of the newspaper in a section entitled, "To the Peasant Woman." One poem, "Mujer te doy por compañera, no sierva" (Woman, you are a companion, not a slave), explained how women were finally treated as equals. The writer exclaimed that "Noble women! Beautiful women! Strong women! . . . [were] the characteristics of the Mexican woman that can be summed up in a few words such as a good wife and a magnificent mother." It urged "women [to] learn to understand life's problems and [education] should be used to offer effective aid to the man who will be her companion."[11] *El Surco* further castigated women who "did not understand her *compañero's* work." These women ceased to be "true *compañeras*." Equality for women, per the larger message of *El Surco*, would stem from women's proper instruction to care for the farm, for animals, for the cultivation of crops, and for the ability to handle business transactions. The editorial argued the importance of these skills in the event that women

Figure 15. Market scene from station, Tampico. Courtesy, Miriam and Ira D. Wallach Division of Art, Prints, and Photographs, New York Public Library.

assumed their husbands' position. If women possessed these skills, coupled with "beauty, caring, and nobility," a "more complete family [would] make a better society."[12]

Thus, a "revolutionary mother," a "*compañera*" as outlined by state-sanctioned literature, was one who through patriotism and loyalty placed the interests of the state before her own, and stood in stark contrast to the way the anarcho-syndicalist movement employed the idea of revolutionary womanhood and motherhood. Throughout the republic, particularly at the regional level, rural education promoted by the state focused on "the instruction in farming methods, citizenship, hygiene, child care, preservation of food, and the more prosaic aspects of education."[13] Specific education for each sex would help to maintain the "proper" place for both men and women, thereby framing "emancipation" in terms of women's domesticity. Compared to the societal critiques launched by anarcho-syndicalist women, the state's use of the revolutionary woman and motherhood discourse was the modernization of gender inequality at its best, and the perpetuation of gender hierarchies at its worst.[14]

By the dawn of the 1930s, Portes Gil's vision of state-controlled organized labor became a reality. His close associates and supporters continued to encourage participation in the PSF and the larger Partido Nacional Revolucionario, placing women at the heart of such efforts. Among Portes Gil's associates was Marte R. Gómez, an agronomist, engineer, politician, and supporter of the PSF who urged the federal government to incorporate women into its sociopolitical and economic agenda. Women in PSF clubs and even those not directly involved in the PSF's political agenda, according to the party platform, were key to transforming Mexico into a real progressive and modern nation. Portes Gil rallied behind further guarantees of labor rights with the passage of the 1931 Federal Labor law during the Pascual Ortiz Rubio administration, codifying an eight-hour workday, vacation, the right to organize, and collective contracts. The labor law included much of the language prevalent in the PSF platform. The law functioned, as Susie Porter and others have explained, "as protective labor legislation." Two articles "prohibited women from working at night and from work in places that dispensed alcoholic beverages for immediate consumption and from dangerous or unhealthy work."[15]

As the project to produce morally sound subjects in Mexico continued in the 1930s, scholars from the Instituto de Derecho Comparado at the University of Paris began a study on women's status around the globe. Gómez, acting as a representative of the Mexican Legation in France, urged the secretary of foreign relations in Mexico City to heed the request for information so as to "include Mexico in this study."[16] The office responded with a lengthy report citing the country's Civil Code of August 30, 1932, that laid the legal foundation for circumscribing women's new position in society. The report maintained that in the years preceding such a legal text, women's social condition was "the same as in civilized countries of the world, particularly in the Latin world."[17] The report acknowledged "the profound inequality between [women] and men, that seeks to portray women as an inferior and implies that she be a subordinate, and one who is condemned by nature to an eternal position of submission and a repugnant slave in and outside her home." The report continued, referencing various studies on women's status that underscored both socially based studies such as John Stuart Mill's work, "that women's status grew from the environment that surrounded her and not due to nature," as well as those citing biology as the root cause for "women's inferiority."[18]

The writers of the report, all government officials with no indication of any women's groups' participation in drafting the statement, pointed to Mexico's progressive stance. The report offered a historical overview and then referenced the Independence period and its subsequent privileges extended to women in the form of "the same principles supported by French law in the aftermath of its great revolution."[19] Authorized by the head of the Departamento Jurídico, the report indicated that the origins of women's equal status to men was the emergence of a secular education in the Positivist tradition during the Porfiriato. Such a path "toward emancipation," the report claimed, was then strengthened by the 1910 Revolution.[20] Yet, there was no mention of women's efforts in labor organizations in the years leading up to the Revolution and immediately afterward.

If the Civil Code of 1932 and its further amendments by 1934, as argued by the foreign relations office, "sanctioned . . . what was essentially already in practice, the legal equality of men and women,"[21] then women had in fact achieved equal status according to the report. The divorce allowances and rights extended to married women after the Ley de Relaciones Familares was implemented in 1932, were indicators of women's equal standing in contemporary Mexican society.[22] After a lengthy assessment, the final verdict regarding women was that "Mexican women work just as much as men. . . . she is not her husband's object to instruct any longer, nor one without will or her own conscience, one who was destined to be enclosed in perpetuity to be the slave of the home."[23] The report was far from the truth; society still did not accept women as full equals as envisioned by anarcho-syndicalists, and suffrage remained elusive for communists and other feminist activists.

Collectively and individually, women from different class and ideological backgrounds had fought for suffrage at the local, state, and national level. A contemporary of Piña and trained medical doctor, Esther Chapa Tijerina, worked to promote women's political rights. Chapa Tijerina hailed from Tampico and became an active member of the Mexican Communist Party and cofounder of the FUPDM while in Mexico City. Tampico emerged with a strong FUPDM chapter that sought to counter the claim that "women lacked the intellectual capacity, the civic training, and the independence from the church required to exercise effective suffrage." Activists such as Chapa Tijerina and other FUPDM members argued that, while critics claimed women were among the adherents of clericalism and were easily persuaded, men too were influenced by clericalism and not necessarily better-prepared or better-informed voters.[24]

The FUPDM was created in 1935 by women from the Partido Nacional Revolucionario (PNR) and Partido Comunista Mexicano (PCM). Its founders include Michoacán native María Refugia "Cuca" García, Matilde Rodríguez Cabo, Consuelo Uranga, Luz Encina, and Chapa Tijerina.[25] While the FUPDM comprised women from various ideological perspectives, it was "dominated by communist women." Their goals ranged from modernizing corn mills through mechanization, "land reform, long-term political aims of securing suffrage," to fighting against fascism.[26] While the historical record does not provide concrete evidence linking Chapa Tijerina or García with Piña or with Velásquez, it is likely that they knew of each other's work, as communist newspapers including *El Machete* frequently reported on Tampico events sponsored by Hermanos Rojos and the CGT, among other organizations. Possibly, Piña knew of García's past history as a supporter of the oil workers. During the El Águila strike, García and her partner visited Tampico-Cecilia and stood in solidarity with the strikers. Other Tampico female groups formed part of the coalition that strengthened the FUPDM. The Liga Femenil Pro Derechos de la Mujer de Tampico y Ciudad Madero, with affiliations to the later Confederación de Trabajadores de México (CTM) organized in early 1934, became affiliated with the FUPDM.[27]

Women from various organizations with distinct ideological orientations worked collaboratively to promote shared class and gender interests. Cuca García had joined forces with Margarita Robles de Mendoza, one of the leaders of the UMA, the Unión de Mujeres Americanas. The UMA, with offices in Mexico City and New York City, was organized in 1934 and employed conservative tactics to achieve suffrage, which was its main organizational goal. Robles de Mendoza emerged as an ardent supporter of suffrage, yet she also took toward it a "gradualist posture," as historian Gabriela Cano has pointed out.[28] Often more progressive than some of her colleagues in the UMA, Robles de Mendoza critiqued heads of state when urging consideration of motherhood in labor laws. She stood out as a feminist who had access to diplomatic channels but included working-class women in her efforts. UMA, the FUPDM, and other organizations collaborated on various occasions, proving once again that while coalitions could be difficult to create, they were often urgent and necessary.[29]

Countering the Rise of State Socialism

Collaborations and tentative alliances between anarchists and communists from urban and rural backgrounds also characterized the early 1930s labor activism in the region among men and, to a certain extent, kept the momentum for both movements in the wake of repressive actions against radical labor.[30] Tampico and the greater Gulf of Mexico region exemplified such alliances, even if these were short-lived. The collective power of oil workers affiliated with different labor organizations as well alliances with the agrarian labor associations provided a moment of hope for all who supported labor. Valentín Campa, an ardent communist, after multiple key roles in promoting the Communist Party in Mexico City among other places, traveled to Tampico in support of the oil workers' strikes. Like his counterparts in the anarcho-syndicalist CGT, he quickly became an enemy of Portes Gil. Campa, like Méndez Guerra and

Rivera, also suffered abuse at the orders of Portes Gil when he attempted to organize the workers from Pederera de Tamatán, an oil company in which Portes Gil had personal interest. He was jailed and pressured to abandon organizing efforts in exchange for a government position. Campa refused. Upon his release, he took to the union halls and, recognizing the urgent need for alliances with other anti–Portes Gil groups, reached out to old anarchist supporters like Rivera and founded the worker-peasant organization Comité Pro-Asamblea Nacional Obrera y Campesina in late 1928. Portes Gil quickly moved to quash any communist momentum. By the close of the decade, Portes Gil and his government supporters had literally declared communism illegal and, much like the repressive wave to which anarchists were subjected during the nineteen teens and early 1920s, a series of assaults on communists followed. Adherents of the PCM were persecuted and subsequently persuaded or pressured to join the PNR. As a sign of goodwill toward Tampico anarchists, the Comité Pro-Asamblea Nacional Obrera y Campesina vowed to "remain exclusively as a labor syndicate" and it "definitively prohibited any committee activity that could be defined as political."[31] Reflecting the commitment to growing agrarian unrest and subsequent formation of agrarian leagues and peasant alliances with urban workers like petroleum workers in Tampico and Veracruz, CGT affiliates supported the new Ligas Campesinas (peasant federations) emerging throughout the country.[32]

Such alliances, however, were contingent upon national developments, some members' hardline ideological positions, class background and strategy, and the state's perception of particular political ideologies. Due to their on-the-ground activism and treatment in the media, anarcho-syndicalist and communist female activists often were regarded with suspicion and perceived differently than mainstream feminists, who were usually cast as less threatening. The Mexican consulate in New York City described the women who comprised the Liga Internacional, such as Elena Arizmendi, as "among the most educated and virtuous of our race."[33] Arizmendi had founded the Cruz Blanca Mexicana during the Francisco Madero presidency and had gained the respect of diplomats and *políticos* as "a talented woman" among Mexicans and in Latin America.[34] Arizmendi and her colleagues, who expressed their ideas and goals for women in the Americas through newsletters and magazines such as *Feminismo Internacional*, practiced a feminism in the context of Pan Americanism and internationalism, often through diplomatic channels.[35] Arizmendi wrote, "[*Feminismo Internacional*] is a practical and efficient system to stimulate our culture and make the fraternal links between sister nations even stronger."[36] Arizmendi's *Feminismo Internacional* took a hemispheric, transnational approach and defended the interests of "Hispanic countries." She had the support of consuls in the United States representing those countries as well as the support of other women's organizations including the Unión Pan-Americana de Washington.

Unlike Arizmendi and other activists from the Liga Internacional, Piña and others articulated labor and gender rights from a transnational, internationalist perspective—but not in diplomatic terms and certainly not to the benefit of any one government or nation. Instead, they promoted worker solidarity from the perspective of a global labor struggle. In this way, Piña and her colleagues' efforts followed a global approach along the lines of the IWW, the PLM, and the COM and differed from some feminist groups operating in the 1920s and 1930s that invested much of their time to gaining suffrage. Piña's Comité did not receive donations from the Mexican Embassy in the United States and consular offices, could not rely on official diplomatic channels to submit protests on behalf of fellow Mexican workers, and could not petition the embassy to protest assaults on members' sexuality and morality or when they were described as women of "ill-repute."[37] Rarely did members of the Comité participate (nor were they asked to represent their respective countries) in some official political capacity, as with the Pan American Union or the FUPDM. The Pan American Union and other organizations such as UMA were conscious of geopolitical borders and, while they engaged in transnational efforts, they recognized the sovereignty of nation-states. Piña and colleagues such as Velásquez not only envisioned a borderless society but engaged in protests as if it were the case.

The Comité's survival and growth was based on modest monetary donations from its members and sympathizers. Despite their commitment to remain on the sidelines of government politics, Comité members were politically engaged but as critical observers of the state and as individuals working to create an alternative way of life, outside the bounds of the state. Women from the Comité and the larger anarcho-syndicalist network worked beyond the confines of formal political channels, in informal circles crafting petitions and engaging in letter-writing campaigns to free colleagues and to promote their idea of a just society. Besides engaging in the writing and sharing of editorials, poems, and commentaries previously discussed, they also engaged in public protests and rallies, strikes, and in numerous meetings or public gatherings employing direct-action tactics. As historian Kirwin Shaffer has argued, anarchist networks survived, recirculated information, and gathered modest donations sent by their readers and members.[38] The Tampico network fit this pattern. For Piña, the sharing of pamphlets and newsletters that detailed their actions was key to the organization's own financial survival. This too was tied to the survival of the very idea of anarcho-syndicalism as a practice that could benefit all, and

ultimately worked to help and in some cases free detainees, such as FelipaVe-
lásquez and Librado Rivera.

Other differences between the anarcho-syndicalist female activists and those
affiliated with organizations such as the FUPDM and the UMA were class background and ideological or political beliefs that shaped the strategies they used.
Yet, as is clear from the petitions submitted by Piña, Velásquez, Rodríguez, Esther Mendoza, and other anarcho-syndicalists, while women and men's social
class status was often underscored (mainly that they all were part of the working, laboring class), the role of women as mothers was not ridiculed, degraded,
or seen as an impediment to labor activism. For anarcho-syndicalists, working
mothers were part of the larger labor family, on par with their male counterparts,
not to serve the purpose of the state or for the promotion of nationalism but for
the advancement of worker solidarity. The petitions submitted to government
officials by Mexican feminists including Arizmendi and Robles de Mendoza,
which referenced and privileged women's status as mothers, while similar to
the privileging of motherhood in Piña's network, made the case for women's
full inclusion in the political system as citizens, worthy of the vote and all of
the other benefits of citizenship. For Piña and colleagues, maternalism was
key to the reproduction of new members of society that would not cater to the
new revolutionary state but who would remain committed to the principles
of anarcho-syndicalism: labor solidarity for the good of labor, for a "just and
better world for all workers," as Piña put it, removed from any political party or
government entity.[39]

Further, women promoting anarchism as well as communism were often
portrayed as immoral, while women such as Arizmendi were described as "talented wom[e]n" among other validating and less-threatening labels.[40] While
the efforts of feminists invested in suffrage as their main goal also faced ridicule
or were described as lacking sufficient knowledge or the capacity to engage
in politics (and in some cases, targets of physical violence), their key role in
the formation of the ruling revolutionary political party and the urgency with
which their collaboration was needed in sustaining a far-reaching and inclusive party forced politicians, often, to begrudgingly accept women as political
equals. Why would politicians such as Portes Gil conciliate female anarchists
and female anarcho-syndicalists who opposed any and all political affiliation?
There simply was no benefit for him or any other politician. While that was a
signature characteristic of anarchists, it also was its Achilles' heel.

Hailing from rural backgrounds but quickly fitting into the urban labor
movement or born into working-class families, Piña, Felipa Velásquez, Esther and María Mendoza, and others worked outside formal politics yet were

deeply political, in the broadest sense of the term. While earlier writings on anarcho-feminists emphasized differences over commitments to the "movement," critiquing "short-term radicals" as opposed to "those who remained in the movement, long-term," these writings downplayed differences based on "class, ethnicity, or educational background."[41] The composition of the Tampico network, however, reveals how differences ranging from social class to race and educational background did in fact matter, perhaps more than the length of commitment. While other feminists framed the advancement of women's rights in diplomatic, internationalist terms, anarcho-feminists emphasized a global worker front that would unite them for the good of their own livelihoods, not in the interests of international diplomacy.

Piña's and Velásquez's outlook was shaped not only by their background but also by their position as residents and workers in border states, as *fronterizas*. This reflected their concern for labor issues beyond Mexico and beyond its immediate borders and shaped their feminismo transfronterizo. Both women had been members of organizations adhered to the CGT that *specifically* had embraced, among other issues, a "reject[ion] in participation in international wars." Adhering to CGT principles, they "aid[ed] political prisoners in the United States (among other places)" and "join[ed] in solidarity movements with other workers engaged in strikes," revealing their deep commitment to labor struggles across borders embracing a transnational, global sense of struggle.[42]

Their nationalism as Mexicanas shaped their outlook, and informed their transnational activism. Piña and Velásquez petitioned for the release of political prisoners, lent support and led agrarian land invasions, promoted gender equity, and pushed for labor rights from a transnational feminist position centered on anarchist principles. In this way, anarcho-syndicalists were anything but parochial and were quite the "internationalists," as Kirwin Shaffer explains for activists elsewhere.[43]

The activism of Piña and Velásquez, nonetheless, had its limits. At the end, it could not contain a corporatist socialism that came to dominate labor politics in the region and in most corners of the country. Organized labor became co-opted through the state party and nationally, through the Partido Revolucionario Institucional (PRI), of which the PSF was a crucial early part.[44] Those who remained committed to rejecting PSF efforts like the CGT were soon overshadowed not only by the sheer numbers of those who eventually pledged loyalty to the PRI but also by the gradual incorporation of labor policies that, while they in general benefitted workers, nonetheless became part of the state. There were some longtime and well-known anarcho-syndicalists such as José Angel Hernández who eventually opted to support the state. Hernández, a former IWW, *magonista* and member of the Texas Socialist Party, organized the Socialist and IWW Party of Tamaulipas, running unsuccessfully in 1921 for the Tamaulipas state congress.[45]

The call to build a multiclass coalition incorporating into the PSF a variety of labor unions to "achieve social justice" was too strong to stop. The PSF urged that "a call will be made to all youth and women as key elements in this new coalition." Two principles would guide women's inclusion. They became integral to the state because "the party would be an apparatus of the state," and would help usher and transform the "morality" of all workers.[46] The new members spoke of a "new Mexican woman," in gendered terms, as it cast the state as the father figure.[47] PSF women could reap real benefits, the PSF explained, if allied to the new state organization.

The PSF relied on support of the national PNR, over which Portes Gil now presided; the PNR would come to dominate politics for the next seventy years. Portes Gil and state authorities had managed to quash long-time supporters of the anarchist tradition—if not through deportation, through arrest, detention, torture, or in some cases, death. Years of radical thought were gradually contained despite the guarantee of political expression in the new revolutionary constitution. Amid profound political transformations, increased urbanization, and subsequent modernization in the form of expanded roads and highways, organized labor had become part of the state. Enduring, yet small, opposing voices continued to reverberate in and outside of the Mexican Gulf Coast region.[48]

Some new groups formed in 1932, such as the Grupo "Rayos de Luz" from Youngstown, Ohio, focused on reviving the movement and reaching across to the old Tampico-Cecilia anarchists. It reminded adherents that what was of immediate urgency was the promotion of "culture and propaganda." The Grupo requested two copies of any labor newspaper that covered local issues. The organization would make these "available in their *mesa de lectura*" (reading room) and "discuss" them despite "finding themselves far from those workers."[49] Contacting such new groups among others, in September 1934, Tampico local organizations representing agrarian and urban workers heeded the call and urged others to join forces and petition the president of the United States, Franklin D. Roosevelt, on behalf of the striking textile workers from "Maine to Alabama." Those strikers, who "paved the road toward Revolution," were confronted by "troops heading to South Carolina," among other places.[50] The plea to join forces, "raise money, hold meetings, and public demonstrations," echoed the calls for unity and solidarity decades earlier, showing continued efforts to promote organized labor via the anarcho-syndicalist path. The call described solidarity as "a way to bring down the barriers . . . the borders" that "surround the struggles" that prevent workers from "getting out of the misery in which they live."[51]

* * *

In the midst of such calls, Michoacán native Lázaro Cárdenas campaigned for the presidency. Cárdenas easily won the election in 1934 as Portes Gil finished his last year as the country's attorney general. Some resistance came from organized labor. Some were committed to keeping organized labor separate from politics, as one of several petitions submitted to the new president indicated: "the state is intent on blocking [the] entrance into a new liberty and justice."[52] The Sindicato Huasteco de Mata Redonda, chauffeurs' unions, as well as some workers from El Águila who had remained affiliated with the CGT put up some resistance to the new administration, although by 1938, Cárdenas's decree nationalizing the oil industry won over the bulk of oil workers as well as huge segments of the working class.

Although not explicitly expressed, Cárdenas's actions with respect to agrarian issues—and his support of agrarian activists, including Felipa Velásquez— likely helped garner anarcho-syndicalist support for his administration. On a Sunday morning, January 27, 1937, agrarian activists invaded lands of the US Colorado River Land Company once again, seven years after their first attempt. The "day of the land assault," however, had a different ending. Earlier that decade in June 1930, Velásquez had participated along with other activists from various ideological orientations in an agrarian invasion in Baja California. The memories of imprisonment in the infamous Islas Marías and her time away from her numerous children had only helped to fuel Velásquez's strong belief in *agrarismo* and the quest for access to arable land. At that time, Piña and the Comité had come to her rescue. Now, in 1937, plans for agrarian control of the lands claimed by the Colorado River Land Company resumed. This time, the arrest of Velásquez and her compatriots later that day was brief; on orders of President Cárdenas, the detainees were released the following day. The Cárdenas administration had consolidated various labor factions throughout the country, further legitimizing him as a "true" revolutionary leader, as he is still remembered by many. In a move that helped to solidify peasant support for Cárdenas, the former Michoacán governor expropriated the Alamo Mocho sector of the company lands, creating the "Ejido Islas Agrarias" in honor of agrarians like Velásquez.[53] This triumph was celebrated among the remaining anarcho-syndicalist circle, as the news was a much-needed shot in the arm after the movement had suffered such great losses. Just five years prior, Librado

Rivera, among the last of the old *magonistas*, died within a month of being hit by a cargo truck.[54] Other activists had retired, joined in support of Cárdenas, remained in jail, or had died.

By the latter part of the Cárdenas administration, the most radical elements of labor had been tamed. The CGT, which had remained loyal to anarcho-syndicalism and had maintained autonomy from the CROM, by the early 1930s had largely been dissolved. Only a handful of individuals, including supporters of the COM and other loyalists who had kept a semblance of anarcho-syndicalism alive via the Federación Anarquista Mexicana (FAM) or other new locals, loosely affiliated groups such as Grupo Femenino 'Rosaura Gortari,' remained. Piña and Velásquez's home, the CGT, went "from a revolutionary movement to one adopting a 'labor politics'/*política laboral* as it agreed to participate in the JLCA [labor boards] and supported the labor politics of the government."[55] While the idea remained, the promulgation of the Labor Law of 1931 had, according to the state, eliminated the usefulness of direct action. Given the CGT's basic tenet of direct action, anarcho-syndicalism "was left out of the political game."[56] Anarcho-syndicalism as the means to achieve labor equality had been tamed and incorporated, at least partly, into state politics.

CHAPTER SEVEN

Finding Closure

Legacies of Anarcho-Feminism in the Mexican Borderlands

In a 2009 summary of annual edicts published by the state of Tamaulipas, government officials included a note on the transfer of property in the town of Ocampo. The property belonged to a resident of Ocampo, registered by a local judge in Xicoténcatl, about a two-hour drive from Tampico. The description of the property outlining the size of the lot identified the property's previous owner as Caritina Piña.[1] The name Caritina was and remains uncommon in Mexico; perhaps a bit more common is the surname Piña. Put together, though, the name is quite rare. In fact, in a recent search of popular names in that country, the name "Caritina" only came up ten times, with different surnames. My discovery of this edict unleashed a series of findings about Piña that provided an ending to Piña's history within the larger regional labor network, but perhaps leaves us with more unanswered questions.

As the anarcho-syndicalist path toward labor equity and unity became, to some, irrelevant since the new revolutionary party had incorporated organized labor and conceded to many labor demands solidified in the 1931 federal labor code, Caritina Piña too took another path. Yet Piña, at least per the historical record, did not adopt another political ideology. That same year, Piña's father, Nicanor Piña Hernández, died in Ocampo. A septuagenarian in 1930, Nicanor lived in Tampico, possibly with his second wife and children including a twenty-something Adela Piña. The following year the family held a wake for him.[2] It is likely Piña left Ciudad Madero, the old Villa Cecilia town, upon her father's death. Despite efforts to locate her voice and presence in the local press after 1930, she is nowhere to be found. Had the death of her father marked the end of her activist years? What had become of Piña in the small town of Ocampo?[3]

Her father's death marked an abrupt end for Piña in the world of labor activism. She had, by the early 1930s, abandoned the region along with the Comité and other political activism in the port. While in Ocampo, in 1937 she married her old housemate and partner, Gregorio Ortiz. He was from a working-class, agrarian background from nearby San Luis Potosí, with no apparent connection to the labor movement. She and Ortiz had lived in free union for at least seven years, and Piña likely acted as stepmother to Ortiz's two children, just as her stepfather had cared for her upon her mother's death. Unlike her anarchist colleagues who had hurled strong attacks on the practice and institution of marriage, Piña's ideology did not include such critiques. Piña had grown up surrounded by her stepsiblings, including the rebel soldier Zenaido Piña, and had been accepted by the family despite the fact that she was living proof of their father's infidelity.

Piña and Ortiz either moved in together in 1930 or began living together shortly after Piña arrived with her family in Tampico by the end of the Revolution. By 1937, upon her return to the countryside, the couple married in Ocampo on Valentine's Day. There is no record of a religious marriage, but their marriage certificate testifies to both parties' union at the local municipal court in the small town.[4] Together, they lived in Ocampo where they shared a home. Piña inherited a house and several rural properties in the outskirts of the town from her father. A property in nearby Morelos, farther south toward Ortiz's home state of San Luis Potosí, appears to have been registered under her name in the 1950s. In a rare twist of fate, between 1950 and 1960, the local *cronista* of Ocampo writes that part of Piña's rural property toward the southwestern part of Tamaulipas near Guadalcazar, San Luis Potosí, together with lands belonging to other individuals, was acquired by the Mexican government and redistributed to peasant families as part of Mexico's agrarian reform. A newly created *ejido* "Lázaro Cárdenas" emerged out of those lands on February 21, 1960.[5] The Mexican government, under Adolfo López Mateos, reversed what had been policies favorable to the landowning class and small-scale owners implemented by the previous administrations. By the late 1950s and into the 1960s, coinciding with the López Mateos agenda, reforms to reinvigorate the countryside resulted in 304 million *campesinos* receiving nearly 11.3 million hectares of land.[6] There is no evidence indicating Piña fought the actions of the government, and she may have been in agreement with the loss of her inheritance, as the land transferred over to landless *campesinos* she herself had vowed to defend.

Had she maintained contact with her old colleagues? Had she shared the recent developments with respect to her inherited property? What had become of the colleagues of her activist years in the Gulf of Mexico region? Méndez Guerra continued publishing in anarcho-syndicalist newspapers in the late 1930s and into the early 1940s, including *La Voz Antifascista* and *Ruta*. He worked with organized labor throughout the 1950s up through the 1970s. Méndez Guerra became a representative on the oil workers' union, the Sindicato de Trabajadores Petroleros de El Águila. There is no evidence he maintained contact with Piña. In 1961, as Méndez Guerra continued his work with the oil workers' union, Piña left her native Ocampo, possibly without Gregorio Ortiz, and headed toward the border town of Reynosa. Given Reynosa's history of oil deposits and the city's expansion of refineries, had she become reengaged in labor activism alongside workers from the state-controlled Petróleos Mexicanos (PEMEX) union? There is no indication she did, nor whether she reengaged Méndez Guerra via his oil union local. By 1979, though, Méndez Guerra had died.[7]

With Méndez Guerra gone, had she informed Felipa Velásquez, her agrarian activist colleague, of her own land dispossession for the creation of an *ejido* in Tamaulipas? Had she seen an editorial published in the 1950s featuring the life of Velásquez and her role in the agrarian struggle in Baja California? The news article described Velásquez with the unflattering label of "*matrona*" to whose calls for action "men listened and obeyed."[8] While the editorial sought to honor Velásquez, it nonetheless emphasized her perceived masculine role in the movement. The gendered label "*matrona*" hinted at a reversal of gender roles, connoting, in this case, Velásquez's strength in promoting agrarian justice to the point where "men . . . obeyed [her]." Similar to the way in which the *mesera libre* leader Paz's leadership qualities were measured by her physical attributes, "thin and cute," but a leader "with beard and all!," Velásquez's accomplishments were overshadowed by the *matrona* label. Yet her accomplishments were real, and Piña knew exactly how hard she had fought and had witnessed her colleague's unfortunate deportation. The first land seizure that Velásquez helped to orchestrate in 1930 deprived her of her freedom. While she participated in the second agrarian assault in Baja California in 1937 and helped to pressure Cárdenas to nationalize the US Colorado River Land property, she had endured a horrific seven months in the infamous Islas Marías, and her health suffered greatly. Piña's petitions, as well as the collaborative effort to free her, however, had made a difference.

In an eerie way, Velásquez had written on the need for a type of solitary confinement to find "the light, to finally know the truth," several years before her deportation and subsequent imprisonment. In 1928 she had published

"Convocatoria a la mujer" (A call to women) in *Avante* in which she asked women to "envision, pretend that you are confined to a dark space for several hours and one will quickly feel the anxiety that moves us to want to escape from such space ... and while the light will blind you at first when you exit, that same light will allow you to see clearly, to see the truth."[9] She literally experienced such darkness while at the brutal Islas Marías. The imprisonment caused Velásquez's health to significantly deteriorate and, by the age of sixty-seven in 1949, as Piña lived with her husband in Ocampo, Velásquez passed away in Mazatlán.[10]

Not until three decades after the first editorial recounted her actions, in 1980, was a ceremony organized to honor "Doña" Felipa Velásquez. She was remembered as a woman "in the halls of honor building Baja California in the name of service to the nation." Velásquez was a working-class woman who taught herself to read and became a poet and supporter of anarcho-syndicalism in the greater fight for worker protections. She dedicated her efforts to improving the livelihoods of the peasantry. Her efforts against the US Colorado River Land Company during the 1930s culminated in 1937 with the return of lands to Mexicans known as "the day of the assault on lands." While her efforts alone did not dismantle a US company, it did help to increase support for Cárdenas's eventual plan to redistribute lands in that state.[11] Velásquez's intention was not to "service . . . the nation." Her service was to fellow workers regardless of borders, gender, and background—urban or those whose lives were rooted in the countryside. Her remains were later transferred to the Ejido las Islas Agrarias in her native Sinaola as requested by former agrarian activists.

What of the other *compañeras*? Aurelia Rodríguez from the Liga Cultural had continued to contribute her profound thoughts on justice and freedom, writing at least four lengthy commentaries about women's status and women's activism and the labor movement more broadly. Sadly, sometime in the 1970s, by that time a mature woman, she committed suicide in the old CGT meeting ground. While her motives are unclear, members of the CGT's numerous affiliates recalled her fighting spirit and deep commitment to workers and fondly shared stories about how Aurelia was always supportive and never liked to be called a lady. She was missed dearly by her former colleagues who later shared the sad story in interviews with scholars.[12] It is unclear whether other Liga Cultural members knew of Aurelia Rodríguez's tragic death. Nor is it clear when the Liga Cultural suspended its activities. Evidence indicates that Liga Cultural members Esther and María Mendoza continued to engage in labor activism while in Mazatlán, Sinaloa. There are similar biographical dead ends in searching for information about the final years of the pioneer activists Isaura Galván and Reynalda González Parra.

Larger Lessons

The abrupt end of Piña's activism coincided not only with her father's death but also with the end of the early industrialization phase in the Tampico-Cecilia region. By the dawn of the 1940s, renewed industrialization efforts driven by new technologies focused on automotive and electronics signaled a new era for the region; labor unionism in associated factories followed. This time, however, while the ideas of anarcho-syndicalism persisted, no real, effective anarcho-syndicalist national organization could compete with what seemed to be an unstoppable shift toward state-sanctioned organizing via the Confederación de Trabajadores de México (CTM) founded in 1936 during Cárdenas's term. By the 1950s, the CTM was almost synonymous with the Mexican government, which still bore the revolutionary label.[13]

The victories of the oil workers—many of whom promoted broader CGT goals during the late nineteen teens up through the early 1930s, particularly the signing of collective contracts—served as a model for new generations of oil and other types of workers. When the oil industry recovered with the opening of new wells farther south of Tampico in Poza Rica, Veracruz, oil workers there created a local of the older Tampico-based El Águila union.[14] While the 1940s brought new challenges despite the nationalization of the oil industry in 1938, the early anarcho-syndicalist ideas that shaped much of Tampico and Villa Cecilia labor culture lived on.

Despite the lack of full biographical details for many of the anarcho-feminists engaged in the regional labor network, we can draw larger lessons from what we *do* know concerning their activism. Radical labor activism in the Mexican borderlands, in the anarcho-syndicalist tradition, was an uneven process in which women's ideological positions did not obey strict boundaries of organizational affiliation. Local, national, and global concerns informed women's activism and deeply influenced their interactions with other women and men as well as their relationships with other organizations. Localized ideas about race, nationalism, and gender norms as well as borders or their decision to engage labor issues as if no geopolitical border existed further shaped women's identities and their activism during the period under examination.

The crucial early organizing on behalf of workers from various backgrounds carried out by Isaura Galván and Reynalda González Parra in the years leading up to and during the Revolution, when Caritina Piña was a teenager, as well as the willingness of some anarcho-syndicalists organizations to open their doors to women, paved the road for other women to follow suit. The tradition of embracing all workers regardless of international boundaries with the principal caveat that workers would unite for their own benefit, not for the benefit of government via an organized political party, defined the early anarcho-syndicalist efforts in the region. While only a handful of women appear on the roster of some of the leading anarchist affiliates such as Hermanos Rojos, Germinal, the Tampico COM, and other CGT affinity groups, the newspapers sponsored by these and other organizations featured numerous female voices. Women's insistence that they too needed to fight for the good of all humanity as well as their commitment to rejecting all political entities was heard loud and clear.

Within anarcho-syndicalist circles, most female supporters, while advocating for liberty and justice as well as the emancipation of all women, framed their struggles and the path toward equality in gendered terms that often privileged the reproductive role of women. Activists promoting other ideological positions differing from anarchism also employed similar gendered discourses that privileged motherhood and maternalism. However, it carried a distinct meaning for anarcho-feminists. This was a political move on the part of women as a way to bolster their argument that they should be entitled to the same benefits and privileges as their male counterparts. The language women employed was informed and guided by the ideas of motherhood and maternalism as a marker of privilege and as a tool with which women could engage in labor activism. But the basic framework within which these rights were couched privileged worker autonomy and human dignity over the interests of the state. Such language further shaped the local, national, and transnational ideas about women's place in society. This gendered language allowed women certain flexibility to express concerns and ideas about how best to improve their social, economic, and political conditions and those of their communities.

While anarchist and anarcho-syndicalist thought as expressed through formal political affiliation (i.e., CGT or Hermanos Rojos) declined by the 1930s in the region in great part due to the rise of the Partido Socialista Fronterizo and to the activism of opposition groups such as the CROM and later via a national state-sanctioned CTM, anarcho-syndicalist organizations and their periodicals served as an outlet for women to express concerns with the status quo, recruit members to their organizations, inform other women from the country and beyond about local efforts, and to assume, in some cases, leadership positions. The emerging socialist platform that also privileged women's reproductive capacities advanced a more moderate agenda and was seen as safer or nonthreatening. As the historian Margaret Marsh wrote during the late 1970s, "women who were dissatisfied with contemporary economic or social conditions had other choices, particularly socialism, which did not threaten the existing (normative) family structure."[15] The anarcho-feminist idea of a revolutionary motherhood was framed using the language of labor equity, whose end result was not self-serving nor in the interest of a political party. Adhering to the basic principle of direct action and avoiding becoming an arm of the state, these activists whose politics transcended regional, state, and international borders did not promote suffrage. To them it only meant that women would become political pawns of the state.

Larger Legacies

When the days of the Mexican Revolution were long gone, its memory stood as a symbol and reminder of the unaccomplished mission of worker autonomy and need for continued direct action. Women and men had claimed those "rights bestowed upon us by the Mexican Revolution [1910]" to demand labor rights, and such historical memory remained a constant reference point framing commentaries and editorials in the local anarchist newspapers.[16] Calls for change had included promoting an entirely new vision for women, which only anarchism could accurately define in a true revolutionary way.

As historian Ana Lau Jaiven has explained, "as feminism developed in different sectors" it took on different meanings. It also developed from multiple perspectives and multiple experiences.[17] The activism of Piña and other women who collaborated in her labor sphere, as well as those who preceded her generation, reveals several things. Their engagement with labor rights was an example of what Gloria Anzaldúa articulated as a a type of *feminismo transfronterizo* that, while it privileged women's status and participation in the larger fight for labor rights within and beyond the Mexican borderlands, did so within a radical labor activist framework that promoted worker unity free from state control. It promoted an anarcho-feminist activism that emerged as a process, crafted during the moment of exchanges between people and their ideas from different regional, cultural (gendered, racial, ethnic, language), class, and historical positionalities.

Piña embodied the shifting of gender politics in Mexico's Gulf Coast region that formed part of a greater transformation unfolding throughout the country and its borders. As she challenged the modern ideals of the new government that sought to use the memory of the Revolution to legitimize its power, she embodied those same modern ideals as a woman whose gendered and class-based activism challenged prescribed boundaries set by the Mexican state. At the same time, she embodied a rejection of state authority, as her activism was further shaped by her deeply rooted commitment to anarchist tradition within a community-based framework. Her use of motherhood, sisterhood, and *compañerismo*, and of the idea of the "great family" to promote labor rights reflected her own type of negotiation. She and others in her ambit decided what those terms meant. While women in other labor movements shaped by socialism and communism also employed the language of maternalism and motherhood as well as anticlerical ideas, those engaged in anarcho-syndicalism rejected any association of maternalism with religion or any type of god or larger being, and rejected state affiliation. Anarcho-syndicalists were indeed among the most radical of female activists in the country at the time.

Piña's vision and articulation of a transnational feminism defied geographical boundaries just as much as ideological, social, and cultural limits. Her own ideas about race and gender shaped her brand of feminism, which placed women's privileged position as reproducers of community at the heart of a labor justice agenda. Her approach helped to sustain the global labor movement through her active role in spreading knowledge about the movement itself. She invoked the language of worker dignity as a way to provide a larger context with which to underscore women as worthy of equal treatment. As Temma Kaplan succinctly noted about the postrevolutionary state efforts to reconstruct society, "new governments . . . [took] women as symbols of what had been wrong with former regimes . . . to alter the conditions of women's lives" in the hopes of reforming society.[18] While there were contradictions and ambiguities in women's use of the language of motherhood, the frequent use of the idea, as well as women's multiple positions as mothers/wives/caregivers and as workers, reveals how it remained a useful tool with which to engage in direct action. References to women's roles as "reproduce[ers] [of] the labor force" and as contributors to the "production" process of labor itself "at low or no cost," continued to shape public discourse.[19]

The state-sanctioned language of motherhood was recognized by anarchist supporters as having roots in anarchist beliefs, yet anarchists' reasons for its use differed from the state's. For anarcho-syndicalist women, women were automatically worthy of equality, especially within the realm of labor. And, if women workers happened to be mothers too, deeply rooted beliefs about equality and libertarian ideals led anarchists to further radicalize motherhood as a tool to claim labor rights and labor autonomy. Women did not need full suffrage because voting, choosing who to place at the helm of the state, was antithetical to real freedom. The anarcho-feminists helping to sustain labor movements challenged normative gender expectations rooted in nineteenth-century Victorian conceptions of morality and decorum. They did not go through proper channels navigating the political system as some of their female contemporaries did to petition for changes in the law or to promote suffrage.

In the case of Piña, in her transnational labor broker role as secretary of correspondence for the Comité Internacional Pro-Presos Sociales, she spread knowledge about the labor movement shaped by her own biases, life experiences, and her subjectivity as a woman, as a Mexicana. She contributed to the aid, in some cases leading to the full liberty, of political prisoners. Defying traditional norms for Mexican women during the 1920s, she had lived with Ortiz in free union for several years. She married him in 1937 and, while in Reynosa or shortly before leaving Ocampo, married once again, this time to José Villarreal Franco, sometime during the late 1960s or 1970s.

The marriage was short-lived. On August 23, 1981, in a hospital along the border, Piña died of a diabetic coma. There was no march in her honor, no homage paid in the press. Her death certificate reported her age of death as eighty-two, married to Villarreal Franco, and her occupation was listed as "a woman dedicated to the *hogar*," echoing the 1930 Mexican Census that defined her as a "woman dedicated to housework," ignoring her role as *secretaria de corespondencia* in the Comité.[20]

Despite Piña's heretofore absence in Latin American, labor, US-Mexican borderlands, and women's historiography, and the brief coverage others like Reynalda González Parra and Felipa Velásquez have received, they all promoted and sustained the greater anarcho-syndicalist movement and shaped the larger question of women's place in the world of labor. Their activism rooted in anarchist ideas lent itself to a transnational feminism that sought labor equity for all, complementing the nationless vision promoted by the PLM, the IWW, the COM, and the CGT. It also was an anarcho-feminism that could complement, compete with, and at times also reinforce ideas about the larger women's movement and women's status. Limits and all, their radical labor activism reveals how the road to real democracy in Mexico involved deep engagement on the part of women from borderlands communities long seen as peripheral. Such activism assumed a central position in the larger labor movement, and while ultimately organized labor became an arm of the state by the mid-1930s, the ideas rooted in anarchist thought lingered for the next several decades and remain part of the legacy of women's labor history.

Notes

Abbreviations

AGET	Archivo General del Estado de Tamaulipas
AGN	Archivo General de la Nación
AHEMG	Archivo Histórico Fondo Esteban Méndez Guerra
AHPEPG	Archivo Histórico Particular de Emilio Portes
AHT	Archivo Histórico de Tampico Carlos González Salas
ALR-HR	Archivo Librado Rivera y Los Hermanos Rojos
ARFM	Archivo Digital Ricardo Flores Magón, INAH
BC	Biblioteca de Catalunya
BPCMRG	Biblioteca Pública Central Ing. Marte R. Gómez (Cd. Victoria)
CEMOS	Centro de Estudios de los Movimientos Obreros Sociales
DGG	Fondo Dirección General de Gobierno
EDRF	E. L. Doheny Research Foundation, Occidental College
IIH-UAT	Instituto de Investigaciones Históricas, Universidad Autónoma de Tamaulipas
NARA	National Archives and Records Administration
NLB	Nettie Lee Benson Latin American Library, University of Texas at Austin
NYPL	New York Public Library
SRE	Secretaría de Relaciones Exteriores
SRKL	Sue & Radcliffe Killam Library, Texas A&M International University
UNAM	Universidad Autónoma de México

Introduction

The chapter epigraph is taken from "Por que saltamos a la lucha," in the November 1929 issue of *El Preso Social*, which closed with these words from the French philosopher Félix Le Dantec (1869–1917). AHEMG, IIH-UAT. All translations are my own.

1. To M. V. Barnhill (Charlotte, NC) from Caritina M. Piña, Comité Internacional Pro-Presos Sociales (Villa Cecilia, Tamps.), September 20, 1929, AHEMG, IIH-UAT. All translations are my own.

2. Ibid.

3. Ibid. In other reports, the local police officer ordering the burning of the homes is identified as Alderholt although he also appears as the local sheriff. For an examination of the strike in Gastonia see Gregory S. Taylor, *History of the North Carolina Communist Party*.

4. The literature on anarchism is extensive. Foundational studies include, but are not limited to, Kropotkin, *Anarchism*; Goldman, *Anarchism and Other Essays*; Berkman, *What Is Anarchism?*; Nettlau, *A Short History of Anarchism*; and Reichert, *Partisans of Freedom*. Other studies on anarchism and anarcho-syndicalism specifically examining a region, country, or anarchist networks include Bookchin, *Spanish Anarchists*; and Avrich, *Russian Anarchists* and *Anarchist Voices*, among his other publications. For other texts on the topic see full bibliography.

5. While there is no evidence indicating Piña left her native Mexico, her ambit was pretty expansive. I draw inspiration from Karl Jacoby's work *The Strange Career of William Ellis*, in which he describes the "alternative borderlands" of Ellis who, like Piña, traversed an expansive area with reach beyond the geopolitical border of the United States and Mexico.

6. "Por los que sufren," *Regeneración*, August 12, 1916, Hispanic American Historical Newspapers.

7. "Acta de Formación del 'Grupo Racionalista' de San Antonio, Tex.," *Regeneración*, October 9, 1915, Hispanic American Historical Newspapers; in some documents, Isaura Galván appears as Rosaura Galván.

8. "México, Censo Nacional 1930: Caritina M. Piña," index and images, Family Search, http://familysearch.org (accessed May 10, 2016); Marvin Osiris Huerta Márquez, "Inició la lucha del feminismo Caritina Piña," *Expreso–La Razón*, December 8, 2019.

9. "Comité Pro-Presos por Cuestiones Sociales," *Sagitario*, May 1, 1927, AHEMG, IIH-UAT. Some sources use Grupo Hermanos Rojos.

10. Alcayaga Sasso, "Librado Rivera y Los Hermanos Rojos en el movimiento social y cultural anarquista en Villa Cecilia y Tampico, Tamaulipas, 1915–1932," 21.

11. Ibid., 24, 34.

12. Ibid., 165. Alcayaga Sasso does not indicate the length of time the organization operated or any further information about its formation. The women appear as members of the Liga Cultural in González Salas, *Acercamiento a la historia del movimiento obrero en Tampico*; see also various newspapers including *Sagitario*, featuring commentaries written by members of the Liga Cultural, IIH-UAT.

13. Aurelio Regalado H., "El combativo grupo Hermanos Rojos," *El Sol de Tampico*, November 23, 2009.

14. To Secretaría de Guerra y Marina from El Aguila, May 3, 1919, caja 7, exp. 40, Serie: Quejas y Reclamaciones, Departamento de Petróleo, in AGN.

15. On maternalism and motherhood (and broader studies that excavate the relationship between gender and class) see the foundational work of Boris and Kleinberg, "Mothers and Other Workers"; Boris and Orleck, "Feminism and the Labor Movement"; and Koven and Michel, eds., *Mothers of a New World*. See also Hagemann, Michel, and Budde, eds., *Civil Society and Gender Justice*. For maternalism along the US-Mexican borderlands see González, *Redeeming La Raza*. Other studies examining the idea of motherhood and maternalism within the context of postrevolutionary Mexico include Olcott, Vaughan, and Cano, eds., *Sex in Revolution*; Hutchison, *Labors Appropriate to Their Sex*, 97–99; and French and James, eds., *The Gendered Worlds of Latin American Women Workers*.

16. Johnson and Graybill, eds., *Bridging National Borders in North America*, 23. Johnson and Graybill caution historians that "the transnational turn in border studies" has had a tendency to "obscure" the local, rich histories of said communities. Such concern for not losing specificity is also a major theme in a published conversation among historians on transnationalism. Bayly, Beckert, Connelly, Hofmeyr, Kozol, and Seed, "AHR Conversation: On Transnational History"; see also various examples of a transnational approach to labor in Fink, ed., *Workers across the Americas*.

17. "AHR Conversation: On Transnational History," 14.

18. Anzaldúa, *Borderlands/La Frontera*.

19. Román-Odio and Sierra, eds., *Transnational Borderlands in Women's Global Networks*, 3.

20. Laughlin, Gallagher, Cobble, Boris, Nadasen, Gilmore, and Zarnow, "Is It Time to Jump Ship?," 93.

21. Fernandes, *Transnational Feminism in the United States*; see also Saldivar-Hull, *Feminism on the Border*; Luibhéid, "Sexual Regimes and Migration Controls"; Anzaldúa, *Borderlands/La Frontera*; Sandoval, *Methodologies of the Oppressed*; Anzaldúa and Moraga, eds., *This Bridge Called My Back*; Rodríguez, "The Fiction of Solidarity"; Hurtado, "Sitios y Lenguas."

22. Porter, *From Angel to Office Worker*, 10–11.

23. Fernández Aceves, Ramos Escandón, and Porter, eds., *Orden social e identidad de género*; Fernández Aceves, *Mujeres en el cambio social en el siglo XX mexicano*; see also her excellent overview on the topic of Mexican women's work, "El trabajo femenino en México." Fowler-Salamini, *Working Women, Entrepreneurs, and the Mexican Revolution*.

24. Historian Premilla Nadasen argues that in some cases, African American female activists did not adopt the term *feminist* because "of the way feminism was popularly represented or how its history was written," in Laughlin et al.,"Is It Time to Jump Ship?," 103.

25. Koven and Michel, eds., *Mothers of a New World*; see also Koven and Michel's article, "Womanly Duties," 1079.

26. De Laforcade and Shaffer, eds., *In Defiance of Boundaries*, 5.

27. Hernández, *Working Women into the Borderlands*.

28. Vella, "Newspapers," 193; see also Kanellos, *Hispanic Immigrant Literature*.

29. See, for example, Shaffer, "Havana Hub," 4; and Aguilar, "The IWW in Tampico."

30. "Correspondencia," *¡Luz!*, July 14, 1917, ALR-HR.

31. Alcayaga Sasso, "Librado Rivera y Los Hermanos Rojos," 166.

32. Ibid., 159.

33. Ribera Carbó, *La casa del obrero mundial*. In some sources Reinalda is used while in others, the full name Reynalda González Parra appears.

34. Wood, *Revolution in the Street*; Fowler-Salamini, *Working Women, Entrepreneurs, and the Mexican Revolution*.

35. Kirwin Shaffer's publications on the topic of anarchism are numerous and have firmly established the importance of anarchist thought in social movements in Latin America with links to the United States, among other countries; these include *Black Flag Boricuas* and *Anarchist Cuba*. Particularly important to the topic of anarcho-feminism is his article "The Radical Muse."

36. Shaffer, "The Radical Muse," 140–142.

37. Suárez Findlay, *Imposing Decency*.

38. Hewitt, "Luisa Capetillo"; Hewitt, *Southern Discomfort*. See also an excellent brief overview of Latina feminist practices by Vicki Ruiz, whose work on another feminist labor activist, Guatemalan native Luisa Moreno (Rosa Rodríguez López), forms part of this larger historiography: "Class Acts."

39. Especially important in re-creating the larger history of Mexican women's organized labor from various ideological perspectives beyond anarchism are works focused on Latin American labor history, including Klubock, *Contested Communities*; Besse, *Restructuring Patriarchy*; and Farnsworth-Alvear, *Dulcinea in the Factory*; While not necessarily focused on anarchist women, the following studies have made important inroads in the study of the development of transnational links between women in Latin America and the United States, particularly as it relates to women's suffrage: Threlkeld, *Pan American Women*; Marino, "Marta Vergara, Popular-Front Pan-American Feminism and the Transnational Struggle for Working Women's Rights in the 1930s," and Marino's recent book *Feminism for the Americas*; and Olcott, *International Women's Year*.

40. Molyneux, "No God, No Boss, No Husband," 120; see also Dore and Molyneux, eds., *Hidden Histories of Gender and the State in Latin America*.

41. While earlier Argentinean writers struggled to entice workers who aspired to rapid concrete material change, as opposed to abstract calls for liberty and emancipation, as scholar Juan Suriano has argued, such anarchist ideals about justice and emancipation had to be fulfilled before any tangible or material change could occur. Suriano, "Las prácticas culturales del anarquismo argentino," 147.

42. Hutchison, "From 'La Mujer Esclava' to 'La Mujer Limón,'" 553. While Hutchison examines anarchism specifically in this article, she places it in broader context and in relation to other ideologies in *Labors Appropriate to Their Sex*, 66–67.

43. *Labors Appropriate to Their Sex*, 66–67.

44. Adelson, "Historia social de los obreros industriales de Tampico, 1906–1919"; González Salas, *Acercamiento a la historia del movimiento obrero en Tampico*. Other earlier histories of Tampico that included discussions of organized labor include Ocasio Melendez, *Capitalism and Development*.

45. Alcayaga Sasso, "Librado Rivera y Los Hermanos Rojos."

46. Goldsmith, "De combativas a conformistas."

47. Myrna Santiago, "Women of the Mexican Oil Fields"; see especially her overview on Tampico. While Santiago's work is focused on Tampico's history as an oil-producing port and not solely on women's participation in its labor force, it nonetheless speaks to important watershed moments in the region's history. See her "Tampico, Mexico: The Rise and Decline of an Energy Metropolis."

48. Aguilar, "The IWW in Tampico," 124–139; see also the recent article by Savala, "Ports of Transnational Labor Organizing," which further documents the extensive reach of anarchist thought in ports of entry like Tampico.

49. Weber, "Keeping Community, Challenging Boundaries" and her more recent "Wobblies of the Partido Liberal Mexicano." Pérez, *The Decolonial Imaginary*, also speaks to the importance of women in the PLM along the border. Some sources use Centro de Estudios Sociales Feministas instead of Centro de Estudios Feministas Sociales.

50. Baena Paz, *La Confederación General de Trabajadores, 1921–1931*, Hemeroteca, UNAM, 5.

51. Ibid.

52. Avrich, *Anarchist Voices*.

53. Truett, "Transnational Warrior."

54. Greene, "Historians of the World," 16.

55. The idea of multiple feminisms and of women's unity based on "contingent solidarity and shifting points of convergence" was also discussed within the context of the historiography of the women's movement (US-based) and its wave analogy in Laughlin et al., "Is It Time to Jump Ship?," 89.

56. Ibid.; Simpson Fletcher, "Teaching the History of Global and Transnational Feminisms," 155; see also Offen, ed., *Globalizing Feminisms, 1789–1945*.

57. To "Grupo Libertario Sacco y Vanzetti," from Caritina Piña, Secretaria de Correspondencia, July 6, 1929, AHEMG, IIH-UAT.

Chapter 1. The Circulation of Radical Ideologies, Early Transnational Collaboration, and Crafting a Women's Agenda

The chapter epigraph is taken from Reynalda González Parra, "Intransigencia," *Tribuna Roja* (Tampico), November 27, 1915, ALR-HR.

1. Lara Orozco, *En el vaivén del Frente Rojo*, 23.

2. Garner, *Goals and Means*; Lara Orozco, *En el vaivén del Frente Rojo*, 32.

3. Hart, *Anarchism and the Mexican Working Class*, 24; Tullis, "Early Mormon Exploration and Missionary Activities in Mexico."

4. Hart, "The Evolution of the Mexican and Mexican-American Working Classes," 24.

5. Lara Orozco, *En el vaivén del Frente Rojo*, 32, 34; Hart, "The Evolution of the Mexican and Mexican-American Working Classes"; see also Carr, *El movimiento obrero y la política en México, 1910–1929*.

6. Kornegger, *Anarquismo*, 5–6.

7. Cuadrat, *Socialismo y anarquismo en Cataluña 1899–1911*; Lara Orozco, *En el vaivén del Frente Rojo*, 22–23.

8. *El Gladiador, Órgano de la Sociedad Progresiva Femenina*, May 26, 1906, BC; *Real protectorado de la Federación Sindical de Obreras, sesión de junta general ordinaria del día 15 de enero, 1913* (Barcelona: Tipografía L. Benaiges, 1913), BC; *Estatuts de la Secció Mútua Feminal del Centre Autonomista de Dependents del Comerçi de L'Industria* (Barcelona, 1922), BC; see also Kaplan, "Female Consciousness and Collective Action," among her numerous publications on the topic.

9. Lara Orozco, *En el vaivén del Frente Rojo*, 22; "Manifiesto de la Internacional Roja de Sindicatos y Uniones de Trabajadores," in *La Confederación General de Trabajadores, 1921–1931*, ed. Baena Paz, 25.

10. Díaz Cárdenas, *Cananea*, BPCMRG; see also the classic work by E. P. Thompson, *The Making of the English Working Class* (New York: Vintage Press, 1966); on the particular characteristics of free and indebted wage laborers see Katz, "Labor Conditions in Haciendas in Porfirian Mexico"; see also Greene, "Rethinking the Boundaries of Class: Labor History and Theories of Class and Capitalism."

11. "A los compañeros de *Páginas Libres*," *Páginas Libres* (Barcelona), April 30, 1908, in To Secretaría de Relaciones Exteriores, Mexico City, from Luis G. Pardo, Legación Mexicana de los Estados Unidos Mexicanos, regarding "Anarchist Plot," Havana, March 2, 1908, SRE, Sección América, Asia y Oceania, Asuntos: Anarquistas que vienen a México, caja 20, exp. 30.

12. "Tampico as a Port," *Oildom* (Bayonne, NJ) 5, no. 2 (April 1915): 16.

13. Ibid., 15.

14. Ceballos Ramírez, "Tamaulipas en el contexto del Noreste Mexicano."

15. Brown, "Domestic Politics and Foreign Investment," 390–392; see also Kuecker, "Public Health, Yellow Fever, and the Making of Modern Tampico."

16. Foreigners such as the Spaniard Casimiro del Valle arrived in Tampico via Mexico City and was one of the cofounders of the COM Tampico branch.

17. For nineteenth-century figures, see Alejandro Prieto, *Historia, geografía y estadística del Estado de Tamaulipas* (Mexico City: Tip. Escalerillas Num. 13, 1873), 276–277, Alejandro Prieto Papers, NLB; for Tampico population figures see Adelson, "Coyuntura y conciencia," 632.

18. Alvarado Mendoza, *El portesgilismo en Tamaulipas*, 126.

19. Brown, "Domestic Politics and Foreign Investment," 412–414; see also specific data on oil production in "The Oil Fuel Outlook," *Nautical Gazette* 90 (July 1916): 4–5; "Conditions Still Unfavorable in Mexico," *Oildom* (Bayonne, NJ) 5, no. 2 (April 1915).

20. Adelson, "Historia social de los obreros industriales de Tampico"; Aguilar, "Peripheries of Power, Centers of Resistance"; Aguilar, "The IWW in Tampico"; Cravey, *Work in Mexico's Maquiladoras*, 64; Brown, *Oil and Revolution in Mexico*.

21. Brown, *Oil and Revolution in Mexico*, 412–414.

22. Carolina Infante Pacheco, "Historia de Cd. Madero—Devenir histórico de Ciudad Madero," ca. 2003, Archivo Histórico Municipal de Ciudad Madero.

23. Hart, "The Historical Roots of Mexican Anarchism"; I thank Professor Hart for providing me a copy of this lecture; see also Saad-Saka, *For God and Revolution*; Cárdenas Herrera, "Aspecto histórico del municipo."

24. Hart, *Anarchism and the Mexican Working Class*, 88–89.

25. To Gilberto Torres, Río Blanco, Veracruz, from José Neyra, October 8, 1906, AGN, Fondo: Revoltosos, caja 1-a, exp. 1; Lomnitz, *Return of Comrade Ricardo Flores Magón*, 237.

26. Guidotti-Hernandez, "Partido Liberal Mexicano."

27. "Agrarismo en Tamaulipas," January 1943, Records of the American Mexican Claims Commission, NARA.

28. Alter, "From the Copper-Colored Sons of Montezuma to Comrade Pancho Villa," 101; Díaz Cárdenas, *Cananea*, 25, 75; Reyna, Palomares, and Cortez, "El control del movimiento obrero como una necesidad del Estado de México (1917–1936)," 786.

29. Lara Orozco, *En el vaivén del Frente Rojo*, 45.

30. Alter, "From the Copper-Colored Sons of Montezuma to Comrade Pancho Villa," 92; De Lara joined the Texas Socialist Party in 1915.

31. "Resoluciones tomadas por el Primer Congreso Liberal de la Republica Mexicana, instalado en San Luís Potosí el 5 de febrero de 1901," as quoted in Huitron, *Orígenes e historia del movimiento obrero en México*, 90.

32. Sandos, *Rebellion in the Borderlands*, 72; Ricardo Flores Magón, "Levantamientos en Texas," *Regeneración* (Los Angeles), October 2, 1915, ARFM.

33. "'Amado G. Hernández,' Diccionario Biográfico," ARFM; Hernández was collaborating with Isaura Galván by 1915.

34. Hernández, *Working Women into the Borderlands*, chaps. 2, 3, and 4; Alvarado Mendoza, *El portesgilismo en Tamaulipas*, 181. The revolutionary factions were led by Alberto Carrera-Torres and his family members.

35. "Por Aldama," *El Cauterio* (Cd. Victoria), October 7, 1911, Hemeroteca, IIH-UAT; Alvarado Mendoza, *El portesgilismo en Tamaulipas*, 181.

36. "Grupos," *Regeneración*, August 17, 1912, ARFM; while *Regeneración* noted that Tanguma had died in battle in 1912, Alvarado Mendoza in *El portesgilismo* cites a 1913 attack by Tanguma, thus the exact date of his death remains unknown.

37. Hernández, *Working Women into the Borderlands*, 70; "Revolución: Juanita Torres de Carrera," in Zorilla, *La mujer en Tamaulipas*, 49.

38. Zorilla, *La mujer en Tamaulipas*, 50–51.

39. Huerta Márquez, *Antiguo Morelos*, 163; Alvarado Mendoza, *El portesgilismo en Tamaulipas*, 145–146.

40. Huerta Márquez, "'Los Pelones' Los Villanos de la Revolución." Venustiano Carranza became leader of the Ejército Consitucionalista in the spring of 1913.

41. "Acta de Bautismo de Victor Piña Hernández," FamilySearch, http://family search.org (accessed December 3, 2019); Huerta Márquez, "'Los Pelones.'"

42. *Diccionario de generales de la Revolución*, vol. 2, *M–Z* (Mexico City: Instituto Nacional de Estudios Históricos de las Revoluciones de México, 2014), 841; Ricardo Flóres Magón, "La bandera roja triunfadora," *Regeneración*, no. 84, April 6, 1912.

43. Hart, *Anarchism and the Mexican Working Class*, 88.

44. Huitron, *Orígenes e historia del movimiento obrero en México*, 84.

45. Díaz Cárdenas, *Cananea*, 8.

46. Montejano, *Anglos and Mexicans in the Making of Texas*; De León, *The Tejano Community, 1836–1900*; Hernández, *Working Women into the Borderlands*; Young, *Catarino Garza's Revolution*.

47. Young, "Imagining Alternative Modernities," 152; Young, *Catarino Garza's Revolution*.

48. Hart, *Revolutionary Mexico*. While ample evidence exists regarding US investment in Mexico, it did not have the same effect everywhere nor were US investors always uncooperative or unwilling to accede to Mexican government demands. See, for example, Kim, *Imperial Metropolis*.

49. Sandos, *Rebellion in the Borderlands*, 74, 188. Basilio Ramos was the ethnic Mexican who was apprehended in McAllen, Texas, in January, 1915, carrying a copy (at least one version) of the failed Plan de San Diego. See also Trinidad Gonzales, "The Mexican Revolution, Revolución de Texas, and Matanza de 1915," 112–113.

50. "La voz de la mujer," *Revolución* (Los Angeles), July 13, 1907, AGN, Fondo: Revoltosos, caja 6, exp. 2. *Revolución* was briefly published to replace *Regeneración*, which had been shut down. *Magonistas*, however, would soon reestablish *Regeneración*.

51. "Por Aldama," *El Cauterio* (Cd. Victoria), October 7, 1911, Hemeroteca, IIH-UAT.

52. List of donors and donations as printed in the January 13, 1912, issue of *Regeneración*, http://www.archivomagon.net/Periódico/Regeneración/.

53. "Administración, entradas," *Avante*, n.m. 1924, AHEMG.

54. "Administración, entradas," *Avante*, n.m. 1924, AHEMG; correspondence between Luz Mendoza and the Comité Internacional Pro-Presos Sociales, AHEMG.

55. "Los mártires de Texas," *Sagitario*, February 1, 1925, ALR-HR. *Sagitario* kept its readers apprised of developments surrounding the imprisoned Mexicans throughout the early 1920s. While *Sagitario*, in its recounting of the events, notes that fifteen individuals participated in the armed insurrection in 1913, including the female Luz Mendoza who had helped found a PLM-affiliated group in Harlingen, Texas, Lomnitz does not mention Mendoza and instead cites "Rangel and a group of over twenty . . ." and "Rangel and his men were arrested . . ." Lomnitz, *Return of Comrade Ricardo*

Flores Magón, 418. Not all of the prisoners received the same sentence: it varied from "nine years, twenty-five years, and ninety-nine years," ibid., 419. It is possible that Luz Mendoza from Harlingen, Texas, who supported the PLM, was confused with a male Luz Mendoza who lived in Smithville, Texas, among other places, and was a PLM member and vice president of the Club Liberal Mexicano of Smithville, "Luz Mendoza," archivomagon.net. The name Luz, however, is more commonly associated with females.

56. To Francisco I. Madero from Pedro Lascuráin, Secretario de Relaciones Exteriores, México, June 25, 1912, AGN, Fondo: Francisco I. Madero, caja. 16, exp. 391; for a robust discussion of the activities of Ricardo Flores Magón and colleagues see Lomnitz, *Return of Comrade Ricardo Flores Magón*. The group was imprisoned in 1910 and once again in 1912, ibid., 312. Lomnitz rightly points out that the Rangers' role in the affair was illegal, as "violation of the U.S. neutrality laws was a federal, and not a state offense," ibid., 419.

57. "¡Basta!," *Regeneración*, October 23, 1915.

58. Alcayaga Sasso, "Librado Rivera y Los Hermanos Rojos."

59. Sonia Hernández, "Women's Labor and Activism in the Greater Mexican Borderlands"; Sandos, *Rebellion in the Borderlands*, 77; see also table 3.

60. "Alida Martínez," 1910 Federal Census, Coleman County, Texas.

61. Sonia Hernández, "Women's Labor and Activism in the Greater Mexican Borderlands," 91.

62. Montejano, *Anglos and Mexicans in the Making of Texas*; Valerio-Jimenez, *River of Hope*. See also Johnson, *Revolution in Texas*.

63. Ribera Carbó, "Mujeres sindicalistas."

64. Hart, *Anarchism and the Mexican Working Class*; Hart, "The Evolution of the Mexican and Mexican-American Working Classes," 18; Fernández Aceves, *Mujeres en el cambio social en el siglo XX mexicano*, 190. Early on, the Tampico branch of the IWW held mass meetings in the evenings as well as gatherings of new mutual aid groups and emerging labor collectives.

65. "Acta de Formación del 'Grupo Racionalista' de San Antonio, Tex."

66. Ibid. Because Guadalupe is a unisex name, I did not include it in the list of female adherents. The full name of this member was Guadalupe Rivero. See "¡Basta!," *Regeneración*, October 23, 1915, on Elisa Alemán Hernández.

67. Hart, *Anarchism and the Mexican-Working Class*; for the Ferrer schools in Cuba, see Shaffer, "Freedom Teaching."

68. "Acta de Formación del 'Grupo Racionalista.'"

69. McKillen, "Hybrid Visions," 81; see also McKillen's *Making the World Safe for Workers*.

70. Reynalda González Parra, "A La Mujer," *Germinal, Periódico Libertario* (Tampico), July 2, 1917, ALR-HR; Hart, *Anarchism and the Mexican Working Class*; Hart, "The Evolution of the Mexican and Mexican American Working Classes," 18; Fernández Aceves, *Mujeres en el cambio social en el siglo xx mexicano*, 190.

71. To Presidente Municipal, from Ricardo Treviño, Secretario General, COM Tampico, May 26, 1917, Fondo: Presidencia, caja 1917, #1, AHT; Carr, "The Casa del Obrero Mundial, Constitutionalism, and the Pact of February 1915," 605.

72. "General Salvador Alvarado," *Forum* 4 (1916): 71, cited in Carlo De Fornaro, *Carranza and Mexico* (New York: Mitchell Kennerley, 1915), 45–46, in EDRF, Life of the People, 1401–1502/L-804-1599; Hart, *Anarchism and the Mexican Working Class*, 18.

73. Hart, *Anarchism and the Mexican-Working Class*; Alcayaga Sasso, "Librado Rivera y Los Hermanos Rojos," 50; "Como pensaba Ferrer: A las Sociedades de Resistencia," *Luz* (Mexico City), April 3, 1918; for the Ferrer schools in Cuba, see Shaffer, "Freedom Teaching."

74. Ribera Carbó, *La Casa del Obrero Mundial.*

75. Lomnitz, *Return of Comrade Ricardo Flores Magón*, 429.

76. "Mexico Handbook on Approaches to San Luis Potosi and Tampico from the North and East through Zone E," prepared by the Military Intelligence Division General Staff, United States War Department (Washington, DC: Government Printing Office, 1920), 35–36, Copy no. 196, Library of Congress, Rare Books and Special Collections.

77. Ibid.

78. Ibid.; for a discussion of the linkages between cultural views of Mexicans held by Americans and Mexican elites see Gilbert Gonzales, *Culture of Empire.*

79. Alter, "From the Copper-Colored Sons of Montezuma to Comrade Pancho Villa," 91.

80. Lomnitz, *Return of Comrade Ricardo Flores Magón*, 419; on the efforts to free the prisoners, see Librado Rivera, "Por la libertad de nuestros Presos en Texas," *Sagitario*, February 17, 1924, ALR-HR. While in *Sagitario* Luz Mendoza appears as female (which is credible given the history of the name in Spanish tradition), in the ARFM, Mendoza appears to be a male *magonista* supporter, "¡Basta!," *Regeneración*, October 23, 1915. See also note 55.

81. Lomnitz, *Return of Comrade Ricardo Flores Magón*, 423.

82. "Mujeres deportadas," September 28, 1911, newspaper clipping without newspaper title, Box 1, 1309-Labor Folder 1674–1685, "Effects of Revolution on Labor Conditions," EDRF.

83. Stern, "Buildings, Boundaries, and Blood," 43–45; see also Mckiernan-González, *Fevered Measures.*

84. As quoted in Christopher Castañeda, "Moving West," 131.

85. Alter, "From the Copper-Colored Sons of Montezuma to Comrade Pancho Villa," 96; the Houston, Texas, PLM branch reference comes from Alcayaga Sasso, "Librado Rivera y Los Hermanos Rojos," 59. The Houston branch was founded in 1913.

86. Alter, "From the Copper-Colored Sons of Montezuma to Comrade Pancho Villa," 96.

87. Lomnitz, *Return of Comrade Ricardo Flores Magón*, 422. Lomnitz notes "121 concerned Tejanos and Mexicans from San Marcos, Texas," while Alter ("From the Copper-Colored Sons of Montezuma to Comrade Pancho Villa") cites 128. The reference

to Hernández's moving to Tampico comes from Alter; it is likely that Elisa was also deported or joined José Angel after his deportation to Mexico, see ARFM.

88. Lewis Spence, *Mexico for the Mexicans*, May 31, 1918, 34, in Box 1, 1309-Labor Folder 1674–1685, "Effects of Revolution on Labor Conditions," EDRF; "Mexican Laborer a Real Autocrat," *Washington Star*, February 3, 1918, Box 1, 1309-Labor Folder 1674–1685, "Effects of Revolution on Labor Conditions," EDRF. See also work by Leif Adelson and Jonathan Brown who examine different aspects of the oil industry based in Tampico: Adelson, "Historia social de los obreros industriales de Tampico, 1906–1919"; Brown, ed., *Workers' Control in Latin America, 1930–1979*.

89. Alcayaga Sasso, "Librado Rivera y Los Hermanos Rojos," 59.

90. *Germinal*, November 1, 1917, ALR-HR.

91. Ibid.; Alcayaga Sasso, "Librado Rivera y Los Hermanos Rojos," 62.

92. *Germinal*, November 1, 1917, ALR-HR.

93. García Flores, *Lo transparente del poder*. I thank Rosario Cárdenas Herrera, director of the Archivo Histórico Municipal de Cd. Madero, for bringing this text to my attention. Cárdenas Herrera is currently the general secretary of the Sindicato Liberal Democrático de Cd. Madero.

94. González Salas, *Acercamiento a la historia del movimiento obrero en Tampico*, 32.

95. Ibid., 32–33; Alcayaga Sasso, "Librado Rivera y Los Hermanos Rojos," 51.

96. Weber, "Keeping Community, Challenging Boundaries," 219.

97. *Germinal*, first issue, June 14, 1917.

98. Alcayaga Sasso, "Librado Rivera y Los Hermanos Rojos," 15.

99. "Report of the Proceedings of the Second Congress of the Pan American Federation of Labor," New York, New York, July 7, 1919, 8–9, originally deposited in the Harvard College Library. The surname Borrán, in some documents, appears without an accent on the *a*. In the conference, Borrán served alongside Samuel Gompers, one of three representatives of the AFL, and Luis N. Morones who represented the CROM; McKillen, "Hybrid Visions," 85; "Hermanos Rojos," 38–39, ALR-HR.

100. Aurelio Regalado H., "El combativo grupo Hermanos Rojos," *El Sol de Tampico*, November 23, 2009; Alcayaga Sasso, "Librado Rivera y Los Hermanos Rojos," 69.

101. Alcayaga Sasso, "Librado Rivera y Los Hermanos Rojos," 16, 36; see also Aguilar, "The IWW in Tampico."

102. Hart, "The Evolution of the Mexican and Mexican-American Working Classes," 18; Caulfield, "Wobblies and Mexican Workers in Mining and Petroleum, 1905–1924," 61; Ribera Carbó, *La Casa del Obrero Mundial*, 158–160.

103. Goldman publicly advocated birth control and was jailed for it, spoke in favor of gender equity, and supported unions. After Goldman's imprisonment, US authoritites deported her to the Soviet Union in 1919 citing violations of the 1918 Alien Act. She nonetheless continued to push for women's and workers' rights and remained in contact with Mexican, Russian, and Spanish intellectuals.

104. *Historia del anarco-feminismo en América Latina*, 3; on the PLM in the region in a comparative context see McKillen, "Hybrid Visions," 78–79. As Martha Eva Rocha

explains, before *Vésper* was published in San Antonio, Texas, it was published in Guanajuato (1901–1902) and Mexico City (1902, 1903, 1905, 1911), *Los rostros de la rebeldía veteranas de la revolución Mexicana, 1910–1939*, 133.

105. Inés Hernández, "Sara Estela Ramírez"; Melero, *Mythological Constructs of Mexican Femininity.*

106. Rocha, *Los rostros de la rebeldía veteranas de la revolución Mexicana, 1910–1939*, 343, 353. Among early feminists promoting a woman's agenda was Hermila Galindo, who directed the La Mujer Moderna (Mexico City), but whose early exposure to radical ideas was in the Mexican North. There is a rich history of women who wrote in support of the Revolution and promoted radical ideology in Mexico and the United States (as exiles).

107. Marsh, "The Anarchist-Feminist Response to the 'Woman Question' in Late-Nineteenth Century America," 539.

108. Merithew, "Anarchist Motherhood," 231–232.

109. Luisa Michel, "Por que soy anarquista," originally published in 1895 in London, *Sagitario*, June 1926, AHEMG, IIH-UAT; Torres Parés, *La revolución imposible*; see also Ellstrand, "Las Anarquistas." Luisa Capetillo, already by 1905, had also been active in labor struggles in Arecibo, Puerto Rico; see Hewitt, "Luisa Capetillo."

110. "Estamos de plácemes," *Sagitario*, November 1, 1928, http://www.antorcha.net /index/hemeroteca/periodico_avante/21.pdf, accessed April 26, 2017. The *grupo* Hermanos Rojos obtained its printing press in 1910 to produce *Sagitario*.

111. "Mexico Handbook on Approaches to San Luis Potosi and Tampico from the North and East through Zone E," 35–36.

112. See, among several examples from the Archivo Histórico de Tampico, "Caso de Regina Villanueva y Hilaria González," Caja: Justicia (1902–1937), #1, exp. "Denuncias, varias, presentadas ante el juez de ramo penal, 1918." See also Peña Delgado, "Border Control and Sexual Policing." Tampico and Villa Cecilia also attracted communists; there were communist organizations and collectives in the region including the FUPDM and the Electrical Workers' Union.

Chapter 2. Gendering Anarchism and Anarcho-Syndicalist Organizations

The original text from *El Porvenir de Tampico*, quoted in the first epigraph, reads, "La mujer de tal modo se hace mala . . . en los talleres, en los convites y en la calle, no en su casa."

1. See the various issues of *Germinal: Periódico Libertario* in www.libradorivera.com; Ricardo Flores Magón, "La huelga de Tampico," *Regeneración*, no. 259, September 1, 1917, http://archivomagon.net/obras-completas/art-periodisticos-1900-1918/ 1917/1917-31/; *Germinal: Periódico Libertario*, June 14, 1917, Archivo Librado Rivera y Los Hermanos Rojos, herefter cited ALR-HR, www.libradorivera.com/inicio.html; Baena Paz, *La Confederación General de Trabajadores, 1921–1931*, 88. Baena Paz lists Galván as the director/administradora of *Germinal* and notes the newspaper's closure in 1927. The

historian José Ángel Solorio Martínez also mentions Rosaura Galván in "En Ciudad Madero realizan foro del movimiento obrero en Tamaulipas," *Red Tampico*, June 20, 2019, https://redtampico.net/?p=230885.

2. Klubock, "Morality and Good Habits," 237.

3. "El Conde Tolstoi y el feminismo," *El Porvenir de Tampico*, March 1, 1907, NYPL, folder "El Porvenir" (1907–1909, incomplete).

4. Ibid.

5. Such a binary was further reinforced as gendered identities and norms experienced a transition along the US-Mexico borderlands as well as in the interior of both countries more generally. State authorities on both sides of the border spent considerable time and effort to limit education on "anatomical knowledge, contraception, and prostitution," or at the very least attempted to control and regulate these practices. Cocks, "Rethinking Sexuality in the Progressive Era," 103.

6. Peña Delgado, "Border Control and Sexual Policing," 161.

7. "La huegla que se inició en Monterrey amenaza propagarse en la frontera," *La Prensa*, July 16, 1918, 1.

8. Ibid.

9. Quote from "La huegla que se inició." See also Ramos, "Understanding Greater Revolutionary Mexico," 314–315. On Monterrey during the Revolution see Snodgrass, *Deference and Defiance in Monterrey*, 204.

10. Sonia Hernández, *Working Women into the Borderlands*.

11. This estimate is based on my previous research on women wage earners in the Mexican Northeast during the 1880–1940 period. As I explain in *Working Women into the Borderlands*, industrial censuses underreported female workers; yet an examination of labor dispute cases after 1918 in the state point to this discrepancy and, overall, indicate that at least one third of the workforce in the state was female. An example of such underreporting is evident from a typical industrial census: "Selected sectors employing women, Tampico Period 1906–1911," in "Anuario 1910–1911," AGET, Fondo Anuarios Estadísticos del Estado de Tamaulipas, caja s.n. This census counted Restaurant/food service N/A, Laundry 293, Sewing and pressing 173. However, we know that more than 293 women were employed in laundry work (in the entire state) given the testimonies of women in labor disputes.

12. "Desde Tampico," *Vida Nueva*, August 1920, CEMOS, Partido Comunista Mexicano, caja 1, exp. 8; Goldsmith, "De combativas a conformistas," 145–146; Sonia Hernández, *Working Women into the Borderlands*.

13. Ramona García, Francisca Orta, Florencia Moctezuma, Emiliano Benitez, Catarino Benitez, Salome Rangel, Patricio Benitez, Lucio Cortazar, Manuel Calvillo, Blas Cerda, Jesús Cafiazales, Roberto Reyes, Petronilo Ruíz, Donato Pérez, and José Juárez, "Casa del Obrero Mundial," *Tribuna Roja*, November 27, 1915, ALR-HR; Alcayaga Sasso, "Librado Rivera y Los Hermanos Rojos," 108.

14. García et al., "Casa del Obrero Mundial," *Tribuna Roja*, November 27, 1915, ALR-HR; Wood, *Revolution in the Street*.

15. Norvell, "Syndicalism and Citizenship," 97, 107; Fowler-Salamini, *Working Women, Entrepreneurs, and the Mexican Revolution*, 148–149.

16. Fowler-Salamini, *Working Women, Entrepreneurs, and the Mexican Revolution*.

17. As quoted in Santiago, "Women of the Mexican Oil Fields," 100; see also Adelson on Tampico oil workers' activism, "Historia social de los obreros industriales de Tampico, 1906–1919."

18. Olcott, *Revolutionary Women in Post-Revolutionary Mexico*, 56.

19. See also literature on female communists and how they were perceived in sexual and gendered terms as "Red Woman (a whore, an engulfing tide) contrasted with the vision of a White Woman (mother, wife, nurse)." As quoted in Rosenberg, "Gender," 121.

20. "La mujer en la lucha emancipadora," *¡Luz!: Semanario Libertario, doctrinario y de protesta, escrito por trabajadores en defensa de la mujer y de los trabajadores mismos*, November 21, 1917, ALR-HR; I thank Romy Natalia Goldberg for her assistance in translating this text.

21. *El Mundo* was founded in 1918 and its first director was Vicente Villasana. Solorio Martínez, *Grupos de gobierno*, 351. See "Caprichos femeninos: Joyas," *El Mundo de Tampico*, July 26, 1928. Similar portrayals of women's expected/normative behavior appear in *El Porvenir* during the first decade of the twentieth century, see, for example, "Al Bello Sexo," November 1, 1907 and "Oficios Femeninos," February 1, 1909, NYPL; "La mujer en la lucha emancipadora."

22. "El marido no se puede conformar con esas cosas," *Diario Periódico Político de la Mañana*, July 4, 1919, AHT.

23. "Mujeres criminales," *El Porvenir de Tampico*, May 1, 1909, NYPL.

24. Ibid.

25. "Se impidió desembarcar a dos mujeres extranjeras," *La Opinión: Diario Independiente de la Tarde* (Tampico), April 12, 1924, Hemeroteca, IIH-UAT.

26. "Mexico Handbook on Approaches to San Luis Potosi and Tampico from the North and East through Zone E"; Ngai, *Impossible Subjects*.

27. Peña Delgado, "Border Control and Sexual Policing," 157.

28. Porter, *Working Women in Mexico City*; Bliss, *Compromised Positions*.

29. Lomnitz, *Return of Comrade Ricardo Flores Magón*, 445.

30. As historian Barbara Reyes has written, "women's socially constructed roles and expectations . . . corresponded to their position in the prevailing social and racial hierarchy," Reyes, *Private Women, Public Lives*, 4–9.

31. Peña Delgado, "Border Control and Sexual Policing." The French American Voltarine de Cleyre, for example, was described as "a veiled advocate of violence," in "Noted Women Anarchists," *Dallas Morning News*, October 27, 1901; Longa, ed., *Anarchist Periodicals in English Published in the United States (1833–1955)*.

32. "Noted Women Anarchists," *Dallas Morning News*, October 27, 1901.

33. R. González Parra, "A la mujer," *Germinal, Periódico Libertario* (Tampico), July 2, 1917, ALR-HR.

34. Huitron, *Orígenes e historia del movimiento obrero en México*, 291.

35. Ibid., 292.

36. "Se impidió desembarcar a dos mujeres extranjeras"; "Invasión de gentes de mal vivir, que ha unos años de esta parte ha inundado la ciudad," *La Opinión: Diario Independiente de la Tarde* (Tampico), April 12, 1924, Hemeroteca, IIH-UAT.

37. "Mexico Handbook on Approaches to San Luis Potosi and Tampico from the North and East through Zone E."

38. Ibid. In neighboring Nuevo León, reports in 1916 in *El Triunfo* and reprinted in *El Regiomontano* featured news on the "radical foreigners" from Tamaulipas, awaiting deportation. The report warned of Monterrey's vulnerability given its many industrial sites with large numbers of urbanized workers susceptible to such "radical" ideas.

39. Hart, *Anarchism and Mexican Working Class*, 158–159. Treviño eventually opted to join the CROM.

40. Flores Magón, "La huelga de Tampico," *Regeneración*, no. 259, September 1, 1917, in *Regeneración 1900–1918*, ed. Bartra.

41. Adelson, "Coyuntura y conciencia," 639; Solorio Martínez, *Grupos de gobierno*, 349.

42. Ribera Carbó, *La Casa del Obrero Mundial*, 224–229; on the pact between the COM and Carranza see Ribera Carbó and Carr, "The Casa del Obrero Mundial."

43. Hart, *Anarchism and the Mexican Working Class*, 183.

44. To Presidente Municipal, Tampico, from COM Tampico, August 10, 1917, Fondo: Presidencia, caja 1917, #1, AHT.

45. Flores Magón, "La huelga de Tampico."

46. See the various issues of *Germinal: Periódico Libertario* in www.libradorivera.com; Flores Magón, "La huelga de Tampico"; see all of the issues in *Germinal: Periódico Libertario*, June 14, 1917, ALR-HR, www.libradorivera.com/inicio.html (accessed March 2019). The COM Tampico, which maintained a busy schedule, had held several sit-ins or demonstration-meetings in the Plaza de la Libertad in early 1917, To Presidente Municipal, from COM Tampico, Ricardo Treviño, February 17, 1917, Fondo: Presidencia, caja 1917, #1, AHT.

47. Transcript of Proceeding in Investigation of Manuel Almedo, US Department of Labor Immigration Service, from Inspector of Immigration, Nuevo Laredo, Tamaulipas, NARA, August 8, 1917, Record Group 84, 962/301, August 8, 1917.

48. Transcript of Proceeding in Investigation of Manuel Almedo, US Department of Labor Immigration Service, from Inspector of Immigration, Nuevo Laredo, Tamaulipas, NARA, August 8, 1917, Record Group 84, 962/301, August 8, 1917.

49. Ibid.

50. "¡Deportados!," *¡Luz!: Semanario Libertario, doctrinario y de protesta, escrito por trabajadores en defensa de la mujer y de los trabajadores mismos*, November 21, 1917, ALR-HR; "Los obreros de Tampico se quejan a la representación nacional," *¡Luz!: Semanario Libertario, doctrinario y de protesta, escrito por trabajadores en defensa de la mujer y de los trabajadores mismos*, November 28, 1917, ALR-HR. On Huitrón see Ribera Carbó, *La Casa del Obrero Mundial*; see also Buffington, *A Sentimental Education for the Working Man*.

51. "Report of the Proceedings of the Second Congress of the Pan American Federation of Labor," New York City, New York, July 7, 1919, 8–9, originally deposited

in the Harvard College Library; McKillen, "Hybrid Visions," 85; Vicenta Cabrera, an anarcho-feminist who had attended the Saltillo labor conference also contributed to *Vida Libre*, Alcayaga Sasso, 330; several issues of *Vida Libre* have been archived in ALR-HR.

52. Alcayaga Sasso, in "Librado Rivera y Los Hermanos Rojos," 120–124, refers to Berkman as Alejandro Berman; Ribera Carbó, *La Casa del Obrero Mundial*, 227–229. On Berkman (his first name appeared as Alejandro in Mexican anarchist newpapers), see Fellner, ed., *Life of an Anarchist.*

53. Interview with Ricardo Treviño as published in González Salas, *Acercamiento a la historia del movimiento obrero en Tampico*, 34.

54. Ibid.; González Salas, *Acercamiento a la historia del movimiento obrero en Tampico*, 34.

55. To Presidente Municipal, from Jefe de la Policía Reservada, Tampico, December 24, 1917, Fondo: Presidencia, caja 1917, #1, AHT; Hart, *Anarchism and the Mexican Working Class*, 157.

56. Alcayaga Sasso, "Librado Rivera y Los Hermanos Rojos," 123; Ribera Carbó, *La Casa del Obrero Mundial*, 222–223; Hart, *Anarchism and the Mexican Working Class*, 155; Lear, *Workers, Neighbors, and Citizens*, 333–336.

57. Alcayaga Sasso, "Librado Rivera y Los Hermanos Rojos," 123; Ribera Carbó, *La Casa del Obrero Mundial*, 222–223; Hart, *Anarchism and the Mexican Working Class*, 155.

58. The philosopher and anarchist died in Barcelona on October 13, 1909. For more on Carranza's role in labor matters from the perspective of Carranza as labor progressive, see Ulloa, *Historia de la Revolución Mexicana, periódo 1914–1917*; for an analysis from the perspective of Carranza as antilabor see Reyna and Cortez, "El control del movimiento obrero como una necesidad del Estado de México (1917–1936)," 785–813.

59. Adelson, "Coyuntura y conciencia," 639.

60. See the references to the Centro in *Sagitario*; Alcayaga Sasso, "Librado Rivera y Los Hermanos Rojos," 50, 60, 123–125; Aguilar, "The IWW in Tampico," 127–128. While Alcayaga Sasso uses "Centro de Estudios Sociales Feministas," Aguilar uses "Centro Femenil de Estudios Sociales." Oikión Solano, *Cuca García (1889–1973)*, 170.

61. Hart, *Anarchism and the Mexican Working Class*, 157–158; among those supporting anarcho-syndicalism against any type of alliance with the state was the Spaniard Jorge Borrán.

62. For all ten points see "Bases del Congreso Obrero reunido en Tampico" in *¡Luz!: Semanario Libertario, doctrinario y de protesta, escrito por trabajadores en defensa de la mujer y de los trabajadores mismos*, November 28, 1917, ALR-HR; these points are also paraphrased in Alcayaga Sasso, "Librado Rivera y Los Hermanos Rojos," 125.

63. "La voz de la mujer," *Revolución* (Los Angeles), July 13, 1907, AGN, Fondo: Revoltosos, caja 6, exp. 2; Guidotti-Hernández, "Partido Liberal Mexicano."

64. Luz Gudiño Marín, "El día de la Navidad," *Sagitario*, February 17, 1924, ALR-HR.

65. Despite the lack of a real female membership, Hermanos Rojos encouraged women like Gudiño to submit creative writing, poems, and commentaries, *Germinal:*

Periódico Libertario in www.libradorivera.com; Flores Magón, "La huelga de Tampico"; see all of the issues in *Germinal: Periódico Libertario* (Tampico), June 14, 1917, ALR-HR, www.libradorivera.com/inicio.html (accessed March 2019).

66. Román Delgado, "Adelante compañeras," *Germinal: Periódico Libertario* (Tampico), June 14, 1917, ALR-HR, www.libradorivera.com/inicio.html (accessed March 2019).

67. Alcayaga Sasso, "Librado Rivera y Los Hermanos Rojos," 52; Reinalda González Parra, "Intransigencia," *Tribuna Roja* (Tampico), November 27, 1915, ALR-HR.

68. González Parra, "Intransigencia."

69. Ibid.

70. Jacinto Huitrón, "Amor sin cadenas," *Revolución Social* (Orizaba), July 1, 1915, as quoted in Ribera Carbó, "Mujeres sindicalistas."

71. Hart, *Anarchism and the Mexican Working Class*, 153–155.

72. R. González Parra, "A la mujer," *Germinal: Periódico Libertario* (Tampico), July 2, 1917, ALR-HR.

73. Reinalda González Parras, "¡Al abordaje!," *Germinal*, June 14, 1917, ALR-HR.

74. Carbó, "Mujeres sindicalistas," In 1915, González Parra participated, along with Paula Osorio Avendaño and Genoveva Hidalgo, in the first Ferrer Rational School sponsored by the Mexico City COM; Hart, *Anarchism and the Mexican Working Class*, 125.

75. Reynalda González Parra, "Para las dos," *Germinal* (Tampico), August 2, 1917, ALR-HR.

76. Reynalda González Parra, "¡Salud!," *Germinal*, October 11, 1917, ALR-HR.

77. Portes Gil would serve as interim governor until early 1921, at which point César López de Lara assumed the governorship. Portes Gil assumed the governorship once again in early 1925. Solorio Martínez, *Grupos de gobierno*, 352; Comité Directivo del Gran Partido "Demócrata Laborista Tamaulipeco," Comisión de Investigación, Administración Principal del Timbre, Tampico, October 19, 1922, AHPEPG, c. 1bis, Serie I, exp. 6, AGN.

78. Reyna, Palomares, and Cortez, "El control del movimiento obrero como una necesidad del Estado de México (1917–1936)," 75; Carr, *Marxism and Communism in Twentieth-Century Mexico*; the party was first organized by 1917 as the Socialist Workers Party.

79. "Federación Local de Tampico: Adherida a la Confederación General de Trabajadores a los obreros de la región petrolera," *Sagitario*, December 11, 1924, http://www.antorcha.net/index/hemeroteca/sagitario/2.pdf, accessed January 26, 2017. Other issues of the newspaper appear in ALR-HR. Caulfield, "Wobblies and Mexican Workers in Mining and Petroleum, 1905–1924," 44.

80. Lara Orozco, *En el vaivén del Frente Rojo*, 22.

81. Hart, *Anarchism and the Mexican Working Class*, 120; Porter, *Working Women in Mexico City*, 113; Caulfield, "Wobblies and Mexican Workers in Mining and Petroleum, 1905–1924," 52.

82. "El Unionismo se intensifica," *Sagitario*, November 1, 1924, ALR-HR; while the CGT counted on the support from the large electrical workers' union, the CROM

relied on its ties to El Águila oil workers. Thus, each national organization had its own locally based large affiliate. The PSF, later, would count on the large dockworkers' union, Alvarado Mendoza, *El portesgilismo en Tamaulipas*, 276.

83. "Manifesto de la Federación Local de Tampico, adherida a la Confederación General de Trabajadores," December 1924, published in *Sagitario*, December 11, 1924, AHEMG.

84. Rose, "'Good' vs. 'Militant' Citizens."

85. As quoted in "La burguesía y la pena de muerte," *Alma Obrera: Quincenal de propaganda sindicalista, Órgano del grupo sindicalista "Alma Obrera" de Zacatecas*, no. 5, November 21, 1929, in AHEMG; see also the work by Oscar Misael Hernández on masculinity in postrevolutionary Tamaulipas, "Estado, cultura y masculinidades en el noreste de México en la posrevolución"; and Guidotti-Hernández, "Partido Liberal Mexicano."

86. "La burguesía y la pena de muerte."

87. "La burguesía y la pena de muerte"; in 1930, Piña petitioned on behalf of Hernández, "Actas de la junta 16 de junio, 1930," June 16, 1930, AHEMG. Alfaro played a crucial role in the development of Portes Gil's PSF.

88. Specific works that address female *magonistas* and/or women supporting the movement include *Las mujeres en la revolución mexicana* and Lau and Ramos, *Mujeres y revolución*. See also Porter and Fernández Acéves, eds., *Género en la encrucijada de la historia social y cultural de México*; Lomas, "Transborder Discourse"; Pérez, *Decolonial Imaginary*; Sonia Hernández, *Working Women into the Borderlands*; Porter, "Working Women in the Mexican Revolution"; Hernández Velásquez, "Mujeres magonistas."

Chapter 3. *Feminismos Transfronterizos* in Caritina Piña's Labor Network

This chapter draws on my article "Revisiting *Mexican(a)* Labor History through *Feminismo Transfronterista*." I use the terms *feminismo/s transfronterista* and *feminismo/s transfronterizos* interchangeably. The chapter epigraph is from "To 'Grupo Libertario Sacco y Vanzetti,'" New York, from Caritina Piña, Secretaria de Correspondencia, Comité, Villa Cecilia, July 6, 1929, AHEMG, IIH-UAT.

1. "Demetria D. Gutiérrez and Nicanor Piña Hernández," Family Tree, Family Search.org., accessed December 1, 2019; "Acta de Bautismo de Victor Piña Hernández," Family Search, http://familysearch.org, accessed December 3, 2019; Marvin Osiris Huerta Márquez, "'Los pelones' los villanos de la revolución," *Expreso.press*, November 25, 2019, accessed December 3, 2019.

2. "Demetria D. Gutiérrez and Nicanor Piña Hernández." It appears Demetria was José Nicanor's second or third wife.

3. Aguilar, "Peripheries of Power, Centers of Resistance." Aguilar provides a good discussion on the connections between US-based anarchists and *magonistas* in Mexico as well as their correspondence with groups around the world that shared similar ideologies and concerns.

4. To Sindicato de la Pierce Oil Co., Arbol Grande, Cecilia, Tamps., from Librado Rivera, January 7, 1925, AHEMG, IIH-UAT; "Esteban Méndez Guerra, 1896–1979," in libcom.org, http://www.libcom.org/history/mendez-guerra-esteban-1896-1979, accessed April 8, 2014; Ricardo Flores Magón, "Tierra y libertad," *Regeneración*, no. 260, October 6, 1917, http://archivomagon.net/category/obras-completas/art-periodisticos-1900-1918/1917.

5. "México, Censo Nacional 1930: Caritina M. Piña," index and images, Family Search.org, http://familysearch.org, accessed May 10, 2016.

6. Ibid.

7. To "Grupo Libertario Sacco y Vanzetti," from Caritina Piña, Secretaria de Correspondencia, July 6, 1929, AHEMG, IIH-UAT.

8. See Santiago, "Women of the Mexican Oil Fields," 88.

9. "Esteban Méndez Guerra, 1896–1979," libcom.org, http://www.libcom.org/history/mendez-guerra-esteban-1896-1979, accessed April 8, 2014; see also the brief description by Alcayaga Sasso on Méndez Guerra based on an interview she conducted with Olga Méndez Velarde, a relative of his, "Librado Rivera y Los Hermanos Rojos," 21.

10. To "Grupo Libertario Sacco y Vanzetti," from Caritina Piña, Secretaria de Correspondencia, July 6, 1929, AHEMG, IIH-UAT; "México, Censo Nacional 1930: Caritina M. Piña." While there is no direct connection between the Comité Pro-Presos of Barcelona and the Comité Pro-Presos in Tampico, it is possible that its members had contact given the updates that each organization received from one another. See "A las víctimas de la represión española," for the Comité Pro-Presos, in *Ideas y tragedia* (Barcelona: Imprenta 'El Trabajo', 1923), BC. In "Entradas: Administración," Caritina M. Piña appears in the list of donors contributing fifty centavos, *¡Avante!*, July 1, 1928, AHEMG, IIH-UAT.

11. "México, Censo Nacional 1930: Caritina M. Piña," 219.

12. González Salas, *Acercamiento a la historia del movimiento obrero*.

13. "Nuevo grupo," *Sagitario*, June 6, 1925, AHEMG, IIH-UAT. Another Edinburg, Texas–based group affiliated with the anarcho-syndicalists of Tampico was Grupo "Vía Libre," Alcayaga Sasso, "Librado Rivera y Los Hermanos Rojos," 168.

14. To Presidente Gral. Porfirio Díaz, from Librado Rivera, St. Louis, MO, November 11, 1906, Fondo: Revoltosos, caja 1-a, exp. 5, "Librado Rivera," AGN. Although the telegram submitted to Josue Benignos identified Rivera as a communist, he was not affiliated with the Communist Party and was in fact a loyal anarchist; Telegram to Secretario de Estado, from Josue Benignos, "Detención de Lider Comunista Librado Rivera," June 12, 1929, Tampico, DGG, exp. #313.1-1729 "Librado Rivera," AGN. While the telegram was written in 1929, this AGN file also contains older notes and letters from Rivera to various government officials.

15. To Presidente Gral. Porfirio Díaz, from Librado Rivera, St. Louis, MO, November 11, 1906; "Telegram to Secretario de Estado from Josue Benignos"; Alcayaga Sasso," Librado Rivera y Los Hermanos Rojos"; Rivera has only recently received in-depth scholarly attention by Alcayaga Sasso in her excellent dissertation.

16. Fallaw, "Eulogio Ortiz," 137.

17. "¡Ricardo ha muerto!," *Sagitario*, December 16, 1923, AHEMG, IIH-UAT.

18. "Los mártires de Texas," *Sagitario*, February 1, 1925, ALR-HR.

19. Ibid.; Alcayaga Sasso, "Librado Rivera y Los Hermanos Rojos," 271; the quote regarding the Texans comes from Lomnitz, *Return of Comrade Ricardo Flores Magón*, 419.

20. "La libertad de Rivera," *Avante* (Monterrey, Nuevo León), November 19, 1927.

21. To Evaristo Rodillo (also appears as Evaristo Badillo), from Caritina M. Piña, June 4, 1930, AHEMG, IIH-UAT.

22. "Carta abierta al presidente de los Estados Unidos Mexicanos Señor Plutarco Elías Calles" (Palacio Nacional de gobierno México, D.F.), from Domingo Loza, secretario provisional, La Antorcha (San Francisco, CA), May 23, 1927. De Lara's story is a sad one. Despite working in support of the Madero government (and later betrayed by it) and then working as "an agent in the United States on behalf of Carranza to sway US support away from Villa, and later becoming an independent agent, he was executed on January 18, 1918," Lomnitz, *Return of Comrade Ricardo Flores Magón*, 500.

23. Alcayaga Sasso, "Librado Rivera y Los Hermanos Rojos," 77.

24. "¡Ricardo ha muerto!," *Sagitario*, December 16, 1923, AHEMG, IIH-UAT; Lomnitz, *Return of Comrade Ricardo Flores Magón*, 418, 420.

25. "Pro-Presos de Texas," *Sagitario*, October 25, 1924, AHEMG, IIH-UAT; reference to 1913 events comes from Alcayaga Sasso, "Librado Rivera y Los Hermanos Rojos," 168.

26. "Cultura proletaria de Nueva York," *Avante* (Monterrey, Nuevo León), November 19, 1927, 4, AGET.

27. See Antonia Castañeda, *Gender on the Borderlands*; on Jaime Vidal; for a global discussion of the Sacco and Vanzetti case and its international supporters see McGirr, "Passion of Sacco and Vanzetti." *Obreros* from Tampico with ties to the labor movement in Mexico City, regardless of orientation, but particularly those sympathetic to communism, also collaborated with other workers on behalf of Sacco and Vanzetti via *El Machete*: "Por Sacco y Vanzetti," *El Machete*, Janaury 15–22, 1925,161, CEMOS. The support for Sacco and Vanzetti crossed ideological and party lines as women in both anarcho-syndicalist and communist organizations petitioned on their behalf. See, for example, the activism of María Refugio "Cuca" García on behalf of the Italian American anarchists, Oikión Solano, *Cuca García (1889–1973)*, 160.

28. "Esteban Méndez Guerra (1896–1979)."

29. Ibid.; Alcayaga Sasso, "Librado Rivera y Los Hermanos Rojos," 277, 280.

30. McGirr, "The Passion of Sacco and Vanzetti," 1088.

31. Rouco Buela, *Historiad de un ideal vivido por una mujer*, Biblioteca Nacional de España; the activist Refugia "Cuca" García, who regularly contributed to *El Machete*, also participated in events that sought to create awareness of the Sacco and Vanzetti ordeal, Oikón Solano, *Cuca García (1889–1973)*, 160.

32. "Trabajadores," *Sagitario*, July 9, 1925, ALR-HR.

33. "Cuarto Congreso de la C.G.T.," *Sagitario*, June 6, 1925, ALR-HR.

34. Alcayaga Sasso, "Librado Rivera y Los Hermanos Rojos," 268.

35. Ibid., 267–268, 293.

36. To "Grupo Libertario Sacco y Vanzetti," from Caritina Piña, Secretaria de Correspondencia, July 6, 1929, AHEMG, IIH-UAT.

37. "Actas de la junta 7 de marzo, 1930," AHEMG, IIH-UAT.

38. "Manifiesto que lanza la Liga Cultural de Mujeres Libertarias 'La Idea' a la Mujer Mundial," *Sagitario*, June 6, 1925, AHEMG, IIH-UAT; González Salas, *Acercamiento a la historia del movimiento obrero en Tampico*, 105–107. While the actual newspaper article includes the names of Alvarado and Mendoza, González Salas does not cite their names. He includes the names of only fourteen women. Citing the AHEMG (although Alcayaga uses the acronym AEM), Alcayaga Sasso lists seventeen women, Alcayaga Saso, "Librado Rivera y Los Hermanos Rojos," 167n82.

39. "Manifiesto que lanza la Liga Cultural de Mujeres Libertarias 'La Idea' a la Mujer Mundial," *Sagitario*, June 6, 1925, AHEMG, IIH-UAT; González Salas, *Acercamiento a la historia del movimiento obrero en Tampico*, 105–107.

40. "A vosotras," *Sagitario*, January 1, 1925, ALR-HR.

41. Ibid.

42. Aurelia Rodríguez, "Insurrección," *Sagitario*, August 16, 1925, ALR-HR.

43. Ibid.

44. Domitila Jiménez, "¡Basta ya tiranos!," *Sagitario*, June, 1926, AHEMG, IIH-UAT.

45. Ibid.

46. Domitila Jiménez, "La jornada de 6 horas," *Sagitario*, September 11, 1926, ALR-HR. Jiménez also contributed funds to *Sagitario*.

47. To Librado Rivera (Tampico, Tamps.), from A. H. Cepeda (Mercedes, Texas), June 21, 1922, AHEMG, IIH-UAT; To Juan Montemayor, from Luz Mendoza (Harlingen, Texas), November 11, 1929, AHEMG, IIH-UAT; "Nuevo Grupo," *Sagitario*, June 6, 1925, AHEMG, IIH-UAT. There were other labor organizations in Texas that were not in direct contact with anarcho-syndicalist organizations on the Mexican side of the border, including organizations such as La Unión Obrera Mexicana, founded in McAllen, Texas, "Nos han llegado algunos fondos mas [*sic*], para las victimas de Veracruz," *La Prensa*, April 7, 1920, Special Collections, SRKL.

48. "Felipa Velásquez: la mujer que encabezó un movimiento," *La Crónica.com,* http://www.lacronica.com/Edicion Enlinea/Notas/Noticias/28012013/664219.aspx, accessed December 2, 2014. It is likely that Velásquez lived in Mexico City for a brief period during the Mexican Revolution as the following document regarding an eviction notice indicates: Caso en contra de Felipa Velásquez presentada por Enrique Sánchez Barquera, November 8, 1912, Fondo: Tribunal Superior de Justicia, caja 1202, exp. 211864, AGN.

49. "El credo," *Avante* (Villa Cecilia), September 1, 1928, 1, AGET. Felipa Velásquez also appears in editorials from Los Mochis, Sinaloa; see "Hacia la Lucha" from Los Mochis, reprinted in *Sagitario*, June 6, 1925, AHEMG, IIH-UAT.

50. "Cuarto Congreso de la C.G.T.," *Sagitario*, June 6, 1925, ALR-HR.

51. "De nuestra correspondencia: Librado Rivera de parte de Felipa Velásquez," July 15, 1928, *Avante*, AHEMG, IIH-UAT. Other examples of Velásquez's atheism include "Carta

a una creyente," *Avante*, December 1, 1928, AHEMG, IIH-UAT; Felipa Velásquez, "Hacia la lucha," reprinted in *Sagitario*, June 6, 1925, AHEMG, IIH-UAT.

52. "La libertad de Rivera," *Avante* (Monterrey, Nuevo León), November 19, 1927, 1, AGET. According to this editorial, the newspaper *Avante*, whose main home was Villa Cecilia, opened another office in 1927 in Monterrey.

53. "Un parásito valiente," *Avante* (Villa Cecilia), September 1, 1928, AGET.

54. Marsh, "The Anarchist-Feminist Response to the 'Woman Question' in Late-Nineteenth-Century America," 539.

55. "Circular del Gremio Unido de Alijadores de Tampico," *El Machete*, March 12–19, 1925, CEMOS.

56. "!A la mujer!," *Avante* (Monterrey), November 19, 1927, AHEMG, IIH-UAT.

57. "La idea," *Avante* (Villa Cecilia), April, 11, 1928, AHEMG, IIH-UAT.

58. María Mendoza, "Lo que prefiero," *Avante* (Villa Cecilia), 1924, AHEMG, IIH-UAT.

59. Ibid.

60. "Administración, Entradas," *Avante*, n.m. 1924, AHEMG, IIH-UAT; To Juan Montemayor, from Luz Mendoza (Harlingen, Texas), November 11, 1929, AHEMG, IIH-UAT; "Nuevo grupo," *Sagitario*, June 6, 1925, AHEMG, IIH-UAT; for "La Unión Obrera Mexicana," founded in McAllen, Texas, see "Nos han llegado algunos fondos más, para las victimas de Veracruz," *La Prensa*, April 7, 1920, SRKL. While terms such as *La dictadura* or *La opresión* took on a female gendered pronoun in Spanish, anarchy, at least according to Mendoza, also took on a female identity.

61. "Margarita Ortega (María Valdez)," *Diccionario biográfico*, ARFM.

62. María Mendoza, "Nuevo grupo," *Sagitario*, July 20, 1927, ALR-HR.

63. Citatoria Urgente a Todas las Organizaciones Obreras de la Localidad, from Caritina Piña, June 10, 1930, AHEMG, IIH-UAT; "Acta de la junta en el salón de actos del H. Sindicato de Obreros y Empleados de la C. de Petroleum La Pierce Oil" Acta: March 7, 1930, Acta: June 16, 1930, AHEMG, IIH-UAT.

64. María Mendoza, "Nuevo grupo," *Sagitario*, July 20, 1927, ALR-HR.

65. "Sedición," *Sagitario*, July 20, 1927, ALR-HR; see also the work of Kirwin Shafer on networks in the Carribean.

66. Citatoria Urgente a Todas las Organizaciones Obreras de la Localidad, from Caritina Piña, June 10, 1930; "Acta de la junta en el salon de actos del H. Sindicato de Obreros y Empleados de la C. de Petroleum La Pierce Oil," June 16, 1930. Piña and others used the terms "social prisoners" and "political prisoners" interchangeably.

67. To Citatoria Urgente a Todas las Organizaciones Obreras de la Localidad, from Caritina Piña, June 10, 1930. While the *Actas* or meeting minutes found in the AHEMG indicate that Felipa had seven children, an editorial in *Periodismo Puntal* written in 2016 notes that four of Felipa's children were underage and were present during her arrest: Francisca, Felipe, Soledad, and Narcizo Arellano Velázquez. Virgina Noriega Ríos, "Felipa Velásquez Viuda de Arrellano, Referente mas importante del asalto a las Tierras," *Periodismo Puntal*, https://periodismopuntual.wordpress.com/2016/01/27/felipa

-velazquez-viuda-de-arellano-referente-mas-importante-del-asalto-a-las-tierras
-virginia-noriega-rios/, accessed April 27, 2017. It is unclear whether or not she had
seven children and was arrested in the presence of all of them, as the meeting minutes
indicate, or whether she was arrested in the presence of her four youngest children, or
if she had only four children.

Chapter 4. The Language of Motherhood in Radical Labor Activism

This chapter is based in part on my essay "Caritina M. Piña and Anarcho-Syndicalism."
The first epigraph is from Aurelia Rodríguez, "A vosotras," *Sagitario* (Villa Cecilia,
Tamps.), January 1, 1925. The second epigraph is from M. C. Guerrero, "Hymn for
the Birth of the People's Son/Canto al nacimiento del hijo del pueblo," *Sagitario* (Villa
Cecilia), July 20, 1927.

1. Gregory S. Taylor, *History of the North Carolina Communist Party*, 23. Taylor does not
indicate if Mexicans were among the mill workers, and it is unclear whether or not
Mexicans or Mexican Americans were among the detained in the Loray Mill Strike.
See also Salmond, *Gastonia 1929*.

2. Fred Beal, "Who Are the Gastonia Prisoners," *Labor Defender* 4 (September 1929):
171, https://www.marxists.org/history/usa/pubs/labordefender/1929/v04n09-sep
-1929-LD.pdf, accessed June 13, 2018.

3. Gregory S. Taylor, *History of the North Carolina Communist Party*, 42; Weisbord, "Gastonia, 1929 Strike at the Loray Mill."

4. As quoted in Gregory S. Taylor, *History of the North Carolina Communist Party*, 35.

5. Weisbord, "Gastonia, 1929 Strike at the Loray Mill." "De Propaganda Anárquica,"
n.d, ca. 1924, AGN, DGG, Asunto: Investigaciones políticas y sociales, caja 7, exp. 3.

6. To M. V. Barnhill (Charlotte, NC), from Comité Internacional Pro-Presos Sociales
(Villa Cecilia, Tamps.), September 20, 1929, AHEMG, IIH-UAT. For an examination
of the strike in Gastonia see Gregory S. Taylor, *History of the North Carolina Communist
Party*.

7. "Alertas trabajadores!," *El Preso Social* (organ of the Comité Internacional Pro-
Presos Sociales [Villa Cecilia, Tamps.]), ca. 1929, AHEMG, IIH-UAT.

8. Ibid.

9. Ibid.; "Comunismo libertario" was adopted as the CGT motto during its third
convention, Baena Paz, *La Confederación General de Trabajadores, 1921–1931*, 47.

10. Laughlin et al., "Is It Time to Jump Ship?," 90.

11. On the ideological positions of the women who comprised the FUPDM see Tuñon
Pablos, "Tres momentos claves del movimiento sufragista en México (1917–1953),"
83–84.

12. "La manifestación de Tampico disuelta por los gendarmes del Lic. Portes Gil,"
Bandera Roja, no. 4, September 30, 1929, CEMOS.

13. Ibid. On Portes Gil see Alvarado Mendoza, *El portesgilismo en Tamaulipas*.

14. Hutchison, *Labors Appropriate to Their Sex*, 101.

15. "El primero de mayo en el puerto de Tampico," *El Machete*, May 15, 1925, CEMOS.

16. Bill Dunne, "Charlotte Press as Judge and Jury," *Labor Defender* 4 (September 1929): 173, https://www.marxists.org/history/usa/pubs/labordefender/1929/v04n09 -sep-1929-LD.pdf, accessed June 13, 2018.

17. Koven and Michel, "Womanly Duties,"1079.

18. Guerrero, "Canto al nacimiento."

19. Ibid.

20. Villanueva, *Teresa Claramunt (1862–1931)*, 226–227, Biblioteca Nacional de España.

21. Dora Andrew, "!Abajo charrateras criminales!," *Sagitario*, October 25, 1924, ALR-HR.

22. Rodríguez, "A vosotras."

23. Alcayaga Sasso, "Librado Rivera y Los Hermanos Rojos," 165.

24. As recalled by fellow labor colleague Francisco Vega Soria in an interview conducted by the Instituto Nacional de Antropología e Historia and quoted in both Baena Paz, *La Confederación General de Trabajadores, 1921–1931*, 87; and Alcayaga Sasso, "Librado Rivera y Los Hermanos Rojos," 251.

25. Hutchison, *Labors Appropriate to Their Sex*, 99.

26. Ibid., 99.

27. The Mexican state also promoted a particular type of masculinity. See Oscar Misael Hernández, "Políticas educativas y formación de identidades culturales en Tamaulipas, 1925–1928."

28. Florinda Mondini, "Escucha, mujer," *Avante* (Villa Cecilia, Tamps.), March 8, 1928, AHEMG.

29. Ibid.

30. Hewitt, "Luisa Capetillo," 124–125.

31. "Boletin de Propaganda Anárquica," n.d, ca. 1924, AGN, DGG, Asunto: Investigaciones políticas y sociales, caja 7, exp. 3.

32. Ibid.

33. "Iguales derechos para las mujeres," *El Mundo*, July 26, 1928, AHT.

34. "La falda corta trae aparejado el dificil problema de sentarse correctamente," *El Mundo*, July 26, 1928, AHT.

35. Ibid. This emphasis on appearance is described by Anne Rubenstein in her work on Mexico City women, "The War on *Las Pelonas*: Modern Women and Their Enemies, Mexico City, 1924," 60–61.

36. Gordillo, *Mexican Women and the Other Side of Immigration*, 61, 126; see also Olcott's discussion on citizenship, in the Mexican context and for women, as a contingent and changing concept and practice, *Revolutionary Women in Post-Revolutionary Mexico*.

37. Sonia Hernández, "Rooted in Place, Constructed in Movement."

38. "Por qué las 'Compañeras' Meseras, cansadas del sindicalismo rompen sus compromisos y se contratan independientemente," *El Mundo*, January 11, 1925, AHT.

Chapter 5. "Leave the Unions to the Men"

The chapter epigraph is a statement from Las Meseras Libres submitted to *El Mundo*, January 11, 1925.

1. To Presidente Municipal, Tampico, from COM Tampico, December 22, 1917, Fondo: Presidencia, caja 1917, #1, AHT; for an in-depth analysis of the use of the labor boards by urban and rural female workers from Nuevo León and Tamaulipas see Sonia Hernández, "Las obreras de Monterrey" and *Working Women into the Borderlands*.

2. "Una sabrosa y pintoresca charla con las 'Compañeras' Meseras," *El Mundo*, January 11, 1925, AHT.

3. Porter, *Working Women in Mexico City*; Suarez-Potts, "The Ambiguity of Labor Justice in Mexico, 1907–1931," 94–95.

4. To Junta Central de Conciliación y Arbitraje, from Obreros: Francisco Contreras, Juan Hernández, and Vidal López, en contra de la Pierce Oil, June 21, 1918, Fondo: JCCA, caja 2, AGET; to Junta Central de Conciliación y Arbitraje, from Pierce Oil Corporation, sucesora de Waters Pierce Oil Company, June 28, 1918, Fondo: JCCA, caja 2, AGET.

5. "Reglamento de Trabajo y Descanso," August 11, 1928, AHT, Fondo: Presidencia, caja 1931, expediente, "Reglamento de Trabajo y Descanso"; "Convención de Organizaciones Obreras y Campesinas Contra la Promulgación de la Ley Federal del Trabajo," prepared for Francisco Castellanos, Governor of Tamaulipas, and Jesus Aguirre Siller, Mayor of Tampico, July 21, 1931, AHT, Fondo: Presidencia, caja 1931, expediente "Obreros sin Trabajo"; Saldaña Martínez and Palacios Hernández, "Entre la reproducción y la producción."

6. Sánchez Gómez, *Proyección histórica de Tampico*, 65. Since the nineteenth century, Tamaulipas has been divided into four sectors with Tampico and outlying areas as the major subsection of this district while other towns, including Xicotencatl and Ocampo, Piña's hometown, comprised the second subsection of the district.

7. For nineteenth-century figures see Alejandro Prieto, *Historia, geografía y estadística del Estado de Tamaulipas* (Mexico City: Tip. Escalerillas Num. 13, 1873), 276–277, Alejandro Prieto Papers, NLB; for Tampico population figures see Adelson, "Coyuntura y conciencia," 632. Tampico's population in 1876 was nearly 5,000.

8. "Así están las cosas y basta," *Sagitario*, July 9, 1925, ALR-HR; Adelson, "Coyuntura y conciencia."

9. "Una sabrosa y pintoresca charla con las 'Compañeras' Meseras," *El Mundo*, January 11, 1925, AHT; included in this labor union were domestic workers employed in the region's restaurants and hotels during the same period, see Goldsmith, "Doméstica, mujer o hija de familia." The SERCS was represented by Eva Ramírez in the FOT; it does not appear that the SDRS had a representative.

10. "Así están las cosas y basta," *Sagitario*, July 9, 1925, ALR-HR; Adelson, "Coyuntura y conciencia," 632–660. It was not until the early 1930s, when the Poza Rica well began to operate, that the industry recovered, Brown, *Oil and Revolution in Mexico*; Olvera Rivera, "Identity, Culture, and Workers' Autonomy."

11. Alvarado Mendoza, *El portesgilismo en Tamaulipas*, 281–283, 303. The leaders of the Dockworkers' Union in consultation with Portes Gil helped negotiate a truce

between radicals like Tito Durán y Huerta and Portes Gil. Durán y Huerta was rewarded with a political position in 1925; "Los obreros sostienen que hubo presión de la policia," *El Mundo*, December 30, 1924, AHT; "Gran Partido Obrero Socialista Tamaulipeco," *El Mundo*, January 2, 1925, AHT; "Huelga de principios: Sindicato Mexicano de Electricistas, División de Tampico: manifiesto al Pueblo Tampiqueño," August 19, 1923, AHT, Fondo: Presidencia, caja 1923 centenario, exp. 'Huelga de electricistas."

12. "Gran Partido Obrero Socialista Tamaulipeco"; "Cual fue la votación total que aparecio," *El Mundo*, January 2, 1925, AHT; "2 Políticos piden amparo al juez de distrito," *El Mundo*, January 1, 1925, AHT; see also Oikón Solano, *Cuca García (1889–1973)*, 198, on repression against communists and the Mexican Communist Party during Portes Gil's administration. Portes Gil also ordered the closing of one of the party's major newspapers—*El Machete*—in Mexico City.

13. Oscar Misael Hernández, "Políticas educativas y formación de identidades culturales en Tamaulipas, 1925–1928."

14. Adelson, "Coyuntura y conciencia," 633. López de Lara served from 1921 to 1923 as governor; Alvarado Mendoza, *El portesgilismo en Tamaulipas*, 28.

15. De la Garza Talavera, *La formación de un cacicazgo regional*, 143; Alvarado Mendoza, *El portesgilismo en Tamaulipas*, 12–13.

16. Alvarado Mendoza, *El portesgilismo en Tamaulipas*, 12–13. It is unclear whether or not there were Catholic groups engaged in labor activism in the region.

17. Quote comes from Oscar Misael Hernández, "Políticas educativas y formación de identidades culturales en Tamaulipas, 1925–1928," 5; Fowler-Salamini, *Working Women, Entrepreneurs, and the Mexican Revolution*, 148. Marriage had been defined as a voluntary union, a "civil contract, not a religious sacrament," and only after the Revolution did civil laws grant liberties including allowing divorced individuals to remarry. Thus, the war helped usher in a wave of civil reforms seeking to eliminate informal unions and promote a morally sound country, what historian Ann Blum calls "public morality." The reforms, which also included divorce, sought to "emancipate women of the middle classes, whose husbands' affairs held them in a condition of slavery." All in all, the civil code reforms proposed by the Revolutionary government were aimed at "disciplining the lower classes and emancipating women." If the Revolution had sparked legislative changes in civil society, then the years following the Revolution worked to consolidate and solidify them but within the context of a modern Mexico. These reforms affected labor policies concerning women workers as well, Blum, *Domestic Economies*, 103–106.

18. *El Cauterio: Semanario Independiente de Combate*, March 31, 1912, IIH-UAT.

19. Alvarado Mendoza, *Tamaulipas*, 19. Portes Gil received his *normalista* degree from Ciudad Victoria in 1910. *El Cauterio: Semanario Independiente de Combate* published in Ciudad Victoria was registered as the "organ of the Student Democratic Association" (Asociación Democrática Estudiantil), founded in 1911. Two years before Carranza initiated a crackdown of radical labor activists, General César López de Lara appointed Portes Gil as subjefe of the department of military justice, Solorio

Martínez, *Grupos de gobierno*, 348, 351; Alvarado Mendoza, *El portesgilismo en Tamaulipas*, 51. Portes Gil was also involved with numerous political projects including cooperative organizations, "Pediran la renuncia de Portes Gil Los Cooperatistas," *El Mundo*, April 4, 1923, AHT; "Ya no es PTE. del Cooperatista el Lic. Emilio Portes Gil," *El Mundo*, April 6, 1923, AHT.

20. For an expanded discussion on the role of Portes Gil in the state's conservative approach to agrarian reform see Alvarado Mendoza, *El portesgilismo en Tamaulipas*, 145.

21. "Federación local de Tampico: Adherida a la Confederación General de Trabajadores a los obreros de la región petrolera," *Sagitario*, December 11, 1924, http://www.antorcha.net/index/hemeroteca/sagitario/2.pdf, accessed January 26, 2017; Caufield, "Wobblies and Mexican Workers in Mining and Petroleum, 1905–1924," 44. Government forces under President Alvaro Obregón ordered the arrest and deportation of key foreign members of the CGT including those from the Tampico branch. The CGT nonetheless pressed on to have a place at the bargaining table, Caufield, "Wobblies and Mexican Workers in Mining and Petroleum, 1905–1924," 44, 62.

22. Alcayaga Sasso, "Librado Rivera y Los Hermanos Rojos," 161.

23. On the local teachers' union strike see various articles dedicated to these developments in *Sagitario*, 1924 issues, ALR-HR; "El Frente Unico en Tampico," *El Machete*, first two weeks of June, 1924, CEMOS; "El conflicto de El Aguila en Tampico," *El Machete*, first two weeks of June, 1924, CEMOS; "Sigue en pie la huelga de el Aguila," *El Machete*, last two weeks of June, 1924, CEMOS; see also Herr, "*El Machete* sirve para cortar la caña."

24. "La moralización de la mujer," *Via Libre* (Tampico), January 4, 1925, AHT. *Vía Libre* was a CGT-sponsored newspaper and one that was read and supported by FOT members, according to its list of monetary contributors.

25. Alcayaga Sasso, "Librado Rivera y Los Hermanos Rojos," 161.

26. Goldsmith, "De combativas a conformistas," 145–146. Goldsmith writes that the UERS did not support the domestic workers as it viewed them "as inferior."

27. "Ecos de la huelga decretada en contra del Café Louisiana: El rebelde propietario, doblego ante la justicia," and "La moralización de la mujer," *Via Libre* (Tampico), January 4, 1925, 1–2, AHT.

28. "Por la CGT," and "Aclaracion," *Sagitario*, October 11, 1924, http://www.antorcha.net/index/hemeroteca/sagitario/2.pdf, accessed April 26, 2017; other issues from *Sagitario* are from the AHEMG.

29. "Segundo Congreso de la CGT (1922)," Baena Paz, *La Confederación General de Trabajadores, 1921–1931*, 44.

30. Ibid.

31. "Reglamento a que deben sujetarse las Meseras que prestan sus servicios en las Cantinas, Cafés, Restaurants y demás Establecimientos similares en el Puerto," Ayuntamiento de Tampico, en sesión celebrada el 1° de los Corrientes, July 1924, AHT.

32. "Reglamento a que deben sujetarse las Meseras," 6th Clause.

33. Bliss, *Compromised Positions*.

34. Cocks, "Rethinking Sexuality in the Progressive Era," 103; for Mexico and Latin America more broadly, see Bliss, *Compromised Positions*; see also Guy, *Sex and Danger in Buenos Aires.*

35. Santiago, "Women of the Mexican Oil Fields," 88.

36. "Proyecto de Reglamento para el ejercicio de la prostitución en la Municipalidad de Tampico," April 20, 1927, AHT, Fondo: Presidencia, caja 1928 (1925–1928) #1, exp. "Oficio girado para ejercer la prostitución," 1927; Bliss, *Compromised Positions.*

37. "Reglamento a que deben sujetarse las Meseras," 7th Clause.

38. To Medical Inspector, from Presidente Municipal, asunto de prostitución clandestina, September 1, 1924, Presidencia, Caja 1924, caja 1, AHT.

39. To Medical Inspector, from Presidente Municipal, asunto actos inmorales, September 1, 1924, Presidencia, Caja 1924, caja 1, AHT. There was great concern about women who practiced prostitution outside of marked zones. Official reports grossly underreported numbers of prostitutes, as evident from records in the AHT; see also Santiago, "Women of the Mexican Oil Fields," 97.

40. "Reglamento a que deben sujetarse las Meseras," 7th, 8th, 9th Clauses.

41. "Las mujeres deben igualarse a los hombres en sus derechos políticos," *El Mundo*, July 10, 1925, 1.

42. Olcott, *Revolutionary Women in Post-Revolutionary Mexico*, 205. It is important to point out that states that have been historically cast as progressive or pro-women, as in the case of Yucatán need to be further complicated in order to deconstruct what were considered prowomen reforms. At the end "Yucatecan women achieved limited concrete gains, but their direct political action and indirect means of negotiation laid the groundwork for the possibility of women's increased opportunities in the years to come." Stephanie Smith, *Gender and the Mexican Revolution*, 50–51, 178–179.

43. Porter, "Working Women in the Mexican Revolution." An earlier conference had also taken place in 1919 in Mexico City, Porter, *Working Women in Mexico City*, 112; see also Piedad Peniche Rivero, "Los Congresos Feministas de 1916." In 1923 women from different parts of the Americas congregated in the Pan American Women's Congress in Mexico City, Olcott, *Revolutionary Women in Post-Revolutionary Mexico*, 39–40.

44. "Las mujeres deben igualarse a los hombres en sus derechos políticos," *El Mundo*, July 10, 1925, 1. Just two years prior to the formation of the *meseras libres* movement, the Pan-American Women's Congress had taken place, attended by Carrillo Puerto, María Sandoval, and like-minded activists María del Refugio "Cuca" García and Elena Torres, both members of the Partido Mexicano Comunista, Peniche Rivero, "Los Congresos Feministas de 1916," 206.

45. "Pleito de comadres," *Sagitario*, November 1, 1924, ALR-HR.

46. Ibid.

47. "En pro de la mujer mexicana," *La Opinión*, May 23, 1924, 3.

48. Ibid.

49. "De Tampa E.U.A.," *El Machete*, 1924, October 30–November 6, 1924, CEMOS.

50. "Por qué las 'Compañeras' Meseras, cansadas del sindicalismo rompen sus compromisos y se contratan independientemente," *El Mundo*, January 11, 1925, AHT.

While little is known about Carmen Aranda and her nickname "Pellandini," we know that the Pellandini family were leading glass dealers in Mexico in the early twentieth century and had a manufacturing site in Tampico.

51. "Por qué las 'Compañeras' Meseras, cansadas del sindicalismo rompen sus compromisos y se contratan independientemente."

52. Rubenstein, "The War on *Las Pelonas*," 58; Rubenstein's reference to the "long limbs" comes from historian Ageeth Sluis's description of a type of "Deco body" which "encompassed a new ideal for women's bodies and women's ways of moving." The Deco body emphasized "long, thin limbs and torsos, short hair, and vigorous (but graceful) physicality."

53. "Por qué las 'Compañeras' Meseras, cansadas del sindicalismo."

54. "La mesera," lyrics by Esteban Navarette, interpreted by Los Alegres de Terán from Nuevo León, among other musical bands.

55. "Por qué las 'Compañeras' Meseras, cansadas del sindicalismo."

56. "Mesa directive de la Sociedad Mutualista 'Hermanos del Trabajo' (1923)," Albúm Centenario de Tampico, April 12, 1823–1923 (México: Tampico, 1923), 7.

57. "El unionismo se intensifica," *Sagitario*, November 1, 1924, ALR-HR.

58. "Las meseras, cansadas ya del sindicato se separan de él y se contratan independientemente," *El Mundo* (Tampico), January 7, 1925, AHT.

59. "Proyecto de Reglamento para el ejercisio de la Prostitución," To Secretario de la Sala de Comisiones del Ayuntamiento, from Presidencia Municipal en consulta del Departamento de Salubridad, August 12, 1927, Fondo: Presidencia, caja 1928 (1925–1928), #1, exp. "Oficio girado . . . para ejercer la prostitución, reglamento, 1927," AHT.

60. "Informe de Trabajo que rinden ante la Presidencia Municipal" submitted by the Consejo de Higiene del Estado de Tamaulipas, Delegación Secretaría, Dr. Enrique García, December 8, 1931, Presidencia, Caja 1931 (caja 1), AHT.

61. Porter, *Working Women in Mexico City*, 114.

62. Ibid., 115. Porter found that in Mexico City waitresses were also subcontracted and thereby did not receive steady wages. Some of the waitresses in Tampico had agreed to verbal contracts, particularly in smaller establishments or those not defined as "first-class restaurants"; see also "A ultima hora: Aviso importante," *La Mujer: Periódico Bi-mensual de Propaganda Feminista*, January 12, 1920, CEMOS, exp. 10, regarding meetings held by waitresses in Mexico City.

63. See issues of *Sagitario* published in 1924, ALR-HR.

64. "Ecos de la huelga decretada en contra del Café Louisiana: El rebelde propietario, doblego ante la justicia," *Via Libre* (Tampico), January 4, 1925, 1–2, AHT; "La moralización de la mujer," *Via Libre* (Tampico), January 4, 1925, 1–2, AHT.

65. There is little evidence of other all-female union members' opting for a mutual aid collective instead of a labor union. There was however, a long tradition of *mutualistas* since the mid-nineteenth century. Some of these *mutualistas* remained in operation in spite of the legalization of unions forming part of the larger collective efforts to improve working and living conditions. With labor protections as one of its goals, the Sociedad Mutualista "Hermanos del Trabajo," founded in 1900, for

example, remained in operation during the 1920s and did not transition/apply for labor union status.

66. The Sindicato de Empleados de Restaurantes participated in a street demonstration in the summer of 1925, "Manifestación del 21 de junio," *Sagitario*, July 9, 1925, ALR-HR. The Sindicato continued activities well into the 1930s, see for example, To Presidente Municipal, Tampico, from Sindicato de Empleados de Restaurantes, April 28, 1931, caja 1928 (1) exp. "Permisos autorizados manifestación primero de mayo," AHT.

67. To Emilio Portes Gil, from Ismael Martínez representing the Unión de Empleados de Restaurants y Similares, February 16, 1930, AHPEPG, AGN, caja 19, exp. "Agrupaciones." The UERS activities were still covered in communist-leaning media outlets in Mexico City. "Pequeñas notas de la Confederación Sindical Unitaria," *Bandera Roja*, no. 4, September 30, 1929, CEMOS.

68. Fowler-Salamini, "De-centering the 1920s," 288–289.

69. To Presidente Municipal, from Presidente del Partido Anti-Reeleccionista in report to Presidente Municipal submitted by Zeferino Fajardo, Secretaría General de Gobernación y Justicia (Cd. Victoria), October 31, 1929, Presidencia, caja 1931 (caja 1), AHT.

70. To Zeferino Fajardo, Secretaría General de Gobernación y Justicia, from Presidente Municipal de Tampico, November 4, 1929, Presidencia, caja 1931 (caja 1), AHT.

71. To Presidente Municipal, Tampico, from Zeferino Fajardo, Secretaría General de Gobernación y Justicia (Cd. Victoria) on behalf of the Partido Anti-reelecionista, October 31, 1929, Presidencia, caja 1931 (caja 1), AHT; To Presidente Municipal, Tampico, from Ciro Sandoval, President of the Partido Anti-reelecionista, November 3, 1929, Presidencia, caja 1931 (caja 1), AHT.

72. Joaquin Cárdenas Noriega, "José Vasconcelos: Caudillo cultural," http://univas .mx/v1/pdf/biojosevasc.pdf, accessed November 17, 2015.

73. "Gran número de mujeres formó en ese desfile," *El Mundo* (Tampico), September 29, 1929, AHT.

74. Ibid.

75. Ibid.

76. Alcayaga Sasso, "Librado Rivera y Los Hermanos Rojos," 283.

77. To Presidente Municipal, Tampico, from Inspector de la Policía, September 10, 1929, AHT, caja 1929, caja 1, expediente "Correspondencia para realizar manifestaciones."

78. Alcayaga Sasso, "Librado Rivera y Los Hermanos Rojos," 283; *Vasconcelista* supporters, women and men, throughout the country were suppressed, jailed, and intimidated as they approached voting sites, Alvarado Mendoza, *El portesgilismo en Tamaulipas*, 68.

79. Skirius, *Jose Vasconcelos y la cruzada de 1929*.

80. "La huelga de la huasteca," *Sagitario*, July 9, 1925, ALR-HR.

Chapter 6. A Last Stand for Anarcho-Feminists in the Post-1920 Period

The chapter epigraph is from Felipa Velásquez, "En las Islas Marías," *¡Paso!*, January 1932, http://www.antorcha.net/index/hemeroteca/paso/9.pdf, accessed April 27, 2017. Original is as follows: "Aquí termino mis versos para entrar en reflexión, devanándome los sesos buscando la solución. ¿Cual ha sido la intención que para corregir el mal se impone la inquisición?"

1. "Convocatoria del 30 de abril de 1924 para la Fundación del PSF," as printed in appendix 1, in De la Garza Talavera, *La formación de un cacicazgo regional*, 133–134.

2. "Discurso inaugural pronunciado por Emilio Portes Gil en la convención fundadora del PSF," as printed in appendix 2, in De la Garza Talavera, *La formación de un cacicazgo regional*, 137; Carr, *Marxism and Communism in Twentieth-Century Mexico*.

3. Solorio Martínez, *Grupos de gobierno*, 56–57.

4. In Alfaro's and González's cases, they had demonstrated their political loyalty since the early days of the dockworkers' union. See, for example, among other evidentiary documents, correspondence between Portes Gil and his colleague (and later political opponent) Luis Ramírez de Alba, April 6, 1922, April 17, 1922, AHEPG.

5. "Discurso inaugural pronunciado por Emilio Portes Gil en la convención fundadora del PSF," as printed in appendix 2, De la Garza Talavera, *La formación de un cacicazgo regional*, 135.

6. Ibid., 137. Other state-level socialist political organizations and/or parties, like the PSF, emerged across the country and also contributed to formation of the PRI, see Fowler-Salamini, "De-centering the 1920s," on Veracruz; and Oikión Solano, *Cuca García (1889–1973)*, on Michoacán.

7. "Cooperación en el campo," *El Surco*, August 1, 1925, NLB; there is one document from the AHT that indicates Piña's perhaps brief involvement in a peasant league, Liga de Poseedores, Villa Cecilia.

8. "Nuevos ejidos," *El Surco*, May 15 1926, NLB.

9. "Las construciones en el campo," *El Surco*, August 1, 1925, NLB.

10. Ibid.

11. "Se necesita hacer de la mujer campesina, la mujer que necesita el agricultor," in "Página para la mujer campesina," *El Surco*, August 1, 1925, NLB.

12. Ibid.

13. Schoenalls, "Mexico Experiments," 29.

14. See also other commentaries exemplifying the state's role in promoting such gender inequality within the context of forging a new nation: "El aseo de la casa," "A la mujer del campo," and "La alimentación," in "Pagina para la mujer campesina," *El Surco*, July 15, 1925; on the modernization of gender inequality see Besse, *Restructuring Patriarchy*.

15. "Manifiesto al Pueblo de Ciudad Madero," from Reveriano Salazar and Santa Ana Cardoso, Presidente en funciones del comite municipal and secretario general

int., respectively, Cd. Madero, February 17, 1932, AHT; Porter, *Working Women in Mexico City*, 184–185.

16. To Secretario de Relaciones Exteriores (Mexico City), from Marte R. Gomez, Legación de los Estados Mexicanos en Francia (Paris), May 28, 1935, SRE, caja 3, #233-8. The report submitted as a response to the University of Paris's request was entitled "Situación Jurídica y Social de la Mujer en la Sociedad Mexicana Contemporanea." On Gomez's background see Ana Garduño, "Marte R. Gomez: ¿El Colecionista de la Revolución?," http://www.academia.edu/10942503/, 466, accessed May 10, 2017.

17. To Secretario de Relaciones Exteriores (Mexico City), from Marte R. Gomez.

18. Ibid., page 2 of report, "Situación Juridica y Social de la Mujer en la Sociedad Mexicana Contemporánea."

19. Ibid.

20. Ibid., 4–6.

21. The original Spanish text reads, "ya era un hecho, la igual capacidad jurídica del hombre y de la mujer."

22. Ibid., 7.

23. "Situación Jurídica y Social de la Mujer en la Sociedad Mexicana Contemporanea," 8; the original reads, "En la actualidad la mujer Mexicana trabaja al igual que el hombre . . . , y no es ya la eternal tutoreada del marido, el ser sin voluntad y sin conciencia propia, que perecia condenada a una clausura perpetua, a ser la sierva del hogar."

24. Olcott, *Revolutionary Women in Post-Revolutionary Mexico*, 173.

25. Ibid., 111.

26. Ibid.; the reference on María Refugio "Cuca" García comes from the excellent work by Oikión Solano, *Cuca García (1889–1973)*.

27. "Liga Femenil Pro Derechos de la Mujer de Tampico y Ciudad Madero, sección del Frente Único Pro Derechos de la Mujer" was adhered to the Federación de Trabajadores de Tamaulipas and eventually became part of the CTM. It was established in 1936 with twenty members. In 1938, the women's section of the Partido de la Revolución Mexicana's (PRM) Sector Popular Femenil was created and thus this earlier league was eliminated, Goldsmith, "De combativas a conformistas," 163. Correspondence in the AHEMG points to communication between anarcho-syndicalist organizations in Tampico and those with communist affiliations.

28. Cano, "Sufragio femenino en el México Posrevolucionario," 40; Oikión Solano, *Cuca García (1889–1973)*; Cuca García was the administrator of La Mujer (Mexico City), January 29, 1920, CEMOS, exp. 10.

29. Olcott, *Revolutionary Women in Post-Revolutionary Mexico*, 173; see also Tuñón Pablos, "Tres momentos claves del movimiento sufragista en México (1917–1953)"; *The Women's Revolution in Mexico, 1910–1953*, 82–84; Oikión Solano, "El Frente Único Pro Derechos de la Mujer de Cara al debate constitucional y en la esfera pública en torno de la ciudadanía de las Mujeres, 1935–1940," 113.

30. As historian Jeffrey Bortz has explained, the industrial labor force from distinct ideological backgrounds "joined the peasant rebellion early, grew stronger through

the years of violent revolution, and continued to challenge authority" during these two decades, "The Genesis of the Mexican Labor Relations System," 44. Collaboration among various groups had also taken place the previous decade particularly among IWW locals and the PCM, see, for example, "La labor de la I.W.W. en México," *El Comunista de México*, June 1920, CEMOS, PCM, caja 1, exp.3; To Executive Bureau of the Third International, Moscow, Russia, from José Refugio Rodríguez, Mexican Administration of I.W.W., July 24, 1920, CEMOS, PCM, caja 1, exp. 4.

31. Gerardo Peláez Ramos, "Valentín Campa Salazar, dirigente obrero comunista," n.d., https://www.lahaine.org/b2-img11/pelaez_campa.pdf, accessed September 1, 2019; on Portes Gil's intent to limit FUPDM activity see Olcott, *Revolutionary Women in Postrevolutionary Mexico*, 171.

32. Lawrence D. Taylor, "Tightening the Reins of Control over the Country's Borders," 102–103. Portes Gil and other political leaders had created Ligas Campesinas as a way to reform the countryside and assist in the larger educational program, see, for example, on the Ligas Campesinas de Mejoramiento in Sonora during the 1930s, Bonfil, *La revolución agraria y la educación en México*, 178–179, BPCMRG; for Portes Gil see chapter 6 in Alvarado Mendoza, *El portesgilismo en Tamaulipas*.

33. To Secretario de Relaciones Exteriores, Mexico City, from F. Roel, Consul General de México, New York City, January 22, 1923, SRE, asunto: Liga Inter. de Mujeres Ibéricas e Hispano Americanas, caja 18-5-274 # 40881; Olcott, *Revolutionary Women in Post-Revolutionary Mexico*, 165.

34. To Secretario de Relaciones Exteriores, Mexico City, from F. Roel, Consul General de México, New York City, January 22, 1923, Archivo de la Secretaría de Relaciones Exteriores, SRE, asunto: Liga Inter. de Mujeres Ibéricas e Hispano Americanas, caja 18-5-274 # 40881.

35. See Marino, "Marta Vergara, Popular-Front Pan-American Feminism, and the Transnational Struggle for Working Women's Rights in the 1930s."

36. To F. Roel, from Elena Arizmendi, New York City, January 16, 1923, SRE, Asunto: Liga Inter. de Mujeres Ibéricas e Hispano Americanas, caja 18-5-274 # 40881.

37. To Secretario de Relaciones Exteriores, Mexico City, from Representative of the Mexican Embassy, New York City, February 27, 1923, SRE, Asunto: Liga Inter. de Mujeres Ibéricas e Hispano Americanas, caja 18-5-274 # 40881.

38. Shaffer, "Havana Hub," 47.

39. To "Grupo Libertario Sacco y Vanzetti," from Caritina Piña, July 6, 1929, AHEMG, IIH-UAT; Marino, "Transnational Pan-American Feminism"; see also Threlkeld, *Pan American Women*.

40. To F. Roel, from Elena Arizmendi, New York City, January 16, 1923, SRE, Asunto: Liga Inter. de Mujeres Ibéricas e Hispano Americanas, caja 18-5-274 # 40881; To Secretario de Relaciones Exteriores, Mexico City, from Representative of the Mexican Embassy, New York City, February 27, 1923, SRE, Asunto: Liga Inter. de Mujeres Ibéricas e Hispano Americanas, caja 18-5-274 # 40881.

41. Marsh, "The Anarchist-Feminist Response to the 'Woman Question' in Late Nineteenth-Century America," 539.

42. Alcayaga Sossa, "Librado Rivera y Los Hermanos Rojos," 159. Detailed information about the CGT as quoted in Alcayaga Sassa comes from Baena Paz, *La Confederación General de Trabajadores, 1921–1931.*

43. Shaffer, "Havana Hub," 74. As Shaffer explains, anarcho-syndicalists were "internationalist" not only in the way they envisioned the movement but also in the way "they migrated between countries."

44. "Acta num 37 del PSF" celebrada por el sub-comité num. 22 del Partido Socialista Fronterizo, October 21, 1931, AHT, Presidencia caja 1931 (caja 1), expediente: PSF Comité Municipal, 1931.

45. I thank Thomas Alter for providing me a copy of a Bureau of Investigation report that outlines some of Hernández's activities in Texas and in Mexico; see also Alter's article "From the Copper-Colored Sons of Montezuma to Comrade Pancho Villa." Ricardo Treviño too had participated in party politics running for the Partido Laborista, the region's Labor Party.

46. Solorio Martínez, *Grupos de gobierno*, 39.

47. Fowler-Salamini, *Working Women, Entrepreneurs, and the Mexican Revolution*, 290–292; Olcott, *Revolutionary Women in Post-Revolutionary Mexico*, 39.

48. To Oficial Mayor de la Secretaría de Gobernación, from Pedro Medina, Tesorero General del Estado de Tamaulipas, October 5, 1928, AGN, AHEPG, caja 23, exp. 7; "Proyecto de Contrato que Celebran Compañía Constructora de Mejoras Materiales, S.A. (represented by Sherman D. Baker and Bartolo Rodríguez, Jr.)," October 5, 1928, AGN, AHEPG, caja 23, exp. 7.

49. "Nuevos Grupos," *¡Paso!,* January 1932, http://www.antorcha.net/index/hemeroteca/paso/9.pdf, accessed April 27, 2017.

50. "Comisión Permanente Pro Unidad Obrera y Campesina," September 4, 1934, caja 6, exp. 14, CEMOS.

51. Ibid.

52. To Lázaro Cárdenas, from Liga de Choferes, Sindicato Empleados Obreros Oficios Varios Cía. Aguila, Gremio Unido Trabajadores Región Petrolera, Sindicato Huasteco Mata Redonda, July 8, 1935, AGN, AHEPG, caja 63, exp. T-C.

53. Lawrence D. Taylor, "Tightening the Reins of Control," 104; Portes Gil in great part was successful because he was able to control southern Tamaulipas (centered in Tula), which had a long history of agrarian activism. In 1924, Portes Gil convinced Gen. Francisco S. Carrera (from the Carrera-Torres family of agrarian activists during the Revolution) to not run for the governorship and support "the Calles-Portes Gil electoral alliance," Alvarado Mendoza, *El portesgilismo en Tamaulipas*, 156. By the end of his presidency, Cárdenas had redistributed over 45 million acres to millions of peasants from across the country. While the "Ejido Islas Agrarias" stood as an example of what could be accomplished with persistence, it was clear that this could not be accomplished without the intervention of Cárdenas, Kerig, "Yankee Enclave"; Lawrence D. Taylor, "Tightening the Reins of Control," 106–110.

54. Alcayaga Sasso, "Librado Rivera y Los Hermanos Rojos," 336.

55. Ibid., 157, 330.

56. Baena Paz, *La Confederación General de Trabajadores, 1921–1931*, 6.

Chapter 7. Finding Closure

1. "'Edicto,' Juzgado de Primera Instancia Mixto, Octavo Distrito Judicial," Xicotén-catl, Tamaulipas, as published in the *Periodico oficial: Organo del gobierno constitucional del estado libre y soberano de Tamaulipas* (Cd. Victoria, October 8, 2009), 5.

2. "Adela Piña Galván," 1930 Mexican Census, Tampico. Caritina's half-sister, Piña Galván (her married name), later became an important figure in the history of south-ern Tamaulipas. She became a schoolteacher and dedicated her life to the recovery of archeological artifacts. The bulk of her findings now form part of a collection on Huastecan life housed in a museum bearing her name in Mante, Tamaulipas.

3. Ocampo remained a small picturesque town, whose population never reached more than 14,000.

4. "Acta de Matrimonio Civil entre Caritina Piña y Gregorio Ortiz," February 14, 1937, I thank Huerta Márquez for providing a copy of the marriage certificate which also appears in his magazine article, "Inició la lucha del feminismo Caritina Piña."

5. Huerta Márquez, "Inició la lucha del feminismo Caritina Piña."

6. Morett Sánchez, *Reforma agraria*, 102.

7. According to an interview with Méndez Guerra's daughter conducted by the historian Mónica Alcayaga Sasso, Méndez Guerra "suffered an accident" and died on January 10 of that year, as quoted in Alcayaga Sasso, "Librado Rivera y Los Hermanos Rojos," 21.

8. "Un grupo de hombres que le seguían y obedecían," Enrique Estrada Barrera, "El asalto a las tierras," *El Mexicano*, January 28, 2008, http://www.periodistasenlinea.org/28-01-2008/14531, accessed April 27, 2017.

9. Felipa Velásquez, "Convocatoria a la mujer," *¡Avante!*, July 1, 1928, AHEMG.

10. "Felipa Velásquez Viuda de Arrellano," Baja California Instituto de Cultura de Baja California, Biblioteca Virtual, http://www.bibliotecavirtualbc.gob.mx/img/pdf-enciclopedia/parte8_v-z.pdf, 665–66, accessed December 2, 2014. In 1936, another land seizure took place led by Concha Michel, a Mexican Communist Party member, see Olcott, *Revolutionary Women in Post-Revolutionary Mexico*, 1–4. In 1937, President Lázaro Cárdenas revoked the US land company's concession.

11. While Taylor does not discuss Velásquez's efforts he provides a good context as to the internal issue surrounding Cárdenas's agrarian efforts on the ground, Law-rence D. Taylor, "Tightening the Reins of Control over the Country's Borders," 104.

12. In an interview with one of Aurelia's colleagues from the CGT, the former union member shared the tragic story of Aurelia's suicide and is quoted in Alcayaga Sasso, "Librado Rivera y Los Hermanos Rojos."

13. As Olvera Rivera points out for the case of the Poza Rica oil workers, while the CTM had become a dominating force within the state aparatus by the 1940s, the Poza

Rica workers were among the last of the organized workers to submit to government control—until the 1950s, "Identity, Culture, and Workers' Autonomy," 134–136.

14. Adelson, "Coyuntura y conciencia," 634–635; Olvera Rivera, "Identity, Culture, and Workers' Autonomy," 127.

15. Marsh, "The Anarchist-Feminist Response to the 'Woman Question' in Late-Nineteenth-Century America," 546–547.

16. Caso del Sindicato de Obreras de la Fábrica de Camisas "La Palma," November 12, 1934, Archivo General del Estado de Nuevo León, JLCA, caja 34, exp. 8.

17. Lau Jaiven, "Lo personal es también político y el feminismo," 11.

18. Kaplan, "Final Reflections," 262.

19. Staudt and Aguilar, "Political Parties, Women Activists' Agendas, and Household Relations," 90.

20. "Acta de defunción de Caritina Piña," August 23, 1981, Reynosa, Tamaulipas, México, #498, APMOH.

Bibliography

Archives

MEXICO

Acervo Histórico Diplomático, México, Secretaría de Relaciones Exteriores
    Archivo Histórico Genaro Estrada
    Biblioteca José María Lafragua. Fondo Reservado
Archivo General de la Nación (AGN), Mexico City
    Archivo Histórico Particular de Emilio Portes (AHPEPG)
    Fondo Dirección General de Gobierno (DGG). Series: Fomento; Sindicatos y Agrupaciones; Petroleros Transitorios
    Fondo Francisco I. Madero
    Fondo Magonistas Revoltosos
Archivo General del Estado de Nuevo León. Fondo Trabajo
    Asunto: Asociaciones, Organizaciones, y Sindicatos
    Asunto: Junta Local de Conciliación y Arbitraje
Archivo General del Estado de Tamaulipas (AGET)
    Fondo Anuarios Estadísticos del Estado de Tamaulipas
    Fondo Junta Central de Conciliación y Arbitraje. Sección: Demandas; Sección: Datos Estadísticos
Archivo Histórico de Tampico Carlos González Salas (AHT). Fondos: Presidencia; Tesorería; Justicia
Archivo Histórico Municipal de Ciudad Madero (formerly Villa Cecilia)
Archivo Librado Rivera y Los Hermanos Rojos, www.libradorivera.com (ALR-HR)

Archivo Personal de Juan Jaime Llarena, Ocampo, Tamaulipas
Archivo Personal de Marvin Osiris Huerta, Antiguo Morelos, Tamaulipas
Biblioteca Pública Central Ing. Marte R. Gómez (BPCMRG), Ciudad Victoria, Tamaulipas
Centro de Estudios de los Movimientos Obreros Sociales (CEMOS)
Instituto de Investigaciones Dr. José María Luis Mora, Mexico City. Biblioteca Ernesto de la Torre Villar
Instituto Nacional de Antropología e Historia
   Archivo Digital Ricardo Flores Magón (ARFM), archivomagon.net
   Archivo Fotográfico
Universidad Autónoma de México (UNAM). Hemeroteca Nacional y Biblioteca Nacional
Universidad Autónoma de Tamaulipas. Instituto de Investigaciones Históricas (IIH-UAT)
   Archivo Histórico Fondo Esteban Méndez Guerra (AHEMG)
   Hemeroteca Histórica

UNITED STATES

Library of Congress, Washington, DC
National Archives and Records Administration (NARA), Washington, DC. State Department Record Group 59
New York Public Library (NYPL)
Occidental College, Los Angeles, CA. E. L. Doheny Research Foundation (EDRF) Library
Tamiment Library. Robert Wagner Labor Archives
Texas A&M International, Laredo. Special Collections, Sue & Radcliffe Killam Library (SRKL)
Texas A&M University, College Station. Hispanic American Historical Newspapers
University of Houston. Consular Dispatches, United States, Record Group 885. Recovering Hispanic Heritage Online Collection
University of Texas, Austin. Nettie Lee Benson Latin American Library (NLB). Center for American History
University of Texas–Pan American, Edinburg. Lower Rio Grande Valley Historical Collection

EUROPE

Archivo Histórico Nacional de España, Madrid, Spain
Archivo Municipal de Barcelona, Spain
Biblioteca de Catalunya (BC), Barcelona, Spain
Biblioteca Nacional de España, Madrid, Spain
International Institute of Social History, Amsterdam, The Netherlands. Photographic Collection, Tampico

Newspapers

VILLA CECILIA

Avante
Germinal
El Preso Social
Sagitario
¡Paso!

TAMPICO

El Mundo
La Opinión: Diario Periódico Pólitico de la Mañana
El Porvenir
El Sol de Tampico
Tribuna Roja
Vía Libre

CIUDAD VICTORIA

El Cauterio
El Surco

MONTERREY

Avante
El Regiomontano
El Triunfo

MEXICO CITY

Bandera Roja
Fuerza y Cerebro
¡Luz! Semanario Libertario, doctrinario y de protesta
El Machete
La Mujer: Periódico Bi-mensual de Propaganda Feminista

ORIZABA, VERACRUZ

Revolución Social

ZACATECAS

Alma Obrera: Quincenal de propaganda sindicalista, Órgano del grupo sindicalista "Alma Obrera"

UNITED STATES

Dallas Morning News (Dallas, TX)
Diogenes (McAllen, TX)
Labor Defender (Charlotte, NC)

La Prensa (San Antonio, TX)
Regeneración (Los Angeles)
Revolución (Los Angeles)

BARCELONA, SPAIN

El Gladiador
Páginas Libres
El Productor
Tierra y Libertad

Secondary Sources

Acosta-Belén, Edna, and Christine E. Bose. "U.S. Latina and Latin American Feminisms: Hemispheric Encounters." *Signs* 25, no. 4, "Feminisms at a Millennium" (Summer 2000): 1113–1119.

Adelson, Leif. "Coyuntura y conciencia: Factores convergentes en la fundación de los sindicatos petroleros de Tampico durante la década de 1920." In *El trabajo y los trabajadores en la historia de México*, edited by Elsa Cecilia Frost, Michael C. Meyer, and Josefina Zoraida Vazquez, 632–660. Mexico City: El Colegio de México; Tucson: University of Arizona Press, 1979.

———. "Historia social de los obreros industriales de Tampico, 1906–1919." PhD diss., El Colegio de México, 1982.

Agostoni, Claudia. "Médicos rurales y brigadas de vacunación en la lucha contra la viruela en el México posrevolucionario, 1920–1940." *Canadian Journal of Latin American and Caribbean Studies* 35, no. 69 (2010): 67–91.

Aguilar, Kevin Antonio. "The IWW in Tampico: Anarchism, Internationalism, and Solidarity Unionism in a Mexican Port." In *Wobblies of the World: A Global History of the IWW*, edited by Peter Cole, David Struthers, and Kenyon Zimmer, 124–139. London: Pluto Press, 2017.

———. "Peripheries of Power, Centers of Resistance: Anarchist Movements in Tampico and the Huasteca Region, 1910–1945." MA thesis, University of California–San Diego, 2014.

Alanis de Salazar, María Antonia. *En el Tampico: Relatos*. Tampico: n.p., 1981.

Alcayaga Sasso, Aurora Mónica. "Librado Rivera y Los Hermanos Rojos en el movimiento social y cultural anarquista en Villa Cecilia y Tampico, Tamaulipas, 1915–1932." PhD diss., Universidad Iberoamericana, 2006.

Alter, Thomas. "From the Copper-Colored Sons of Montezuma to Comrade Pancho Villa: The Radicalizing Effect of Mexican Revolutionaries on the Texas Socialist Party, 1910–1917." *Labor: Studies in Working-Class Histories of the Americas* 12, no. 4 (2015): 83–109.

Alvarado Mendoza, Arturo. *El portesgilismo en Tamaulipas*. Mexico City: Colegio de México, 1992.

———. *Tamaulipas: Sociedad, economía, política y cultura*. Mexico City: UNAM, 2004.

Andrés, Benny. *Power and Control in the Imperial Valley*. College Station: Texas A&M University Press, 2015.

Anzaldúa, Gloria. *Borderlands/La Frontera: The New Mestiza*. San Francisco: Aunt Lute, 1987.

Anzaldúa, Gloria, and Cherríe Moraga, eds. *This Bridge Called My Back: Writings by Radical Women of Color*. Latham, MD, and New York: Kitchen Table/Women of Color Press, 1983.

Avrich, Paul. *Anarchist Voices: An Oral History of Anarchism in America*. Oakland, CA: AK Press, 2005.

———. *The Russian Anarchists*. 1967. Reprint, Oakland, CA: AK Press, 2005.

Baena Paz, Guillermina. *La Confederación General de Trabajadores, 1921–1931: Antología*. 1982. Reprint. Mexico City: Ediciones HL, 2006.

Baer, James A. *Anarchist Immigrants in Spain and Argentina*. Urbana: University of Illinois Press, 2015.

Bartra, Armando, ed. *Regeneración 1900–1918: La corriente más radical de la Revolución de 1910 a través de su periódico de combate*. Mexico City: Hadise, 1972.

Bayly, C. A., Sven Beckert, Matthew Connelly, Isabel Hofmeyr, Wendy Kozol, and Patricia Seed. "AHR Conversation: On Transnational History." *American Historical Review* 111, no. 5 (December 2006): 1441–1464.

Bennett, Vivienne. "Gender, Class, and Water: Women and the Politics of Water Service in Monterrey, Mexico." *Latin American Perspectives* 22, no. 22, "Women in Latin America" (Spring 1995): 76–99.

Berg, Allison. *Mothering the Race: Women's Narratives of Reproduction, 1890-1930*. Urbana: University of Illinois Press, 2001.

Berkman, Alexander. *What Is Anarchism?* 1929. Reprint. Oakland, CA: AK Press, 2003.

Besse, Susan K. *Restructuring Patriarchy: The Modernization of Gender Inequality in Brazil, 1914–1940*. Chapel Hill: University of North Carolina Press, 1996.

Blackwell, Maylei. *¡Chicana Power! Contested Histories of Feminism in the Chicano Movement*. Austin: University of Texas Press, 2011.

Blanton, Carlos, ed. *A Promising Problem: The New Chicana/o History of the Twenty-First Century*. Austin: University of Texas Press, 2016.

Bliss, Katherine E. *Compromised Positions: Prostitution, Public Health, and Gender Politics in Revolutionary Mexico City*. University Park: Penn State University Press, 2010.

Blum, Ann S. *Domestic Economies: Family, Work, and Welfare in Mexico City, 1884–1943*. Lincoln: University of Nebraska Press, 2010.

Bonfil, Ramón G. *La revolución agraria y la educación en México*. Mexico City: Instituto Nacional Indigenista y Consejo Nacional para la Cultura y las Artes, 1992.

Bookchin, Murray. *The Spanish Anarchists: The Heroic Years 1868–1936*. 1977. Reprint. Oakland, CA: AK Press, 2001.

Boris, Eileen, and S. J. Kleinberg. "Mothers and Other Workers: (Re) Conceiving Labor, Maternalism, and the State." *Journal of Women's History* 15, no. 3 (Autumn 2003): 90–117.

Boris, Eileen, and Annelise Orleck. "Feminism and the Labor Movement: A Century of Collaboration and Conflict." *New Labor Forum* 20, no. 1 (Winter 2011): 33–41.

Bortz, Jeffrey. "The Genesis of the Mexican Labor Relations System: Federal Labor Policy and the Textile Industry, 1925–1940." *The Americas* 52, no. 1 (July 1995): 43–69.

Brown, Jonathan. "Domestic Politics and Foreign Investment: British Development of Mexican Petroleum, 1889–1911." *Business History Review* 61, no. 3 (Autumn 1987): 387–416.

———. *Oil and Revolution in Mexico*. Berkeley: University of California Press, 1993.

———, ed. *Workers' Control in Latin America, 1930–1979*. Chapel Hill: University of North Carolina Press, 1997.

Buffington, Robert M. *A Sentimental Education for the Working Man: The Mexico City Penny Press, 1900–1910*. Durham, NC: Duke University Press, 2015.

Calderón, Roberto R., and Emilio Zamora. "Manuela Solis Sager and Emma Tenayuca: A Tribute." In *Chicana Voices: Intersections of Class, Race, and Gender*, edited by Teresa Cordova et al. Albuquerque: University of New Mexico Press, 1990.

Cano, Gabriela. "Sufragio femenino en el México Posrevolucionario." In *La revolución de las mujeres en México*. Mexico City: INEH, 2016.

Cappelletti, Ángel J. *Anarchism in Latin America*. Translated by Gabriel Palmer-Fernán-dez. Chico, CA: AK Press, 2018.

Cárdenas Herrera, Rosario. "Aspecto histórico del municipo." In *Ciudad Madero*. Ayuntamiento de Cd. Madero, Tamps., n.d.

Carr, Barry. "The Casa del Obrero Mundial, Constitutionalism, and the Pact of February 1915." In *El trabajo y los trabajadores en la historia de México*, edited by Elsa Cecilia Frost, Michael C. Meyer, and Josefina Zoraida Vásquez, 603–632. Mexico City: El Colegio de México; Tucson: University of Arizona Press, 1979.

———. *Marxism and Communism in Twentieth-Century Mexico*. Lincoln: University of Nebraska Press, 1992.

———. *El movimiento obrero y la política en México, 1910–1929*. Mexico City: Sep-Setentas, 1976.

Castañeda, Antonia, with Susan H. Armitage, Patricia Hart, and Karen Weathermon, eds. *Gender on the Borderlands: The Frontiers Readers*. Lincoln: University of Nebraska Press, 2007.

Castañeda, Christopher J. "Moving West: Jaime Vidal, Anarchy, and the Mexican Revolution, 1904–1918." In *Writing Revolution: Hispanic Anarchist Print Culture and the United States, 1868–2015*, ed. Christopher J. Castenada and Montse Feu, 121–135. Urbana: University of Illinois Press, 2019.

Castañeda, Christopher J., and Montse Feu, eds. *Writing Revolution: Hispanic Anarchist Print Culture and the United States, 1868–2015*. Urbana: University of Illinois Press, 2019.

Caulfield, Norman. "Wobblies and Mexican Workers in Mining and Petroluem, 1905–1924." *International Review of Social History* 40 (1995): 51–75.

Ceballos Ramírez, Manuel. *Encuentro en la frontera: Mexicanos y norteamericanos en un espacio común*. Mexico City: El Colegio de México, Centro de Estudios Históricos, 2001.

——. "Tamaulipas en el contexto del Noreste Mexicano." *Historia Humanitas* (2013–2014): 49–56.

Cerutti, Mario. *Economía de guerra y poder regional en el siglo XIX*. Monterrey: AGENL, 1983.

Cobble, Dorothy Sue, Linda Gordon, and Astrid Henry, eds. *Feminism Unfinished: A Short Surprising History of American Women's Movements*. New York: Norton, 2014.

Cocks, Catherine. "Rethinking Sexuality in the Progressive Era." *Journal of the Gilded Age and Progressive Era* 5, no. 2 (April 2006): 93–118.

Cole, Peter, David Struthers, and Kenyon Zimmer, eds. *Wobblies of the World: A Global History of the IWW*. London: Pluto Press, 2017.

Cornell, Andrew. *Unruly Equality: U.S. Anarchism in the Twentieth Century*. Berkeley: University of California Press, 2016.

Cotera, Martha P. *Diosa y Hembra: The History and Heritage of Chicanas in the U.S.* Austin: Information Systems Development, 1976.

Cravey, Altha J. *Work in Mexico's Maquiladoras*. Lanham, MD: Rowman and Littlefield, 1998.

Cuadrat, Xavier. *Socialismo y anarquismo en Cataluña 1899–1911: Los orígenes de la CNT*. Madrid: Ediciones de la Revista de Trabajo, Serie historia, 1976.

De Haan, Francisca. "'Tapestries of Contacts': Transnationalizing Women's History." *Journal of Women's History* 26, no. 2 (Summer 2014): 200–208.

De Laforcade, Geoffroy, and Kirwin R. Shaffer, eds. *In Defiance of Boundaries: Anarchism in Latin American History*. Gainesville: University of Florida Press, 2015.

De la Garza Talavera, Rafael. *La formación de un cacicazgo regional: Emilio Portes Gil en Tamaulipas (1924–1929)*. Cd. Victoria: Comisión Organizadora para la Conmemoración en Tamaulipas, 2010.

De León, Arnoldo. *The Tejano Community, 1836–1900*. Dallas: Southern Methodist University Press, 1997.

——, ed. *War along the Border: The Mexican Revolution and the Tejano Communities*. College Station: Texas A&M University Press, 2012.

Díaz Cárdenas, León. *Cananea: Primer brote del sindicalismo en México*. 3rd ed. Mexico City: Departamento de Bibliotecas de la Sec. de Educación, 1935.

Dicochea, Perlita R. "Chicana Critical Rhetoric: Recrafting La Causa in Chicana Movement Discourse, 1970–1979." *Frontiers: A Journal of Women Studies* 25, no. 1 (2004): 77–92.

Dore, Elizabeth, and Maxine Molyneux, eds. *Hidden Histories of Gender and the State in Latin America*. Durham, NC: Duke University Press, 2000.

Dwyer, John J. *The Agrarian Dispute: The Expropriation of American-Owned Rural Land in Postrevolutionary Mexico*. Durham, NC: Duke University Press, 2008.

Elenes, C. Alejandra. "Reclaiming the Borderlands: Chicana/o Identity, Difference, and Critical Pedagogy." *Educational Theory* 47, no. 3 (Summer 1997): 359–375.

Ellstrand, Nathan K. "Las Anarquistas: The History of Two Women of the Partido Liberal Mexicano in Early 20th Century Los Angeles." MA Thesis, University of California–San Diego, 2011.

Erickson, Jennifer, and Caroline Faria. "'We Want Empowerment for Our Women': Transnational Feminism, Neo-Liberal Citizenship, and the Gendering of Women's Political Subjectivity in South Sudan." *Signs* 36, no. 3 (Spring 2011): 627–652.

Fallaw, Ben. "Eulogio Ortiz: The Army and the Anti-Politics of Post-Revolutionary State Formation, 1920–1935." In *Forced Marches: Soldiers and Military Caciques in Modern Mexico*, edited by Ben Fallaw and Terry Rugeley, 136–174. Tucson: University of Arizona Press, 2012.

Farnsworth-Alvear, Ann. *Dulcinea in the Factory: Myths, Morals, Men, and Women in Colombia's Industrial Experiment, 1905–1960.* Durham, NC: Duke University Press, 2000.

Fellner, Gene, ed. *Life of an Anarchist: The Alexander Berkman Reader.* 1992. Reprint. New York: Seven Stories Press, 2005.

Fernandes, Leela. *Transnational Feminism in the United States: Knowledge, Ethics, Power.* New York: New York University Press, 2013.

Fernández Aceves, María Teresa. *Mujeres en el cambio social en el siglo XX mexicano.* Mexico City: UNAM, 2012.

———. "El trabajo femenino en México." In *Historia de las mujeres en España y América Latina: Del siglo XX a los umbrales del XXI*, edited by Isabel Morant, Guadalupe Gómez-Ferrer, Gabriela Cano, Dora Barrancos, and Asunción Lavrin, 845–859. Madrid: Cátedra, 2006.

Fernández Aceves, María Teresa, Carmen Ramos Escandón, and Susie S. Porter, eds. *Orden social e identidad de género: México, siglos XIX y XX.* Guadalajara: Universidad de Guadalajara, 2006.

Fink, Leon, ed. *Workers across the Americas: The Transnational Turn in Labor History.* New York: Oxford University Press, 2011.

Flores, Lori A. "An Unladylike Strike Fashionably Clothed: *Mexicana* and Anglo Women Garment Workers against Tex-Son, 1959–1963." *Pacific Historical Review* 78, no. 3 (August 2009): 367–402.

Fowler-Salamini, Heather. "De-centering the 1920s: Socialismo a la Tamaulipeca." *Mexican Studies/Estudios Fronterizos* 14, no. 2 (Summer 1998): 287–327.

———. *Working Women, Entrepreneurs, and the Mexican Revolution: The Coffee Culture of Córdoba, Veracruz.* Lincoln: University of Nebraska Press, 2013.

French, John D., and Daniel James, eds. *The Gendered Worlds of Latin American Women Workers: From Household and Factory to the Union Hall and Ballot Box.* Durham, NC: Duke University Press, 1997.

García Flores, Modesto. *Lo transparente del poder.* N.p.: Sindicato de Trabajadores Petroleros de la República Mexicana, 1990.

Garner, Jason. *Goals and Means: Anarchism, Syndicalism, and Internationalism in the Origins of the Federación Anarquista Ibérica.* Oakland, CA: AK Press, 2016.

Goldman, Emma. *Anarchism and Other Essays.* 1917. Reprint. New York: Dover, 1969.

Goldsmith, Mary. "De combativas a conformistas. El Sindicato de Domésticas y Similares de Tampico y sus colonias." *Revista de Estudios de Género* 1, no. 11 (2000): 144–164.

——. "Doméstica, mujer o hija de familia: Identidades en entredicho." *Debate Feminista* 22 (October 2000): 16–25.

——. "Política, trabajo y género: La sindicalización de las y los trabajadores domésticos y el Estado mexicano." In *Orden social e identidad de género: México, siglos XIX y XX,* edited by María Teresa Fernández Aceves, Carmen Ramos-Escandón, and Susie Porter, 215–244. Mexico City: CIESAS, Universidad de Guadalajara, 2006.

Gonzales, Gilbert. *Culture of Empire: American Writers, Mexico, and Mexican Immigrants, 1880–1930.* Austin: University of Texas Press, 2004.

Gonzales, Trinidad. "The Mexican Revolution, Revolución de Texas, and Matanza de 1915." In *War along the Border: The Mexican Revolution and the Tejano Communities,* edited by Arnoldo De Léon, 107–133. College Station: Texas A&M University Press, 2012.

González, Gabriela. *Redeeming La Raza: Transborder Modernity, Race, Respectability, and Rights.* New York: Oxford University Press, 2018.

González Salas, Carlos. *Acercamiento a la historia del movimiento obrero en Tampico: 1887–1983.* Cd. Victoria: Autónoma de Tamaulipas, IIH, 1987.

Gordillo, Luz María. *Mexican Women and the Other Side of Immigration: Engendering Transnational Ties.* Austin: University of Texas Press, 2010.

Graybill, Andrew, and Benjamin Johnson, eds. *Bridging National Borders in North America: Transnational and Comparative Histories.* Durham, NC: Duke University Press, 2010.

Greene, Julie. "Historians of the World: Transnational Forces, Nation-States, and the Practice of U.S. History," in Leon Fink, ed. *Workers Across the Americas: The Transnational Turn in Labor History* (New York: Oxford University Press, 2011).

Greene, Julie. "Rethinking the Boundaries of Class: Labor History and Theories of Class and Capitalism," *Labor: Studies in Working-Class History,* Vol. 18, Issue 2 (2021): 92–112.

Guerra Manzo, Enrique. "La Confederación General de Trabajadores y la lucha política, 1921–1925." PhD diss., UNAM, 1989.

Guerrero, M. C. "Hymn for the Birth of the People's Son/Canto al nacimiento del hijo del pueblo." *Sagitario* (Villa Cecilia, Tamps.), July 20, 1927.

Guidotti-Hernández, Nicole. "Partido Liberal Mexicano: Intimate Betrayals: Enrique Flores Magón, Paula Carmona, and the Gendered History of Denunciation." *Southern California Quarterly* 101, no. 2 (Summer 2019): 127–162.

Guy, Donna. *Sex and Danger in Buenos Aires: Prostitution, Family, and the Nation in Argentina.* Lincoln: University of Nebraska Press, 1991.

Hagemann, Karen, Sonya Michel, and Gunilla Budde, eds. *Civil Society and Gender Justice: Historical and Contemporary Perspectives.* New York: Berghahn Books, 2008.

Hart, John Mason, *Anarchism and the Mexican Working Class.* Austin: University of Texas Press, 1978.

——. "The Evolution of the Mexican and Mexican-American Working Classes." In *Border Crossings: Mexican and Mexican-American Workers,* edited by John Mason Hart. Wilmington, DE: Scholarly Resources, 1998.

———. *Revolutionary Mexico: The Coming and Process of the Mexican Revolution*. Berkeley: University of California Press, 1987.

———, ed. *Border Crossings: Mexican and Mexican-American Workers*. Wilmington, DE: Scholarly Resources, 1998.

Heidenreich, Linda, with Antonia I. Castañeda, original interviews by Luz María Gordillo and a conclusion by Deena J. González. *Three Decades of Engendering History: Selected Works of Antonia I. Castañeda*. Denton: University of North Texas Press, 2014.

Hernández, Inés. "Sara Estela Ramírez: Sembradora." *Legacy* 6, no. 1 (1989): 13–26.

Hernández, Oscar Misael. "Estado, cultura y masculinidades en el noreste de México en la posrevolución." *Gazeta de Antropología* 25 (2009), article #38.

———. "Políticas educativas y formación de identidades culturales en Tamaulipas, 1925–1928." In *Identidad nacional: Sus fuentes plurales de construcción*, edited by Héctor M. Capello and Michelle Recio Saucedo, 165–185. Mexico City: Autónoma de Tamaulipas–Plaza y Valdés, 2011.

Hernández, Sonia. "Caritina M. Piña and Anarcho-Syndicalism: Labor Activism in the Greater Mexican Borderlands, 1910–1930." In *Writing Revolution: Hispanic Anarchism in the United States*, edited by Christopher J. Castañeda and Montse Feu López, 136–152. Urbana: University of Illinois Press, 2019.

———. "Las obreras de Monterrey: Trabajo y activismo femenino en la industria de ropa, 1930–1940." In *Género en la encrucijada de la historia social y cultural de México*, edited by Susie S. Porter and María Teresa Fernández Aceves, 149–178. Mexico City: Colegio de Michoacán and CIESAS, 2015.

———. "Revisiting *Mexican(a)* Labor History through *Feminismo Transfronterista*: From Tampico to Texas and Beyond, 1910–1940." *Frontiers: A Journal of Women Studies* 36, no. 3, Transnational Feminism Special Issue (2015): 107–136.

———. "Rooted in Place, Constructed in Movement: Transnational Labor Solidarities in the Texas-Mexico Borderlands." *Labor: Studies in Working Class History* 18, no. 1, Special Issue on Global Labor Solidarities (2021): 38–53.

———. "Women's Labor and Activism in the Greater Mexican Borderlands." In *War along the Border: The Mexican Revolution and Tejano Communities*, edited by Arnoldo De León, 176–204. College Station: Texas A&M University Press, 2012.

———. *Working Women into the Borderlands*. College Station: Texas A&M University, 2014.

Hernández Elizondo, Roberto. *Empresarios extranjeros, comercio y petróleo en Tampico y la Huasteca, 1890–1930*. Cd. Victoria: UAT, 2006.

Hernández Velásquez, María Remedios. "Mujeres magonistas: Una participación política activa en las Filas del PLM, 1900–1911." Tésis de licenciatura, Universidad Autónoma Metropolitana Unidad Iztapampa, 1994.

Herr, Robert. "'El Machete sirve para cortar la caña': Obras literarias y revolucionarias en 'El Machete' (1924–1929)." *Revista de Crítica Literaria Latinoamericana* 33, no. 66 (2007): 133–153.

Hewitt, Nancy A. "Luisa Capetillo: Feminist of the Working Class." In *Latina Legacies: Identity, Biography, and Community*, edited by Vicki L. Ruiz and Virginia Sánchez Korrol, 120–134. New York: Oxford University Press, 2005.

———. *Southern Discomfort: Women's Activism in Tampa, Florida, 1880s–1920s*. Urbana: University of Illinois Press, 2001.

Historia del anarco-feminismo en América Latina. Mexico City: Santocho Taller Encuadernaciones Huacal, Marea Negra Ediciones, 2014.

Huerta Márquez, Marvin Osiris. *Antiguo Morelos: Historia de un pueblo huasteco*. Monterrey: Geoformas, 2011.

———. "Inició la lucha del feminismo Caritina Piña." *Expreso–La Razón*, December 8, 2019.

———. "Los Pelones' Los Villanos de la Revolución." *Expreso.press*, November 25, 2019.

Huitron, Jacinto. *Orígenes e historia del movimiento obrero en México*. Mexico City: Editores Mexicanos Unidos, 1974.

Hurtado, Aída. "Sitios y Lenguas: Chicanas Theorize Feminisms." *Hypatia* 13, no. 2 (Spring 1998): 149–150.

Hutchison, Elizabeth Quay. "From 'La Mujer Esclava' to 'La Mujer Limón': Anarchism and the Politics of Sexuality in Early-Twentieth-Century Chile." *Hispanic American Historical Review* 81, no. 3–4 (2001): 519–553.

———. *Labors Appropriate to Their Sex: Gender, Labor, and Politics in Urban Chile, 1900–1930*. Durham, NC: Duke University Press, 2001.

Jacoby, Karl. *The Strange Career of William Ellis: The Texas Slave Who Became a Mexican Millionaire*. New York: Norton, 2016.

Joffory, Michelle. "El espacio relacional/Las relaciones espaciales: La práctica del feminismo chicano en la literatura fronteriza contemporánea." *Revista Iberoamericana* 71, no. 212 (July–September 2005): 801–814.

Johnson, Benjamin. *Revolution in Texas: How a Forgotten Rebellion and Its Bloody Suppression Turned Mexicans into Americans*. New Haven: Yale University Press, 2003.

Johnson, Benjamin, and Andrew Graybill, eds. *Bridging National Borders in North America: Transnational and Comparative Histories*. Durham, NC: Duke University Press, 2010.

Kanellos, Nicolás. *Hispanic Immigrant Literature: El Sueño del Retorno*. Austin: University of Texas Press, 2011.

———. "Spanish-Language Anarchist Periodicals in Early Twentieth-Century United States." In *Protest on the Page: Essays on Print and the Culture of Dissent since 1865*, edited by James L. Baughman, Jennifer Ratner-Rosenhagen, and James P. Danky, 59–84. Madison: University of Wisconsin Press, 2015.

Kaplan, Temma. "Female Consciousness and Collective Action: The Case of Barcelona, 1910–1918." *Signs* 7, no. 3 (Spring 1982): 545–566.

———. "Final Reflections: Gender, Chaos, and Authority in Revolutionary Times." In *Sex in Revolution: Gender, Politics, and Power in Modern Mexico*, edited by Jocelyn H. Olcott, Mary Kay Vaughn, and Gabriela Cano, 261–276. Durham, NC: Duke University Press, 2006.

Katz, Friedrich. "Labor Conditions in Haciendas in Porfirian Mexico: Some Trends and Tendencies." *Hispanic American Historical Review* 54, no. 1 (February 1974): 1–47.

———. *The Secret War in Mexico: Europe, the United States, and the Mexican Revolution*. Chicago: University of Chicago Press, 1983.

Kerig, D. P. "Yankee Enclave: The Colorado River Land Company and Mexican Agrarian Reform in Baja California, 1902–1944." PhD diss., University of California–Irvine, 1988.

Kessler-Harris, Alice. *Out to Work: A History of Wage-Earning Women in the U.S.* New York: Oxford University Press, 1982.

———. *A Woman's Wage: Historical Meanings and Social Consequences.* Lexington: University of Kentucky Press, 1990.

Kim, Jessica M. *Imperial Metropolis: Los Angeles, Mexico, and the Borderlands of American Empire, 1865–1941.* Chapel Hill: University of North Carolina Press, 2019.

Klubock, Thomas M. *Contested Communities: Class, Gender, and Politics in Chile's El Teniente Copper Mine, 1904–1951.* Durham, NC: Duke University Press, 1998.

Knight, Alan. *The Mexican Revolution.* 2 vols. Lincoln: University of Nebraska Press, 1990.

Kornegger, Peggy. *Anarquismo: La conexión feminista.* Coyoacán: Marea Negra Ediciones, 2014.

Koven, Seth, and Sonya Michel. "Womanly Duties: Maternalist Politics and the Origins of Welfare States in France, Germany, Great Britain, and the United States, 1880–1920." *American Historical Review* 95, no. 4 (October 1990): 1076–1108.

———, eds. *Mothers of a New World: Maternalist Politics and the Origins of Welfare States.* New York: Routledge, 1993.

Kraut, Julia Rose. *Threat of Dissent: A History of Ideological Exclusion and Deportation in the United States.* Cambridge, MA: Harvard University Press, 2020.

Kropotkin, Peter. *Anarchism: A Collection of Revolutionary Writings.* 1927. Reprint. New York: Dover, 2002.

———. "Morality and Good Habits: The Construction of Gender and Class in the Chilean Copper Mines, 1904–1951." In *The Gendered Worlds of Latin American Women Workers: From Household and Factory to the Union Hall and Ballot Box*, edited by John D. French and Daniel James, {Pages?}. Durham, NC: Duke University Press, 1997.

Kuecker, Glenn David. "Public Health, Yellow Fever, and the Making of Modern Tampico." *Urban History Review* 36, no. 2 (Spring 2008): 18–28.

Lara Orozco, Marycarmen. *En el vaivén del Frente Rojo: La escena anarquista en la ciudad de Veracruz en 1922 y 1923.* Mexico City: Coedición Redez–Marea Negra, 2015.

Lau Jaiven, Ana. "Lo personal es también político y el feminismo, ¿Llegó para quedarse?" In *Mujeres y constitución: De Hermila Galindo a Griselda Álvarez, 231–246.* México: INEHRM, 2017.

Lau [Jaiven], Ana, and Carmen Ramos. *Mujeres y revolución: 1900–1917.* Mexico City: INEHRM, 1993.

Laughlin, Kathleen A., Julie Gallagher, Dorothy Sue Cobble, Eileen Boris, Premilla Nadasen, Stephanie Gilmore, and Leandra Zarnow. "Is It Time to Jump Ship? Historians Rethink the Waves Metaphor." *Feminist Formations* 22, no. 1 (Spring 2010): 76–135.

Lear, John. *Workers, Neighbors, and Citizens: The Revolution in Mexico City.* Lincoln: University of Nebraska Press, 2001.

Ledesma, Irene. "Texas Newspapers and Chicana Workers' Activism, 1919–1974." *Western Historical Quarterly* 26, no. 3 (Autumn 1995): 309–331.

Lida, Clara E., and Pablo Yankelevich, comp. *Cultura y política del anarquismo en España e Iberoamérica*. Mexico City: El Colegio de México, 2012.

Lim, Julian. *Porous Borders: Multiracial Migrations and the Law in the U.S.-Mexico Borderlands*. Chapel Hill: University of North Carolina Press, 2017.

Lomas, Clara. "Transborder Discourse: The Articulation of Gender in the Borderlands in the Early Twentieth Century," *Frontiers: A Journal of Women Studies* 24, no. 2–3, "Gender on the Borderlands" (2003): 51–74.

Lomnitz, Claudio. *The Return of Comrade Ricardo Flores Magón*. New York: Zone Books, 2014.

Longa, Ernesto A., ed. *Anarchist Periodicals in English Published in the United States (1833– 1955), An Annotated Guide*. Lanham, MD: Scarecrow Press, 2010.

Luibhéid, Eithne. "Sexual Regimes and Migration Controls: Reproducing the Irish Nation-State in Transnational Contexts." *Feminist Review*, no. 83, "Sexual Moralities" (2006): 60–78.

Lytle-Hernández, Kelly. "Borderlands and the Future History of the American West." *Western Historical Quarterly* 42, no. 3 (Autumn 2011): 325–330.

———. *Migra! A History of the U.S. Border Patrol*. Berkeley: University of California Press, 2010.

Marchand, Marianne H. "Engendering Transnational Movements/Transnationalizing Women's and Feminist Movements in the Americas." *Latin American Policy* 5, no. 2 (November 2014): 180–192.

Marino, Katherine M. *Feminism for the Americas: The Making of an International Human Rights Movement*. Chapel Hill: University of North Carolina Press, 2019.

———. "Marta Vergara, Popular-Front Pan-American Feminism, and the Transnational Struggle for Working Women's Rights in the 1930s." *Gender & History* 26, no. 3 (November 2014): 642–660.

———. "Transnational Pan-American Feminism: The Friendship of Bertha Lutz and Mary Wilhelmine Williams, 1926–1944." *Journal of Women's History* 26, no. 2 (Summer 2014): 63–87.

Marsh, Margaret. "The Anarchist-Feminist Response to the 'Woman Question' in Late-Nineteenth-Century America." *American Quarterly* 30, no. 4 (1978): 533–547.

Martínez Sánchez, María Luisa, comp. *Mujeres, trabajo y vida cotidiana en el Noreste México*. Monterrey: UANL, 2014.

McGirr, Lisa. "The Passion of Sacco and Vanzetti: A Global History." *Journal of American History* 93, no. 4 (March 2007): 1085–1115.

Mckiernan-González, John. *Fevered Measures: Public Health and Race at the Texas-Mexico Border, 1848–1942*. Durham, NC: Duke University Press, 2012.

McKillen, Elizabeth. "Hybrid Visions: Working-Class Internationalism in the Mexican Borderlands, Seattle, and Chicago, 1910–1920." *Labor: Studies in Working-Class History of the Americas* 2, no. 1 (2005): 78–79.

———. *Making the World Safe for Workers: Labor, the Left, and Wilsonian Internationalism*. Urbana: University of Illinois Press, 2013.

Melero, Pilar. Mythological Constructs of Mexican Femininity. New York: Palgrave Macmillan, 2015.

Merithew, Caroline Waldron. "Anarchist Motherhood: Toward the Making of a Revolutionary Proletariat in Illinois Coal Towns." In *Women, Gender, and Transnational Lives: Italian Workers of the World*, edited by Donna R. Gabaccia and Franca Iacovetta, 217–246. Toronto: University of Toronto Press, 2002.

Mitchell, Stephanie, and Patience A. Schell, eds. *The Women's Revolution in Mexico, 1910–1953*. Lanham, MD: Rowman and Littlefield, 2007.

Molyneux, Maxine. "No God, No Boss, No Husband: Anarchist Feminism in Nineteenth-Century Argentina." *Latin American Perspectives* 13, no. 1, "Latin American Ninteenth-Century History" (Winter 1986): 119–145.

Montejano, David. *Anglos and Mexicans in the Making of Texas*. Austin: University of Texas Press, 1986.

Morett Sánchez, Jesús Carlos. *Reforma agraria: Del latifundio al neoliberalismo*. Mexico City: Plaza y Valdés, 2003.

Las mujeres en la revolución mexicana: Biografía de mujeres revolucionarias. Mexico City: INEHRM, 1992.

Mujeres y constitución: De Hermila Galindo a Griselda Álvarez. Mexico City: INEH, 2017.

Muñoz Martínez, Monica. *The Injustice Never Leaves You: Anti-Mexican Violence in Texas*. Cambridge, MA: Harvard University Press, 2018.

———. "Recuperating Histories of Violence in the Americas: Vernacular History-Making on the U.S.-Mexico Border." *American Quarterly* 66, no. 3 (September 2014): 661–689.

Nettlau, Max. *A Short History of Anarchism*. London: Freedom Press, 1996.

Ngai, M. Mae. "The Future of the Discipline: Promises and Perils of Transnational History." *Perspectives*, December 1, 2012.

———. *Impossible Subjects: Illegal Aliens and the Making of Modern America*. Princeton, NJ: Princeton University Press, 2004.

Norvell, Elizabeth Jean. "Syndicalism and Citizenship: Postrevolutionary Worker Mobilizations in Veracruz." In *Border Crossings: Mexican and Mexican-American Workers*, edited by John Mason Hart, 93–116. Wilmington, DE: Scholarly Resources, 1998.

Nunzio, Pernicone. *Italian Anarchism 1864–1892*. Princeton, NJ: Princeton University Press, 1993.

Ocasio Melendez, Marcial E. *Capitalism and Development: Tampico, Mexico, 1876–1924*. New York: Peter Lang, 1998.

Offen, Karen, ed. *Globalizing Feminisms, 1789–1945*. New York: Routledge, 2010.

Oikion Solano, Verónica. *Cuca García (1889–1973): Por las causas de las mujeres y la revolución*. Mexico City: Colegio de Michoacán; Colegio de San Luis, 2018.

———. "El Frente Único Pro Derechos de la Mujer de Cara al debate constitucional y en la esfera pública en torno de la Ciudadanía de las Mujeres, 1935–1940." In *Mujeres y constitución: De Hermila Galindo a Griselda Álvarez*, 107–136. Mexico City: INEH, 2017.

Olcott, Jocelyn. *International Women's Year: The Greatest Consciousness-Raising Event in History*. New York: Oxford, 2017.

———. *Revolutionary Women in Post-Revolutionary Mexico*. Durham, NC: Duke University Press, 2006.

Olcott, Jocelyn, Mary Kay Vaughan, and Gabriela Cano, eds. *Sex in Revolution: Gender, Politics, and Power in Modern Mexico*. Durham, NC: Duke University Press, 2006.

Olivares Arriaga, Ma. De Carmen, and Altair Tejeda de Tamez. *Mujeres que han dejado testimonio en Tamaulipas: Compendio biográfico*. Cd. Victoria: UAT, 1998.

Olvera Rivera, Alberto. "Identity, Culture, and Workers' Autonomy: The Petroleum Workers of Poza Rica in the 1930s." In *Border Crossings: Mexican and Mexican-American Workers*, edited by John Mason Hart, 117–138. Wilmington, DE: Scholarly Resources, 1998.

Orozco, Cynthia. *No Mexicans, Women, or Dogs Allowed: The Rise of the Mexican American Civil Rights Movement*. Austin: University of Texas Press, 2010.

Ortiz-Ortega, Adriana, and Mercedes Barquet. "Gendering Transition to Democracy in Mexico." *Latin American Research Review* 45, Special Issue: Living in Actually Existing Democracies (2010): 108–137.

Palomo Acosta, Teresa, and Ruthe Winegarten. *Las Tejanas: 300 Years of History*. Austin: University of Texas Press, 2003.

Peláez Ramos, Gerardo. "Valentín Campa Salazar, dirigente obrero comunista." https://www.lahaine.org/b2-img11/pelaez_campa.pdf, n.d. Accessed September 1, 2019.

Peña Delgado, Grace. "Border Control and Sexual Policing: White Slavery and Prostitution along the U.S.-Mexico Borderlands, 1903–1910." *Western Historical Quarterly* 43, no. 2 (Summer 2012): 157–178.

Peniche Rivero, Piedad. "Los Congresos Feministas de 1916: El obsequio legal y la denegación del sufragio a las congresistas por el General Alvarado." In *Mujeres y constitución: De Hermila Galindo a Griselda Álvarez*, 23-50. Mexico City: INEH, 2017.

Pernicone, Nunzio. *Italian Anarchism 1864–1892*. Princeton, NJ: Princeton University Press, 1993.

Pérez, Emma. *The Decolonial Imaginary: Writing Chicanas into History*. Bloomington: Indiana University Press, 1999.

———. "'She Has Served Others in More Intimate Ways': The Domestic Service Reform in Yucatán, 1915–1918." In *Las Obreras: Chicana Politics of Work and Family*, edited by Vicki Ruiz, 41–64. Aztlán Anthology Series Vol. 1. Los Angeles: UCLA Chicano Studies Research Center Publications, 2000.

Porter, Susie. *From Angel to Office Worker: Middle-Class Identity and Female Consciousness in Mexico, 1890–1950*. Lincoln: University of Nebraska Press, 2018.

———. *Working Women in Mexico City: Public Discourses and Material Conditions, 1879–1931*. Tucson: University of Arizona Press, 2003.

———. "Working Women in the Mexican Revolution." *Oxford Research Encyclopedia of Latin America Online*. May 2016. http://oxfordre.com/.

Porter, Susie, and María Teresa Fernández Acéves, eds. *Género en la encrucijada de la historia social y cultural de México*. Zamora: Michoacán: Colegio de Michoacán, CIESAS, 2015.

Pratt, Joseph A., Martin Melosi, and Kathleen A. Brosnan, eds. *Energy Capitals: Local Impact, Global Influence*. Pittsburgh: University of Pittsburgh Press, 2014.

Ramos, Raúl. "Understanding Greater Revolutionary Mexico: The Case for a Transnational Border History." In *War along the Border: The Mexican Revolution and Tejano Communities*, edited by Arnoldo De León, 310–317. College Station: Texas A&M University Press, 2012.

Reichert, William O. *Partisans of Freedom: A Study of American Anarchism*. Bowling Green, OH: Bowling Green University Popular Press, 1976.

La revolución de las mujeres en México. Mexico City: INEH, 2016.

Reyes, Barbara. *Private Women, Public Lives: Gender and the Missions of the Californias*. Austin: University of Texas Press, 2009.

Reyna, Laura Palomares, and Guadalupe Cortez. "El control del movimiento obrero como una necesidad del Estado de México (1917–1936)." *Revista Mexicana de Sociología* 34, no. 3–4 (July–December 1972): 785–813.

Ribera Carbó, Anna. *La Casa del Obrero Mundial: Anarcosindicalismo y revolución en México*. Mexico City: INAH, 2010.

———. "Mujeres sindicalistas: Las trabajadoras de la Casa del Obrero Mundial (1912–1916). Una aproximación a las fuentes para su estudio." https://anarkobiblioteka3 .files.wordpress.com/2016/08/mujeres_sindicalistas_las_trabajadoras_de_la _casa_del_obrero_mundial_1912-1916_-_anna_ribera_carbc3b3.pdf. Accessed October 1, 2019.

Rivera Garza, Cristina. "Una emigración extraña." *Tierra Adentro*, http://www.tierra adentro.cultura.gob.mx/una-emigracion-extrana1/. Accessed April 21, 2017.

Rocha, Martha Eva. *Los rostros de la rebeldía veteranas de la revolución Mexicana, 1910–1939*. Mexico City: INEHRM, 2016.

Rocha, Rodolfo. "The Influence of the Mexican Revolution on the Texas-Mexico Border." PhD diss., Texas Tech University, 1981.

Rodríguez, Ana Patricia. "The Fiction of Solidarity: Transfronterista Feminisms and Anti-Imperialist Struggles in Central American Transnational Narratives." *Feminist Studies* 34, no. 1–2 (Spring/Summer 2008): 199–226.

Román-Odio, Clara, and Marta Sierra, eds. *Transnational Borderlands in Women's Global Networks: The Making of Cultural Resistance*. New York: Palgrave Macmillan, 2011.

Rosenberg, Emily. "Gender." *Journal of American History* 77, no. 1 (June 1990): 116–124.

Rouco Buela, Juana. *Historia d de un ideal vivido por una mujer*. Madrid: LaMalatesta–Tierra de Fuego, 2012.

Rubenstein, Anne. "The War on *Las Pelonas*: Modern Women and Their Enemies, Mexico City, 1924." In *Sex in Revolution: Gender, Politics, and Power in Modern Mexico*, edited by Jocelyn Olcott, Mary Kay Vaughn, and Gabriela Cano, 57–80. Durham, NC: Duke University Press, 2006.

Rugley, Terry, and Ben Fallaw, eds. *Forced Marches: Soldiers and Military Caciques in Modern Mexico*. Tucson: University of Arizona Press, 2012.

Ruiz, Vicki L. *Cannery Women, Cannery Lives: Mexican Women, Unionization, and the California Food Processing Industry, 1930–1950*. Albuquerque: University of New Mexico Press, 1987.

———. "Class Acts: Latina Feminist Traditions, 1900–1930." AHA Presidential Address delivered on January 8, 2016. *American Historical Review* 121, no. 1 (February 2016): 1–16.

———. *From Out of the Shadows: Mexican Women in Twentieth-Century America*. New York: Oxford University Press, 1998.

Saad-Saka, Mark. *For God and Revolution: Priest, Peasant, and Agrarian Socialism in the Mexican Huasteca*. Albuquerque: University of New Mexico Press, 2013.

Saldaña Martínez, Moisés A., and Lylia I. Palacios Hernández. "Entre la reproducción y la producción: Discurso social sobre la mujer en publicaciones regiomontanas (1920–1950)." In *Mujeres, trabajo y vida cotidiana en el Noreste México*, edited by María Luisa Martínez Sánchez, 85–114. Monterrey: UANL, 2014.

Saldivar-Hull, Sonia. *Feminism on the Border: Chicana Gender Politics and Literature*. Berkeley: University of California Press, 2000.

Salmond, John. *Gastonia 1929: The Story of Loray Mill Strike*. Chapel Hill: University of North Carolina Press, 1995.

Sánchez Gómez, María del Pilar. *Proyección histórica de Tampico*. 2nd ed. Cd. Victoria: Universidad Autónoma de Tamaulipas, IIH, 1998.

Sandos, James. *Rebellion in the Borderlands: Anarchism and the Plan of San Diego, 1904–1923*. Norman: University of Oklahoma Press, 1992.

Sandoval, Chela. *Methodologies of the Oppressed*. Minneapolis: University of Minnesota Press, 2000.

Santiago, Myrna. "Tampico, Mexico: The Rise and Decline of an Energy Metropolis." In *Energy Capitals: Local Impact, Global Influence*, edited by Joseph A. Pratt, Martin Melosi, and Kathleen A. Brosnan, 147–158. Pittsburgh: University of Pittsburgh Press, 2014.

———. "Women of the Mexican Oil Fields: Class, Nationality, Economy, Culture, 1900–1938." *Journal of Women's History* 21, no. 1 (Spring 2009): 87–110.

Savala, Joshua. "Ports of Transnational Labor Organizing: Anarchism along the Peruvian-Chilean Littoral, 1916–1928." *Hispanic American Historical Review* 99, no. 3 (2019): 501–531.

Schiavo, Leda, ed.. *La Mujer española y otros artículos feministas*. Madrid: Editora Nacional, 1976.

Schmitt, Karl M. *Communism in Mexico: A Study in Political Frustration*. Austin: University of Texas Press, 1965.

Schoenhals, Louise. "Mexico Experiments in Rural and Primary Education: 1921–1930." *Hispanic American Historical Review* 44, no. 1 (1964): 22–43.

Shaffer, Kirwin. *Anarchism and Countercultural Politics in Early Twentieth-Century Cuba*. Oakland, CA: PM Press, 2005.

——. *Anarchist Cuba: Countercultural Politics in the Early Twentieth Century.* Los Angeles: PM Press, 2019.

——. *Black Flag Boricuas: Anarchism, Antiauthoritarianism, and the Left in Puerto Rico, 1897–1921.* Urbana: University of Illinois Press, 2013.

——. "Freedom Teaching: Anarchism and Education in Early Republican Cuba, 1898–1925." *The Americas* 60, no. 2 (October 2003): 151-183.

——. "Havana Hub: Cuban Anarchism, Radical Media, and the Trans-Caribbean Anarchist Network, 1902–1915." *Caribbean Studies* 37, no. 2 (July–December 2009): 45–81.

——. "The Radical Muse: Women and Anarchism in Early-Twentieth-Century Cuba." *Cuban Studies* 34 (2003): 130–153.

Simpson Fletcher, Yaël. "Teaching the History of Global and Transnational Feminisms." *Radical History Review*, no. 92 (Spring 2005): 155–163.

Skirius, John. *José Vasconcelos y la cruzada de 1929.* Mexico City: Siglo Veintiuno Editores, 1978.

Smith, Andrea. "Indigenous Feminism without Apology." *Unsettling Ourselves: Reflections and Resources for Deconstructing Colonial Mentality*, September 8, 2011. http://unsettling america.wordpress.com/2011/09/08/indigenous-feminism-without-apology/. Accessed March 1, 2015.

Smith, Stephanie. *Gender and the Mexican Revolution: Yucatán Women and the Realities of Patriarchy.* Chapel Hill: University of North Carolina Press, 2009.

Snodgrass, Michael. *Deference and Defiance in Monterrey: Workers, Paternalism, and Revolution in Mexico, 1890–1950.* Cambridge: Cambridge University Press, 2003.

Solorio Martínez, José Ángel. *Grupos de gobierno: Tamaulipas, 1919–1992.* Mexico City: Amacalli Editores, 1997.

Solorio Martínez, José Ángel, and Raul Sinencio Chávez. *La huelga de la Waters–Pierce Oil Corporation, 1919: La primavera de Villa Cecilia y Tampico, Tamaulipas.* http://libros .histomex.com/product/la-huelga-de-la-waters-pierce-oil-corporation/. Accessed February 1, 2019.

Staudt, Kathleen, and Carlota Aguilar. "Political Parties, Women Activists' Agendas, and Household Relations: Elections on Mexico's Northern Frontier." *Mexican Studies/Estudios Mexicanos* 8, no. 1 (Winter 1992): 87–106.

Stern, Alexandra Minna. "Buildings, Boundaries, and Blood: Medicalization and the Nation-Building on the U.S.-Mexico Border, 1910–1930." *Hispanic American Historical Review* 79, no. 1 (February 1999): 41–81.

Suárez Findlay, Eileen J. *Imposing Decency: The Politics of Sexuality and Race in Puerto Rico, 1870–1920.* Durham, NC: Duke University Press, 2000.

Suriano, Juan. *Paradoxes of Utopia: Anarchist Culture and Politics in Buenos Aires 1890–1910.* Oakland, CA: AK Press, 2010.

——. "Las prácticas culturales del anarquismo argentino." In *Cultura y política del anarquismo en España e Iberoamérica*, edited by Clara E. Lida and Pablo Yankelevich, 145–174. Mexico City: Colegio de México, 2012.

Talpade Mohanty, Chandra. "Under Western Eyes: Feminist Scholarship and Colonial Discourses." *Feminist Review*, no. 30 (Autumn 1988): 61–88.

———. "Transnational Feminist Crossings: On Neoliberalism and Radical Critique." *Signs* 38, no. 4,"Intersectionality: Theorizing Power, Empowering Theory" (Summer 2013): 967–991.

Taylor, Gregory S. *The History of the North Carolina Communist Party*. Columbia: University of South Carolina Press, 2009.

Taylor, Lawrence D. "The Magonista Revolt in Baja California." *Journal of San Diego History* 45, no. 1 (Winter 1999).

———. "Tightening the Reins of Control over the Country's Borders: The Role of Governor Rodolfo Sánchez Taboada in the Implementation of the Plan Cardenista in Baja California." *Meyibó*, new ser., no. 2 (July–December 2010): 95–123.

Threlkeld, Margaret. "The Pan American Conference of Women, 1922: Succesful Suffragists Turn to International Relations." *Diplomatic History* 31, no. 5 (November 2007): 801–828.

———. *Pan American Women: U.S. Internationalists and Revolutionary Mexico*. Philadelphia: University of Pennsylvania Press, 2014.

Tomchuk, Travis. *Transnational Radicals: Italian Anarchists in Canada and the U.S., 1915–1940*. University of Manitoba Press, 2015.

Torres Pares, Javier. *La revolución imposible: La difusión anarquista de la Revolución Mexicana en el periódico francés Les Temps Nouveaux (1906–1914)*. Mexico City: UNAM, 2013.

———. *La revolución sin frontera: El Partido Liberal Mexicano y las relaciones entre el movimiento obrero de México y el de Estados Unidos, 1900–1923*. Mexico City: UNAM, 1990.

Truett, Samuel. *Fugitive Landscapes: The Forgotten History of the U.S.-Mexico Borderlands*. New Haven: Yale University Press, 2008.

———. "Transnational Warrior: Emilio Kosterlitzky and the Transformation of the U.S.-Mexican Borderlands, 1873–1928." In *Continental Crossroads: Remapping U.S.-Mexico Borderlands History*, edited by Samuel Truett and Elliott Young, 241–272. Durham, NC: Duke University Press, 2004.

Tullis, F. LaMond. "Early Mormon Exploration and Missionary Activities in Mexico." *Brigham Young University Studies* 22, no. 3 (Summer 1982): 289–310.

Tuñón Pablos, Esperanza. *Mujeres que se organizan: El Frente Único pro Derechos de la Mujer, 1935–1938*. Mexico City: Universidad Nacional Autónoma de México, 1992.

Tutino, John, ed. *Mexico and Mexicans in the Making of the United States*. Austin: University of Texas Press, 2012.

Ulloa, Bertha. *Historia de la Revolución Mexicana, periódo 1914–1917: La Constitución de 1917*. Mexico City: Colegio de México, 1983.

Valadés, José C. *Sobre los orígenes del movimiento obrero en México*. Mexico City: Centro de Estudios Históricos del Movimiento Obrero en Mexicano, 1979.

Valerio-Jiménez, Omar. *River of Hope: Forging Identity and Nation in the Rio Grande Borderlands*. Durham, NC: Duke University Press, 2012.

Van der Linden, Marcel. *Workers of the World: Essays toward a Global Labor History*. Leiden: Brill, 2008.

Vargas, Zaragosa. "*Tejana* Radical: Emma Tenayuca and the San Antonio Labor Movement during the Great Depression." *Pacific Historical Review* 66, no. 4 (November 1997): 553–580.

Vella, Stephen. "Newspapers." In *Reading Primary Sources: The Interpretation of Texts from Nineteenth- and Twentieth-Ccentury History*, edited by Miriam Dobson and Benjamin Ziemann, 192–208. New York: Routledge, 2009.

Villanueva, Laura Vicente. *Teresa Claramunt (1862–1931): Pionera del feminiso obrerista, anarquista*. Madrid: Fundación de Estudios Literarios Anselmo Lorenzo, 2006.

Weber, Devra. "Keeping Community, Challenging Boundaries: Indigenous Migrants, Internationalist Workers, and Mexican Revolutionaries, 1900–1920." In *Mexico and Mexicans in the Making of the United States*, ed. John Tutino, 208–235. Austin: University of Texas Press, 2012.

———. "Wobblies of the Partido Liberal Mexicano: Reenvisioning Internationalist and Transnational Movements through Mexican Lenses." *Pacific Historical Review* 85, no. 2 (2016): 188–226.

Weisbord, Vera Buch. "Gastonia, 1929 Strike at the Loray Mill," edited and with introduction by Dan McCurry and Carolyn Ashbaugh, *Southern Exposure* 1, no. 3–4 (Winter 1974).

Weiss, Holger. *International Communism and Transnational Solidarity: Radical Networks, Mass Movements, and Global Politics, 1919–1939*. Leiden: Brill, 2016.

Wood, Andrew Grant. *Revolution in the Street: Women, Workers, and Urban-Protest in Veracruz, 1870–1927*. Wilmington, DE: Scholarly Resources, 2001.

Young, Elliott. *Catarino Garza's Revolution on the Texas-Mexico Border*. Durham, NC: Duke University Press, 2004.

———. "Imagining Alternative Modernities: Ignacio Martínez's Travel Narratives." In *Continental Crossroads: Remapping U.S.-Mexico Borderlands History*, edited by Samuel Truett and Elliott Young, 151–182. Durham, NC: Duke University Press, 2004.

Zamora, Emilio. *Mexican Workers and Job Politics during World War II: Claiming Rights and Righting Wrongs in Texas*. College Station: Texas A&M University Press, 2009.

———. *The World of the Mexican Worker in Texas*. College Station: Texas A&M University Press, 1993.

Zavella, Patricia. *Women's Work and Chicano Families: Cannery Workers of the Santa Clara Valley*. Ithaca, NY: Cornell University Press, 1987.

Zavella, Patricia, and Denise A. Segura, eds. *Women and Migration in the U.S.-Mexico Borderlands: A Reader*. Durham, NC: Duke University Press, 2007.

Zimmer, Kenyon. *Immigrants against the State: Yiddish and Italian Anarchism in America*. Urbana: University of Illinois Press, 2015.

Zorilla, José Fidel. *La mujer en Tamaulipas*. Cd. Victoria, Tamps.: Universidad Autónoma de Tamaulipas, 1976.

Index

Page numbers followed by f indicate a figure and t indicate a table.

"¡Abajo charrateras criminales!" (Andrew), 105–106
Acuña, Elisa, 52
Adelson, Leif, 1–16, 17
Administración Mexicana de la IWW, 52
agrarian movement, 36, 143, 146
agrarismo, 133; gendered rhetoric, 133
El Águila, 7, 32; collective contract, 114; Portes Gil connections, 132; strikes, 1916 and 1917, 66, 137
Aguilar, Kevin, 16
"¡Al abordaje!" (González Parra), 74
Alaniz, Elvira, 46
Alcayaga Sasso, Aurora Mónica, 16, 17, 128
Alemán Hernández, Elisa, 42
Alfaro, Isauro, 77–78, 131
Alfaro, Pedro, 6
Alma Obrera, 77–78
Almazán, Lorenza, 91
Almedo, Manuel, 67
Altamira, Rafael, 6
Alter, Thomas, 35
de Alva, E. Martínez, 133

de Alva, Esther, 91
Alzalde, Eugenio, 87
anarchism, 10, 156n4; among port workers, 51; Argentina, 15; Chile, 15; free love and, 44, 82–83; gender equity, 38–39; immigrants and, 15, 19; introduction and spread in Latin America, 26–29; Mexican borderlands, 26; quashed by the state, 142; in Spain, 28; women's involvement in, 14, 25, 39–40
anarchist circles, 57–58
anarchist press: *Ariete* (Mexico City), 47; *Avante*, 12, 107; *Avante*, women's involvement with, 88, 90, 93–95, 148; *Casa del Obrero Mundial* (Mexico City), 11; CGT newspapers, 78; cross-border exchanges, 11; *Cultura Obrera* (New York), 11; *El Galeote*, 12; gendered language and, 14, 16, 18; *Germinal* (Tampico), 11–12, 47, 50–51; *Germinal: Periódico Libertario*, 56; *La Humanidad*, 12; *El Niño Libre*, 12; *Nuestra Palabra*, 12; *El Preso Social*, 12; *El Productor*, 105; *Pro Vida* (Havana), 11; *El Rebelde* (Los Angeles), 11; on religion, 93–94, 95; reprinting from other papers, 15, 53; Rivera's involvement with, 17, 89–90; *Sagitario*, 12, 43, 118;

anarchist press (*continued*): *Tierra y Libertad,* 105; *Tribuna Roja,* 12, 61; *Verbo Rojo,* 12; *Vía Libre,* 12, 118; *La Voz de la Mujer* (Buenos Aires), 15–16; women's involvement with, 4, 6, 19, 25, 147

anarchists: Chilean, 102; collaborations with communists, 137; imprisonment of, 84; Spanish, 105

anarchists, women: de Cleyre, Voltairine, 53; Goldman, Emma, 52–53, 64, 107, 165n103; Jiménez, Domitila, 90, 92–93, 97; Michel, Luisa, 53; writing campaigns, 97. *See also compañeras en la lucha;* Galván, Isaura; Piña Montalvo, Caritina; Rodríguez, Aurelia; Velásquez, Felipa

anarcho-feminism, 8, 15, 57–58, 158n35; in anarchist organizations, 52; anarcho-syndicalism in Veracruz, 12; Casa del Obrero Mundial, 12–13; direct action, 16, 40, 129–130; global worker front, 138–140; Mexico, 12–13; Partido Liberal Mexicano (PLM), 12; perceptions by radical labor, 129–130; rejection of religiosity, 40–41; Rio Grande Valley and, 41

anarcho-feminists: direct action, 97; lost to the historical record, 147–148; organizations, 43–45, 46; writers, 52–54

anarcho-maternalism, 10, 40, 58, 64. *See also* maternal rhetoric

anarcho-syndicalism, 6, 28, 33; Casa del Obrero Mundial (COM), 6; defined, 21–22, 76; demise of, 143–144; distinct from anarchism, 2, 70; equality of genders, 140; female activists (*see* anarcho-feminism); female collectives, 5; Grupo Germinal, 7; Hermanos Rojos, 6; labor equity and, 2; maternal rhetoric, 97, 98, 109, 140; during Mexican Revolution, 111; organizations, 6–7; relationship with communist and prolabor organizations, 94; rise of, 2; women and, 2, 4–5, 9–10, 18, 149; women's increased participation, 58; women's labor movement and, 76–80

anarcho-syndicalist organizations, 57–70; Confederación General de Trabajadores, 57; Hermanos Rojos, 57

anarchy, 2; labor unions and, 3

Andrade, José, 68–69

Andrew, Dora, 105–106

Angel Hernández, José, 44, 46, 47, 49–50, 141–142; San Marcos resident support of, 49–50

anticlericalism, women and, 38

Antonio Aguilar, Kevin, 18

Anzaldúa, Gloria, 8–9, 151

Aranda, Carmen, 122–123, 126

Archivo Histórico de Esteban Méndez Guerra, 83

Argentina, 15

Ariete (Mexico City), 47

Arizmendi, Elena, 138–139, 140

Arredondo, Pablo, 62

Article 123, 111

Avante, 15, 53, 88, 93–94, 107, 148. *See also Sagitario*

Ayala, Carmen, 119–120

Ayala, Josefa, 62

Baena Paz, Guillermina, 21

Bakunin, Mikhail, 28

Barnhill, M. V. (judge, Gastonia), 1, 101

Battle of El Ebano (1915), 6, 21

Beal, Fred E., 99

Berkman, Alejandro (Alexander), 68

Blanco, Lucio, 35

Bliss, Katherine, 119

Boris, Eileen, 23

Borrán, Jorge D., 6, 52, 67–68

boycotts, 89

Buch, Vera, 99–100

Buenos Aires, 15

Burkett, Texas, 44

Café Louisiana (Tampico), 125–126

Calles, Plutarco E., 90, 129

Camacho, Cristina, 64

Campa, Valentín, 137–138

Cano, Gabriela, 137

Capetillo, Luisa, 14–15, 107

de Cárdenas, Isidra T., 42

Cárdenas, Lázaro, 142–144, 149; agrarian redistribution, 188n53; anarcho-syndicalist support for, 143–144

Caribbean anarchist influence, 14–15

Carillo Puerto, Elvia, 120–121

Carillo Puerto, Felipe, 120
Carpenters' Union, 51
Carranza, Venustiano, 37, 65f; administration, 20; crackdowns on labor activism, 61, 65–69; surveillance of labor organizations, 68–69
Carrera Muñoz, Candelario, 36–37
Carrera-Torres family, 36–37
Carta de Amiens (1906), 76
Casa del Obrero Mundial (COM), 4, 11; Batallones Rojos, 69; Centro de Estudios Sociales Feministas, 18; Comité General de Defensa de los Presos, 87; expansion across Mexico and into Texas, 45–46; female membership, 150; gender and, 39–40; González Parra, Reynalda, 70; growth of, 45–47; oil strikes, 66–67; Rational School of Thought, 45; Tampico, 47–48, 50, 61, 64; visibility of women's issues, 25–26. *See also* Casa del Obrero Mundial; Tampico
Castillo, Rosa, 120
Catarino Garza revolt, 49
El Cauterio, 116
Cayaso, Anita Contreras, 104
Center for Rational Studies. *See* Grupo Racionalista
Centro de Estudios Feministas Sociales, 5, 6–7, 18, 70–71
Centro de Estudios Sociales Feministas. *See* Centro de Estudios Feministas Sociales
Centro de Obreros, 67–68
Centro Sindicalista Libertario, 12
CGT, 57, 68; aid to political prisoners, 141; congresses, 5, 68, 69–71, 75–76, 89; creation of, 76–77; demise of, 144; embodiment of anarcho-syndicalism, 118; Federación Local, 57; gendered analysis of, 57; gendered rhetoric, 121; Grupo Afinidad, 57; Grupo Hermanos Rojos, 57; Hermanos Rojos and, 20; Huitrón, Jacinto, 75–76; IAW association, 76; inclusion of women, 77; newspapers endorsed by, 12; in opposition to CROM, 77; pacifism, 141; Piña's membership in, 6; A. Rodríguez's involvement with, 106; role in union-based anarchism, 12; Sindicato de Constructores de Tanques, 57; Sindicato de Dragas, 57; Sindicato de la Continental, 57; Sindicato de O. del Petróleo, 57; Sindicato El Porvenir de Campesinos, 57; solidarity with workers, 141; support for Tampico regulation of women, 118; umbrella organization for anarcho-syndicalism, 57, 61, 76–77, 104, 138; Velásquez's involvement with, 93
Chapa Tijerina, Esther, 101–102, 136, 137
Children's Miners Relief Committee of New York, 99–100
Chile, 15–16
cigarrera work sites, 13
círculos, 33
Cisneros, Abraham, 43, 87
Ciudad Madero, 5. *See also* Villa Cecilia
Civil Code of 1932, 135–136
Claramunt, Teresa, 105
Cline, Charles, 43, 48, 87
Clubs Femeniles Vasconcelistas, 112
Colquitt, Oscar, 49–50
Comisión Inter-Americana de Mujeres, 108
Comité de Defensa Pro-Presos Sociales, 87
Comité Internacional Pro-Presos Sociales, 21, 104; distribution of anarchist newspapers, 90; financials, 139; focus on political prisoners, 83, 99, 102; links to Liga Cultural, 91; Piña as secretaria, 1–2, 6, 96, 153; support for Gastonia Mexicans, 101
Comité Nacional del Partido Comunista, 94
Comité Pro-Asamblea Nacional Obrera y Campesina, 138
communism, 2, 94; Communist Federation of the Mexican Proletariat, 76; female activists, 138; Mexico City, 75–76, 117, 136, 137
compañeras, societal judgement and impacts of, 54–55
compañeras en la lucha, 20, 25, 56–58, 65, 78, 97
Confederación de Trabajadores de México (CTM), 137, 149

Confederación General de Trabajadores (CGT). *See* CGT
Confederación Nacional del Trabajo, 28
Confederación Regional de Obrera Mexicana. *See* CROM
Congreso Feminista (1925), 120; gendered rhetoric, 121
Congreso Internacional de Mujeres de la Raza (1925), 120; gendered rhetoric, 121
Connelly, Mary Goldsmith, 16, 17, 118
Consejo Feminista Mexicano, 120–121
Constitution (Mexico, 1917), 111; Article 123, 111; women's right in, 112; worker's rights in, 112
"Convocatoria a la mujer" (Velásquez, 1928), 147–148
"Cooperación en el campo," 133
Córdova, César, 121
La Corregidora, 52–53
correspondence as activism, 9
Cortés, Felipa, 62
Cortina uprising, 49
Cristero Rebellion, 85
CROM: opposition to GCT, 12, 76–77, 94, 124, 150; organized labor and, 13, 66, 75; Treviño's involvement with, 68
La Crónica, 52
cross-border collaborations, 2, 19, 47. *See also* transnationalism
Cruz, María, 91
Cruz Blanca Mexicana, 138
CTM, 150. *See also* Confederación de Trabajadores de México
Cuba, 14, 16; anarchist press, 14
Cuban influence in US labor circles, 14
Cuellar, Rómulo, 29
Cueto, Manuel, 42
Cultura Obrera (New York), 11
Cultura Proletaria de Nueva York, 88

Dawson, Ellen, 99
Debbs, Eugene, 115. *See* also Partido Obrero Socialista Tamaulipeco (POST)
Delgado, Román, 6, 50, 52, 72
del Valle, Casimiro, 160n16
El Demócrata Fronterizo, 52
"El día de Navidad," (Gudiño Marín, 1924), 72

Diario Periódico Pólitico de la Mañana (El Mundo), 62
Díaz, Porfirio, 19, 29, 34, 49
Díaz Cárdenas, León, 39
direct action, 103f, 114; anarchist preference for, 60; anarcho-feminist support for, 97; at Colorado River Land Company (1937), 143; COM support of, 47; *lavanderas*, 129; May Day protests, 125; oil strikes, 7, 66–67, 84, 112; Veracruz rent strike, 61
Doheny, Edward, 30–31
Dueñas, Emeteria, 62
Durán y Huerta, Tito, 115, 179n11

education, equal instruction, 13
"Ejido Islas Agrarias," 143
Encina, Luz, 136
Escuela Racionalista, 4
Esteban Méndez Guerra collection, 17, 21
export-driven industries and strong labor collectives, 13

FAM, 144
Fanelli, Giuseppe, 28
Federación Anarquista Ibérica, 28
Federación Anarquista Mexicana (FAM), 144
Federación de Trabajadores de Tamaulipas, 186n27
Federación Local, 57
Federación Obrera de Tamaulipas, 101. *See also* Gastonia strike
Federación Obrera de Tampico. *See* FOT
Federación Sindical de Obreras, 28
Federal Labor Law (Mexico, 1931), 113, 135. *See also* Labor Law of 1931
female activist organizations, in workers organizations, 70
female anarchists, 64
female labor activists, 61, 90–93; mainstream perceptions of, 57–65, 78
feminism: and labor activism, 15–16, 23–24; and labor movement, 21; in Latin America, 106; transnationalism and, 23. *See also* anarcho-feminism varieties in, 157n24, 158n38, 159n55, 166n106
Feminismo Internacional, 138–139

Fernández Aceves, María Teresa, 10

Ferrer i Guardia, Francisco, 4, 5, 13, 28, 56, 69–70; Escuela Racional (*see* Rational School of Thought); influence on COM, 45–46, 47

Figueroa, Martina, 91

Fletcher, Yaël Simpson, 24

Flores, Francisca, 46

Flores, María, 82

Flores Magón, Ricardo, 4, 5, 12, 44f; assassination of, 87; call for revolution, 37; imprisonment, 43; influences, 34; playwright, 82; support for gender equality, 38

Florida, 14, 15

FOT, 117, 126; affiliated unions, 118; women's agenda within, 117–118

Fowler-Salamini, Heather, 10, 13, 61

free love, 82–83, 153

free waitress movement, 22–23, 112, 113–114; causes, 118–123; direct action, 125; waitresses break from SDRS, 114, 124

Frente Unico Pro-Derechos de la Mujer, 101–102, 136–137, 139; Tampico branch, 101, 136, 137

Fuerza Consciente (San Francisco), 62

FUPDM. *See* Frente Unico Pro-Derechos de la Mujer

El Galeote, 12

Galván, Amparo Lopez, 46

Galván, Concepción B., 46

Galván, Isaura: activism of, 4, 78–79, 87, 149; association with González Parra, 54, 56–58; detention of, 67–68; Grupo Racionalista, 46–47, 50–51; importance for women in anarcho-synidicalist movement, 72; leadership at *Germinal* (Tampico), 72; lost to the historical record, 148

Galvan, Piña, 189n2

Galveston, 26

García, Elena, 119–120

García, Isabel, 62

García, Juana, 62

García, María, 119–120

García, María (Cuca) Refugia, 136–137, 174n27

García, María Encarnación, 94

García, María P., 42

García, Ramona, 61

García, Rosa, 46

Garza, Catarino, 34

Gastonia strike, 1, 99–100, 102, 156n3; arrests, 99–101; and Federación Obrera de Tamaulipas, 101–102; Mexicans involved and incarcerated, 101, 103; racial issues, 100

gender: and labor activism, 3; wage discrepancies, 107–108

gendered rhetoric: activism, 71; compañera and compañerismo language, 23, 62, 94; free waitress movement, 112; in labor movement, 58, 77–78; Liga Cultural de Mujeres Libertarias, 90–91; in mainstream media, 122–123, 127–129, 132–134, 147; in mainstream politics, 108; maternal rhetoric and *agrarismo*, 133; use by women in anarcho-syndicalism, 7. *See also* anarchist press

gender equality, ideal, not goal, 16

Germinal (Tampico), 4, 11–12, 47, 56, 64, 150; destruction of office, 68

Goldman, Emma, 52, 64, 107, 165n103

Goldsmith, Mary. *See* Connelly Goldsmith, Mary

Gómez, Marte R., 135

González, Isabel, 46

González, Jesús, 87

González, Nicolás, 131

González Parra, Reynalda: anarchist activism, 56–57, 64, 78–79; association with Isaura Galván, 4–5, 56–58; Centro de Estudios Sociales Feministas, 18; CGT congresses, 70; Congreso Obrero Regional del Sindicalismo Revolucionario (Tampico, 1917), 70–71; educational work, 57; founder of COM Tampico, 13, 47, 64; lack of biographical data, 148; women's emancipation, 73–75; writings, 25–26, 72–75

González Salas, Carlos, 16, 51, 83

Gori, Pietro, 82

Granados, Teresa, 46

Gremio Unido de Alijadores (Tampico), 77–78, 86t, 94

Grupo Afinidad, 57
Grupo Avante, 44
Grupo Cultural Libertario "Margarita
  Ortega," 95–96
El Grupo de Propaganda Anárquica,
  107–108
Grupo Femenino "Rosaura Gortari," 144
Grupo Germinal, 4, 43, 46, 50–52
Grupo Hermanos Rojos, 57t, 86t. *See also*
  Hermanos Rojos
Grupo Libertario Sacco and Vanzetti, 83,
  84, 88
Grupo Luz, 45
Grupo Praxedis Guerrero, 43
Grupo Racionalista (San Antonio), 4, 46,
  49, 51, 68
Grupo "Rayos de Luz," 142
Grupo Redención, 4, 95
Grupo Tierra y Libertad "Librado Rivera,"
  104
Gudiño, Pedro, 6, 52, 89
Gudiño Marín, Luz, 6, 71–72
Guerrero, M. C., 97, 104–105
Guillen, Concepción, 91
Gulf of Mexico, 3f1; transatlantic ties,
  26–28
Gutiérrez de Lara, Lázaro, 35, 40f, 87
Gutiérrez de Mendoza, Juana Belén, 52
Guzman, Eduardo, 84

Harlingen, Texas, 4
Hart, John Mason, 37
Havana, 26
hembra, 121–122
Hermanos Rojos, 5–7; creation of, 50, 52;
  female membership, 71, 150, 171n65; oil
  strikes, 66; opposition to CROM, 94;
  support for gender equality, 71. *See also*
  Grupo Hermanos Rojos
Hernández, Amado G., 36
Hernández, Elisa A., 43–44, 46–47
Hernández, Esteban, 77–78
Hernández, José Barragan, assassination
  of, 69
Hernández, José H., 6, 51
Hewitt, Nancy A., 14, 15, 107
Hofmeyr, Isabel, 8
Hoover, Herbert, 1, 101, 104

Huasteca Oil Company, 32
de la Huerta, Adolfo, 75
Huitrón, Jacinto, 68, 73, 75–76
La Humanidad, 12
human rights violations, 49
Hutchison, Elizabeth, Q., 15, 16, 20, 102, 106

immigrants, 15, 19; labor activism, 32, 33
imprisonment: of anarchists and labor ac-
  tivists, 84–85; in the United States, 62,
  84, 85–86; of women, 62; and work to
  release, 85–87
Industrial Workers of the World (IWW).
  See IWW
Inés Mena, José, 85
Instituto de Derecho Comparado, Univer-
  sity of Paris, 135
International Association of Workers, 76
International Labor Defense, 101
IWW: Administración Mexicana de la
  IWW, 52; multiple membership, 46; oil
  strikes, 66; support of COM, 13, 18, 47;
  transnational nature, 18

JCA. *See* Juntas de Conciliación y Arbitraje
  (JCA)
del Jesús Alvarado, María, 82, 90, 96
Jiménez, Domitila, 90, 92–93
Junta Central de Conciliación y Arbitraje,
  132
Junta Organizadora del Partido Liberal
  Mexicano, 34–35, 39, 47–48, 52
Juntas de Conciliación y Arbitraje (JCA).
  See labor arbitration boards

Kaplan, Temma, 151–152
Koven, Seth, 10

labor action (strikes), 45; Huasteca Petroleum, 129; National Textile Workers
  Union (Gastonia), 99–100; oil workers,
  61; oil worker strike (1917), 66–67, 137.
  See also direct action
labor activism, 10, 18–19, 28, 35, 125–126;
  anarcho-feminism, 16; artisan trades,
  47; association with Mexicans, 48–49;
  crackdowns on, 65–69, 180–181n19; domestic workers, female, 17; economics

and, 9; gendered dimensions, 9, 54–55, 57–65, 109–110, 121; ideas of reciprocity, 9; men and, 62; Mexican regulation of, 20, 23; mining, 35; multiple membership, 47; nationals and locals, 171–172n82; oil production and, 7; propaganda plays, 82; race and, 9; spread across Mexican borderlands, 32–35; treatment by state authorities, 49–50; women's movement within, 1–21, 25, 62, 95; worker collectivism, 38
labor arbitration boards, 112–113; acceptance of, 111; rejection by COM, 111
labor collectives, rise in Mexico, 27
Labor Law of 1931, 144. *See also* Federal Labor Law (Mexico, 1931)
labor movement: coopted by the state, 141–142, 143–144; and feminism, 21; importance to Portes Gil, 115. See also *compañeras en la lucha*
labor organizations, 86t. See also *individual organizations*
labor reforms in Constitution (1917), 111
labor unions, 7; anarchy and, 3; rejection by some after the Revolution, 112; supporting Portes Gil, 116–117
de Laforcade, Geoffroy, 10
Lara, Blas, 87
Lárraga Orta, Leopoldo, 37
Las Meseras Libres, 111
Las Rusias Hacienda, 35
Lau Jaiven, Ana, 151
lavanderas, 129, 130f
Le Dantec, Félix, 156no
de León, Federico, 5
Liberal Congress (1901, San Luís Potosí), 37, 39
Libertarian Women of Veracruz, 61
Liga Campesinas, 187n32
Liga Cultural de Mujeres Libertarias, 6, 15, 90–93, 117, 148; associated organizations, 91t; membership, 91t; writings, 91–92, 91t
Liga de Comunidades Agrarias, 133
Liga Femenil Pro Derechos de la Mujer de Tampico y Ciudad Madero, 137, 186n27
Liga Internacional, 138
Ligas Anti-alchólicas, 116

Ligas Campesinas, 138
Ligas Femeninas, 116
location, as intersectional identity, 9
Lomnitz, Claudio, 47
López, Francisca, 62
López, Melchora, 46
López de López, Ester, 62
López Mateos, Adolfo, 146
Loray Mill. *See* Gastonia strike
Lozano, Francisca, 46
Lozano, Rita, 91
Lucio, Ortiz, 87
Luna, Francisca, 91
Luz del Esclavo, 82, 88; anarcho-syndicalism, 111
Luz y Verdad, 64
!Luz!, 11, 62

El Machete, 117, 137
Madero, Francisco I., 5, 37
Magón, Ricardo Flores, 29, 77; correspondence with Goldman, 52
magonistas and *magonismo*, 40f, 42–43, 48; armed operations, 43; as "bandits," 48–50; imprisonment in US, 43; Luz Mendoza, 8; newspapers, 29; support for laborers, 35; support for women's issues, 19; Tanguma and, 36; women soldiers, 40f
Marcos Tristan, J., 66
María Rangel, Jesús, 43, 48, 85–86
Maritime Workers Union, 69
Marsh, Margaret, 53, 94, 150
Martínez, Alida, 44–45
Martínez, María, 91
maternalism, 1, 7, 10, 14, 22, 157n15
maternal rhetoric, 10, 104–107, 150–152; among non-anarchists, 150, 152; among radical women laborers, 10, 97, 98–110, 150; by anarchists, 99; in anarcho-syndicalism, 7, 10, 97–98, 109, 140; *compañeras en la lucha*, 97; in mainstream media and politics, 7, 58–59, 99, 116; Piña's use of, 104, 151–152; state use of, 78; women's critiques of, 64
May Day, Mexico City (1931), 125
McGirr, Lisa, 88
Melvin, Sophie, 99–100

Méndez Guerra, Esteban: anarcho-syndicalism, 88, 147; archive, 17, 21; brief biography, 5–6; Comité membership, 2, 101; imprisonment and torture, 85, 87, 90; Luz del Esclavo, 82; membership in Hermanos Rojos, 83
Mendoza, Bernardino, 4
Mendoza, Esther, 148; anarchist writings, 82, 140; compañera and compañerismo language, 94–95; Liga Cultural de Mujeres Libertarias, 6, 90
de Mendoza, Jesús, 6
Mendoza, Luz, 162–163n55; anarcho-syndicalist, 4; fought Texas Rangers, 85; founded Grupo Redención, 42–43; influenced by María Mendoza, 95
Mendoza, María: anarchist activism, 79, 82, 148; correspondence, 96; Liga Cultural de Mujeres Libertarias, 6; reach of influence of writings, 95
meseras libres. See free waitress movement
Mexican American War, 48
Mexican borderlands, 3–4, 3f, 30–31, 48, 151; foreign capital investment in, 41–42; spread of labor activism, 32–35; state abuse in, 49–50; Treaty of Guadalupe-Hidalgo (1848), 41
Mexican Communist Party, 75–76, 117, 136
Mexican constitution. *See* Constitution (Mexico, 1917)
Mexican National Labor Congress (1876), 28
Mexican Revolution, 4, 32, 34, 47; crackdown on radical labor activists, 111; divorce and remarriage, 180n17; impact on women, 76, 182n42; symbol for worker's rights, 151
Mexico, rise of anarchist activism, 26–35
Mexico City, 5, 25, 45, 66–67; Comisión conference, 69; González Parra, Reynalda, 56–57, 64; May Day parade, 125
Michel, Sonya, 10
mill strike, 1–2
Mirbeau, Octave, 82
Mireles, Eduwiges, 62
Moctezuma, Florencia, 61
Modotti, Tina, 129
Molyneux, Maxine, 15
Mondini, Florinda, 15, 107
Montero, Luz, 62

Morado, Josefa, 91
morals purity, 62
Morones, Luis, 68
movimiento de las meseras libres, 112. *See also* free waitress movement
"A la mujer," (Claramunt), 105
Mujer Moderna, 52–53
El Mundo (Tampico) 62, 108, 122–123
Murray, John, 35
mutual aid societies, 7, 123–124; anarcho-syndicalism and, 58; women's, 183–184n65

Narváes, Maura, 91
nationless world, 3
New Orleans, 26
New York, 14, 21
El Niño Libre, 12
Nuestra Palabra, 12

Obregón, Alvaro, 69, 90
Obreras de la Fábrica, 62
El Obrero, 52–53
obrero/obrera identities, 13, 14, 16, 18
Ocampo, Melchor, 5
oil production, 16; El Águila, 7; expansion in 1920s and 20s Tampico, 113; labor activism and, 2, 7, 61, 66; *lavanderas*, 129; life in camps, 17; nationalization of oil industry, 143; new labor unions, 149; Poza Rica oil workers, 189–190n13; Tampico, 7, 66; unionization, 138; and women, 119, 159n47
La Opinión, 121–122
Orta, Francisca, 61
Ortega, Margarita, 95–96
Ortiz, Eulogio, 85
Ortiz, Gregorio, 82, 146, 147
Ortiz Rubio, Pascual, 128, 129
Oyervides, Macedonio, 68

Páginas Libres (Barcelona), 29
"Para las dos" (González Parra), 74
Parsons, Lucy, 64
Partida, Elena, 64
Partido Comunista Mexicano (PCM). *See* PCM
Partido de la Revolución Mexicana's (PRM) Sector Popular Femenil, 186n27

Partido Laborista Mexicano, 75–76
Partido Nacional Revolucionario. *See* PNR
Partido Obrero Socialista Tamaulipeco
  (POST), 114–115
Partido Revolucionario Institucional, 115,
  141
Partido Socialista Fronterizo. *See* PSF
Paz, 122–123, 126
PCM, 136, 138
Peasant League, 13
"To the Peasant Woman," 133
Pederera de Tamatán, 137
Pellandini. *See* Aranda, Carmen
Peña, Herminia, 46
Perales, Pedro, 43, 87
periodicals promoting women's issues,
  52–53; *La Corregidora,* 52–53; *La Crónica,*
  52; *El Demócrata Fronterizo,* 52; *El Obrero,*
  52–53; *Vesper,* 52
petición, 11
Pierce Oil Company, 32, 66, 96, 116
Piña, Zenaido, 37, 39f
Piña Hernández, Nicanor, 5, 37, 38f, 80–81,
  145
Piña Montalvo, Caritina, 81f, 96; absence
  from the record, 21; activism of, 2, 102,
  139–140, 141–142; adulthood in Villa
  Cecilia, 82–83; brief biography, 82–83;
  childhood, 80–82; death of, 153; dis-
  tancing from women's rights movements, 7, 9–10; erasure from official
  history, 83, 146; free union, 82–83, 153;
  interest in incarcerated striking mothers
  and children, 101, 103; letter regarding
  Gastonia mill strike, 1–2, 101–102, 104;
  life with Ortiz, 146; maternal rhetoric, 104, 109, 151–152; media coverage, 3; multiple memberships, 111, 118;
  Ocampo, 145–147; parents, 5; prisoner
  release activism, 85, 87; religion, lack of,
  82–83; report at Pierce Oil union hall
  (1930), 96–97; Reynosa, 147; rhetoric
  of motherhood, 97; secretaria de correspondencia for Comité Internacional
  Pro-Presos Sociales, 84–85, 153; transnational exchange, 23, 78, 93, 139–140;
  transregional activism, 21; work to
  release political prisoners, 87–88; writings, 90

Pizaña, Aniceto, 36, 42
Plan de Agua Prieta, 75
Plan of San Diego, 43
Plaza de la Libertad, 61
PLM: anarcho-feminist organizations
  spread across Mexican borderlands,
  35–37, 46; direct action and, 3, 34–35;
  Emilia Rodríguez and, 42; Houston, 49;
  Junta Organizadora del Partido Liberal
  Mexicano, 47–48; mining sites and, 35;
  Regeneración, 52; relationship to IWW, 18;
  South Texas women-founded branches,
  43–44; women and, 4, 25–26, 38, 39
PNR, 115, 135, 136, 138, 142
political prisoners, 1, 21–22, 79, 82
Porfirio Díaz regime (Mexico), 19, 28
Porter, Susie, 9–10, 125, 135
Portes Gil, Emilio, 1, 102; anti-Carranza,
  75–76; anti-communism, 138; anti-so-
  cialism, 116; building agrarian support,
  188n53; crackdowns on labor activism, 89–90; interest in state controlled
  organized labor, 134–135; opposition
  to anarchism, 131; political biography,
  114–117; PSF, 23; socialism, state-sponsored, 131–132; use of women's political
  engagement, 23; Vasconcelistas and PSF,
  126–128
El Porvenir (Tampico), 3, 56, 58–59, 62
POST. *See* Partido Obrero Socialista Tamaulipeco (POST)
postrevolutionary period, and female activists, 78
Praxedis Guerrero, 46
El Preso Social, 12
PRI. *See* Partido Revolucionario Institucional
Prismas Anarquistas (Burkett, Texas),
  44–46
prostitution, 61, 119, 124–125, 167n5
Proudhon, Pierre-Joseph, 28
Pro Vida (Havana), 11
PSF, 131, 134–135; attack on Vasconcelista
  Club, 126–127; feminized ridicule by
  Sagitario, 121; origins in PRI, 141; political
  clubs, 116; Portes Gil, 23; rise of, 98, 114–
  118; social reform of families, 132–133;
  unification of labor unions, 142; women
  and, 116, 142

racialized rhetoric, 63–64
racism, 45, 48–49
racism against Blacks in America, 100
radical labor culture, 32
Ramírez, Sara Estela, 52
Ramos, Basilio, 42
ranchero class, 41
Rangel, Jesús María, 87, 162–163n55
Rational School of Thought, 5, 57; gender
    equity and, 45. *See also* Escuela Racio-
    nalista
Rebelde (Barcelona), 29
El Rebelde (Los Angeles), 11
Red Brothers. *See* Hermanos Rojos and
    Grupo Hermanos Rojos
Redención, 43
Regeneración, 29, 35–36, 42–43, 45, 71
Reglamento de Meseras, 118–120, 122, 128
renters' movement, 13, 61
report on the status of women in Mexico,
    135–136
reproductive rights, 120–121
Revolución, 42
Revolución Social, 73
revolution, calls for, 37
rhetoric of separatism, 25
Rhodakanaty, Plotino, 27–28
Ribera Carbó, Anna, 12–13, 47
Ricaut, Alfredo, 66
Rio Grande Valley, anarchist women's
    movement and, 41
Rivera, Librado, 44f, 138; brief biography,
    5–6; Comité work to release, 87; death
    of, 143; Hermanos Rojos, 16–17; im-
    prisonment and torture, 84–85, 89–90;
    Sagitario, 12; transnationalism, 9
Robles de Mendoza, Margarita, 102, 137,
    140
Rodríguez, Aurelia, 91–92, 97, 106–107,
    109, 111, 140, 148; "Insurrección," 91–92
Rodríguez, Emilia, 42
Rodríguez Cabo, Matilde, 136
Roman-Odio, Clara, 9
de la Rosa, Carmen, 42–43
de la Rosa, Luis, 43
Rose, Sonya O., 77
Rouco Buela, Juana, 89
Rubenstein, Anne, 122–123

Ruíz, Concepción, 91
Ruiz Carillo, Gonzalo, 89

Sacco and Vanzetti, 1, 88–89
Sagitario, 129, 162n55; feminist commen-
    taries in, 43, 53, 72, 91–93, 105; gendered
    rhetoric, 121; Rivera and, 12; transna-
    tional exchange, 87–88. *See also Avante*
Salazar, Ignacia, 64
Salazar, María, 42–43
"¡Salud!" (González Parra, *Germinal*), 75
San Antonio, Texas, 4, 46; Galván, Is-
    aura, 4; Grupo Racionalista, 46–47, 49;
    Hernández, Elisa A., 44; Treviño, Ri-
    cardo, 51, 68
Sánchez, Elena, 64
Sánchez, María, 42
Sanchez, Susana, 46
Sandoval, María, 121
Sanger, Margaret, 120
San Juan, 26
San Marcos signers, 49–50
Santiago, Myrna, 16, 17
Santos, Francisco, 37
Santos, Fulgencio, 37
Sarabia, Manuel, 35
Saucedo, Cecilia, 62
SDRS, 114. *See also* Sindicato de Depen-
    dientas de Restaurantes y Similares
    (SDRS)
Secció Mútua Feminal del Centre Autono-
    mista de Dependents del Comerçi de la
    Industria, 28
Segura, Gustavo, 133
SERCS. *See* Sindicato de Empleadas
    de Restaurantes, Cafés y Similares
    (SERCS)
sexism. *See* gendered rhetoric
Shaffer, Kirwin, 10, 14–16, 20, 139, 141
Sierra, Marta, 9
Sinaloa, 6
Sindicato de Campesinos del Estado, 133
Sindicato de Constructores de Tanques, 57
Sindicato de Dependientas de Restauran-
    tes y Similares (SDRS), 109–110, 114
Sindicato de Dragas, 57
Sindicato de Empleadas de Restaurantes,
    Cafés y Similares (SERCS), 114

Sindicato de la Continental, 57
Sindicato de Obreros, 62
Sindicato de O. del Petróleo, 57
Sindicato de Trabajadores del Petróleo y de la Construcción, 52
Sindicato El Porvenir de Campesinos, 57
Sindicato Feminista Josefa Ortíz de Domínguez, 94
Sindicato Huasteco de Mata Redonda, 143
Sindicato Mexicano de Electricistas, 115
Sixth International American Conference, 108
La Social (Mexico City), 27–28
socialism, state-sponsored, 2
socialist activism, 20
Socialist and IWW Party of Tamaulipas, 141–142
Socialist Border Party, 131
Socialist Party (US), 99–100
Sociedad Mutualista "Hermanos del Trabajo," 123–124
Sociedad Progresiva Femenina, 28
Socorro Rojo, 101
Solis, Francisca, 91t
Solis, María, 91
Sosa, Soledad, 28
Soto, María, 91
South Texas radical and anarchist women, 42–43
state reconstruction, women and, 131
state socialism, 137
strikes. *See* direct action; labor action (strikes)
Suárez Findlay, Eileen J., 14–15
suffrage, 120; support of, 14
El Surco, 132–134

Tamaulipas, 17, 26, 179n6
Tampico, 3–5, 26, 29–35; Casa del Obrero Mundial, 6–7, 13, 18, 47; demographics, 113; diversity, 65–66; labor organizations, 2; oil industry, 19, 29–33; photo, 84f, 103f, 134f; population growth, 1876–1915, 32–33; regulation of prostitution, 120; regulation of women, 118–120; transport hub, 30–31; US intelligence reports, 65–66; working class women, 17. *See also* Tampico-Villa Cecilia entries

Tampico-Cecilia, 13–14; anarchist hub, 4, 16, 32–33; anarchist movements and, 6, 140–141; community and mutual aid, 33; free waitress movement, 113–114; women in radical labor activism, 18
Tampico Petroleum Workers Union, 69
Tampico-Villa Cecilia labor movement: and feminism, 54; gender and, 22; labor activism, 7–8, 19–20
Tanguma, Higinio, 36, 116, 161n36
"Texas martyrs," 87
Texas Rangers, 43, 48–50, 85
Texas Socialist Party, 49, 142
Texas-Tamaulipas border region, 9, 11, 49
theater, 6, 82
Tierrra y Libertad, 89
Torres Carrera (Alberto), 65f
Torres de Carrera, Juana, 36–37
torture, 85, 90
transborder activism, 2, 7–8
transnationalism, 9, 10–11, 13, 18, 157n16; diplomatic approaches, 138–139; feminism and, 23, 149–150; global labor struggle, 138–139; solidarity of anarchist groups cross-border, 142–143; theoretical frameworks, 8
travel restrictions on women, 62
Treviño, Ricardo, 46–47, 51, 66, 68–69, 75–76; leadership at *Germinal* (Tampico), 72
Tribuna Roja, 12, 61
Trowbridge, Elizabeth, 35
El Tulteco, 37
Tuxtepec Revolution, 49

UERS. *See* Unión de Empleados de Restaurantes y Similares (UERS)
UMA. *See* Unión de Mujeres Americanas
Unión de Empleados de Restaurantes y Similares, 102, 114, 118, 126
Unión de Mujeres Americanas, 137
Unión Industrial de Trabajadores del Transporte Marítimo, 52
Union of Anarchist Women in Mexico, 77
Uranga, Consuelo, 136

Valadez, Severa C., 46
Valdés, María. *See* Ortega, Margarita

Vanzetti, Bartolomeo, 1
Vasconcelista clubs, 126–127, 129; attacks by men, 126–127, 129; direct action, 127–128
Vasconcelos, José, 112, 126–127
Vásquez, Leonardo M., 87
Vega, Julia, 91
Velásquez, Felipa, 111, 140, 176n67; activism of, 141–142; brief biography, 6; female anarcho-syndicalist activists network, 79, 82; FOT support of, 117; incarcerations with her children, 97, 99, 131, 143, 147–148; maternal rhetoric, 109; overview of her life, 147–148; transnationalism, 9; writings, 93–94, 131, 147–148
Venegas, Serapio, 132
Veracruz, 12, 13–14, 17, 26, 61
Verbo Rojo, 12
Vernon Harris, 62
Vesper, 52
Vía Libre, 12
Vidal, Jaime, 48, 49, 88
Villa Cecilia, 1, 5, 7, 29; labor radicalism and influence on Piña, 83; radical labor media, 82. *See also* Tampico-Cecilia
Villareal, Andrea, 52–53
Villareal, Teresa, 52–53
Villarreal, Cecilia, 29
Villarreal Franco, José, 153
Villasana Ortiz, Manuel, 37

"La Voz de la mujer," (as printed in *Revolución*, California), 42
La Voz de la Mujer (Buenos Aires), 15–16

wage discrepancies, 167n11
waitresses: break from SDRS, 114; conflation with prostitution, 61, 119, 123, 124–125; free waitress movement, 22–23, 112–114, 118–123; Reglamento de Meseras, 118–120, 122; sexism against, 123
Weber, Devra, 12, 18, 51
"Why I Am an Anarchist" (Michel, 1895), 53
women in the labor movements, 59–60, 129, 149, 158n39; direct action, 60–62; domestic workers, 17; gendered relationship, 118; mainstream perceptions of, 20, 112, 140, 183n57. *See also compañeras en la lucha*
"women of ill-repute," 54–55. *See also compañeras en la lucha*
women's suffrage in Mexico, 7,9–10, 14, 39, 40, 77, 102, 108, 120, 122, 136, 137, 139, 140, 151–152
Wood, Andrew Grant, 12, 13
working class women, 28, 42

Yaquis, torture and cover-up, 90
Young Pioneers of America, 99–100

Zambrano, Governor (Nuevo León), 59

SONIA HERNÁNDEZ is an associate professor of history at Texas A&M University and the author of *Working Women into the Borderlands*.

The University of Illinois Press
is a founding member of the
Association of University Presses.

———————————————

University of Illinois Press
1325 South Oak Street
Champaign, IL 61820-6903
www.press.uillinois.edu